In the Cathedral of the Plains is a collection of stories of individuals—Indigenous and non-Indigenous—who meet and became dear friends. The chronicled events occur mainly in the 1950s and 60s, but the author also shares personal memories of interactions with the people as time moved on. The reader is not only taken on a journey through Blackfoot Country in southern Alberta—and along the eastern slopes on the Rockies—but into the heart of the new territory of 'Reconciliation' and building a better world. Unconscious prejudices and erroneous understandings of history become exposed, and the author's learning journey deepens into profound love, with a heightened sense of the 'Sacred', as it can be experienced under the wide-open skies of the plains.

In the Cathedral of the Plains

Joan Young

"They will… show forth a tenderness
which is not of this world…"

'Abdu'l-Bahá, *Selections from
the Writings of 'Abdu'l-Bahá*, p.117

In the Cathedral of the Plains

Cover photo credit

Mickey Shannon Photography, www.mickeyshannon.com.

Disclaimer

The author accepts full responsibility for the information written and unknowing errors that will be made. In all stories about individuals, consents were obtained from the family or person involved in the story. Copyright of excerpts and quotes remain with the original authors. Care has been taken to trace ownership of copyright material. The author will gladly receive information that will enable her to rectify any credit line in subsequent editions.
All queries should be addressed to: joan.gwen@gmail.com.

Library and Archives Canada Cataloguing in Publication

Title: In the cathedral of the plains / Joan Young.
Names: Young, Joan (Author of In the cathedral of the plains), author.
Description: Includes bibliographical references.
Identifiers: Canadiana 20240477391 | ISBN 9781068964008 (softcover)
Subjects: LCSH: Indigenous peoples—Alberta—Religion.
| LCSH: Bahai Faith—Alberta. | LCSH: Alberta—Religion.
Classification: LCC E98.R3 Y58 2024 | DDC 971.23/00497—dc23

bixbooks@agromedia.ca · Calgary AB Canada

Dedication

This book is dedicated to those who shared their stories with me, and to the members of my family—my son, David, and daughter, Dermai—in particular. May their hopes and dreams for a better world be realized.

Contents

Preface

Picture it. Soft sunlight warming the south-facing ochre walls of a state-of-the-art museum. The building hugs the rim of a wide river valley on Siksika, a prairie First Nation. In the visitors parking lot nearby, two white ladies and a dog are eating sandwiches in their car. Admittedly, the dog, isn't eating sandwiches but wishes it was. They appear to be the only guests this autumn afternoon at Blackfoot Crossing Historical Park, an hour's drive east of Calgary.

The women are my long-time friend and me, there to learn about the history and culture of the Blackfoot people. If possible, I also want to check out their library for information about individuals whose stories I have encountered in my efforts to write about cross-cultural friendships between Blackfoot and settler individuals. I have a certain amount of knowledge that I am keen to share with my friend, but I am blissfully unaware of how little I actually know.

We are there on a damp fall day, with a slight breeze bringing the mildly acrid smell of wet poplar leaves from the gullies beyond. The silence is broken by the sudden rush of the dog bursting from behind the driver's seat, out the open door. She pursues a big gray sheep dog which has appeared at the window. Her long leash clatters across the parking lot as she races after him towards the crest of a hill. Dreading the scene of a dog fight, or of my dog tangled up and hanging over a precipice by her leash, I follow. But there is no precipice, and no sound of dogs fighting. By the time I reach the edge of the of the parking

lot, the dog is coming back and her visitor is nowhere in sight.
So much for our initial encounter of the day on Siksika First
Nation.

I am aware, despite my colonial education, that the land
we are on is a tiny remnant of what was once a vast Blackfoot
territory including southern Alberta up to the North
Saskatchewan River, the south eastern portion of the province
of Saskatchewan, and down through Montana to Yellowstone
National Park. As I look out over the scene, a sense of
melancholy seems to hang in the air. I am aware that the signing
of Treaty Seven happened in the valley below in September of
1877. It purported to be a nation-to-nation agreement, though
the First Nations were in a vastly weakened position with the
buffalo—essential to every aspect of their way of life—gone, and
disease having ravaged many of their people. The true motives
of the colonial powers were also less than explicit in the poorly
translated discussions. The signing of the treaty included more
than the three Blackfoot Nations—the Siksika (Blackfoot),
Kainai (Blood), and Piikani (Peigan)—and the representatives
of the Crown. Also present were the Stoney-Nakoda, including
the Goodstoney, Bearspaw, and Chiniki bands from nearer the
mountains, and the Tsuut'ina (Sarcee) from nearer Calgary
(Mohkinstsis). It isn't hard to imagine the camps of the people
gathered in the flats below, with the Blackfoot nations on the
south side of the river and the others on its north side.

I have checked out the Historical Park's website before
coming and noticed the name of its director, Jack Royal. If it is
the same person I am thinking of, I knew his parents when he
was a child. They were friends from Siksika who often stopped
in to visit in Calgary in the 1970s, sometimes spending the
night at my home. I also remember coming out to visit Jack's
grandmother, Alfreda Bearhat. She served a blend of black tea
steeped with wild mint collected in the river valley. She called
it by its Blackfoot name, áísiksikimi. I have tried to replicate it
since though with minimal success.

My thoughts are brought back to the present by the plaintive cry of Indigenous song that greets us on the sound system as we enter the building. The long walkway to the entrance has given us the sensation of entering another world and time. The singing and drumming alerts us further to another way another way of being, another way of seeing. Beyond the wall of windows ahead of us, the Bow River flows steadily towards far-off Hudson Bay. This far downstream from Calgary and its source in the mountains, the Bow has become a mighty river carving out a great valley in a wide floodplain. Below, is the spot in the river known as Blackfoot Crossing where for thousands of years, Indigenous people crossed as they journeyed along an ancient trail.

I ask the lady who takes our entrance fee if I can speak to Jack Royal. She hesitates, so I explain how I know him. She smiles and picks up the phone. A tall, confident man in his forties is soon striding across the foyer toward us. He breaks into a smile and extends his hand in welcome, greeting me by name. "You remember me?" I ask in surprise. "Of course. I used to love coming to your house."

He has not seen me since he was eight or nine years old. He invites my friend and me to join him for a cup of coffee in the cafeteria overlooking the valley. "You know this is the site of the signing of Treaty Seven," he says and points out the window. "And the University of Calgary's archeological dig of Mandan earth dwellings is on-going over there." We catch up on family and what's happened since those visits of long ago. I discover he helped coordinate efforts to rescue and house hundreds of Siksika residents during historic flooding in 2013. "It was basically an inland sea out there," he says, gesturing to the valley below.

So how did a white woman like me come to have friends among the Niitsitapi, the Blackfoot word meaning 'the real people'? The explanation has much to do with my membership in a young, little known, Faith community, the Bahá'í Faith, which numerous First Nations individuals also joined during the 1960s on the prairies. It seems they found in it a recognition and acceptance of their traditional spiritual beliefs, and the Bahá'ís they met treated them as friends and equals.

I enrolled in it for social justice reasons involving its central teachings about the oneness of mankind. I was relieved to hear it did not have a clergy, and that it viewed all the great spiritual traditions of the past as coming from the same sacred source. Some of the Indigenous people who became Bahá'ís possessed a spiritual perceptiveness that caused them to accept it through the guidance of their dreams. Some saw in it a path to a hopeful future in which all the 'tribes' would unite, and the Great Peace foretold in their prophecies would come to pass.

Back in 1970 when I arrived in Calgary as a university student, I was invited to join some of those early Bahá'ís at Siksika for a Feast. I caught a ride with a fellow white Bahá'í who knew the hosts, and we arrived on a mild spring evening. Walking towards our host's door, we could see off to one side, silhouetted against the glow of the setting sun, a gnarled cottonwood tree with pieces of fabric tied to its branches. Higher up, was the remnant of a platform fixed to its limbs. Even before my companion identified it as a 'burial tree', I felt my breath catch in unfamiliar awe. Here was the unknown, and I sensed I needed to walk quietly.

Before that day, I had never set foot on a First Nation. I had met a single Indigenous person once, just months earlier, beginning a journey in which I would encounter and interact with First Nations people in a variety of ways. Some would become close personal friends over time. Others, I visited with at pow-wows and picnics in the summertime. I must have discomfited some of them with exaggerated gestures of friendliness as I tried to demonstrate what a 'nice' person I was. There was much for me to both learn, and unlearn. After fifty years, I am still stunned at moments, by my ignorance of historical (and current) truths I encounter, and how drenched my own viewpoints can be in colonial thinking.

A large part of what has been most meaningful to me in this process, are the moments I have been able to get off my high (white) horse and cross the frontiers of my cultural conditioning, to connect with First Nations individuals and really learn something. I have had to step through unknown waters, rather like crossing the river at Blackfoot Crossing. There are rocks beneath the surface to stumble over, but it can be done.

In the summer of 2021, when news appeared that hundreds (soon it was thousands) of unmarked graves of children who had attended Turtle Island's notorious residential schools were being found, the reality of the experience for First Nations shook me to the core, and it did so in a whole new way. It seems to have shaken the consciousness of the nation as well.

The knowledge of such graveyards across the country focused my desire to understand the meaning of 'Truth and Reconciliation' in a new way. Accepting the truth of our collective history, is uncomfortable enough. Learning the truth of my own viewpoints and attitudes can at times be even more disconcerting. Reconciliation, or what will hopefully become an entirely new and generous way of relating on a collective level, is a condition I can only dimly conceive of. However, it may even be essential to our survival, and certainly to the flourishing of our nation.

'Blackfoot Crossing' has become my metaphor for continued learning and exploration. It reminds me there are new experiences to be had, and that my fears are the river that need to be crossed. Like at the spot along the Bow River on Siksika First Nation, I will look, pause, take a breath, and wade in, going someplace new.

Introduction

Treaty Seven Territory is an area which covers southern Alberta from the mountains in the west, extending eastward almost to the Saskatchewan border. It includes the cities of Calgary and Lethbridge, rural areas as far north as the Red Deer River, current First Nations, and it stretches as far south as the international border with the United States. Most people simply refer to the area as southern Alberta. I have used its treaty name because it recognizes both the colonial powers and the original inhabitants, and that what should have been sacred treaties, were once signed between them. In fact, the province of Alberta was only named 'Alberta' in 1905, almost thirty years after the 1877 signing of Treaty Seven.

The people I feature in this collection of life stories, are an assortment of individuals who became friends with one another as a result of their associations in the small Bahá'í Community that existed during in the 1950s and 60s. Some were First Nations individuals, others, settlers of European background. The notable exception to these two groups was a descendant of enslaved Africans, brought to North America against their will.

I met many of the individuals I write about, as a student after arriving in Calgary in the fall of 1970, participating in the Bahá'í community that existed at the time. I began collecting their stories in 2015. My intention at first, was to simply share the lives of remarkable individuals with the hope that their examples would be inspiring. I soon realized that their friendships with one another and their willingness to reach across the cultural divide between Indigenous and non-Indigenous people, was more significant than I had imagined.

In the summer of 2021, I was affected by almost daily by images of ground penetrating radar searching the grounds of former Residential schools for unmarked graves of children and hearing the number of 'anomalies' they were finding. These images were compounded by frequent instances of weeping aunties of missing or murdered Indigenous women and girls on the nightly news. Sometimes the weeping was for vulnerable young men or two-spirit youth. New, were splashes of red paint on church doors and a number of churches being burned to the ground. The pain and anger of a people was becoming unbearable.

I realized that what I was writing about, was more than just the stories of individuals who had channeled spiritual inspiration into real world friendships across barriers. I was writing my own response to these individuals and their stories, and documenting my learning journey about the experiences of Indigenous people in my country. I was deepening my understanding of the nation's need for truth and healing, 'reconciliation' being the commonly used term.

The individuals I write about had an unusual independence of thought. They remind me of the lone limber pines growing in scattered locations in the nearby landscape. My son and I discovered one of these pines in the Livingstone Range of southwestern Alberta several years ago. It stood so high above the rest of the forest and was so unusual in its configuration of branches, that

Limber pine near Piikani First Nation. photo source: Joan Young

my son slammed on the brakes and pulled over to get a better look. We marvelled that we had never seen one before, despite having spent our summers hiking and camping in the foothills and mountains.

Limber pines are found in the Rockies and foothills of southwestern Alberta (the northern end of their range) down through the United States and into Mexico. According to the 2014 report of the Committee on the Status of Endangered Wildlife in Canada, they are an endangered species. They are also a keystone species, having a disproportionately large effect on the living things around them. They are often quite solitary, sometimes fifty kilometers apart, not unlike the Bahá'ís in those years. The trees live to be very old—a few being documented to be as much as two thousand years of age. Longevity is not a characteristic they have in common with people, but it does make them exceptional, as were the Bahá'ís, though for other reasons.

In the years leading up to 2015, the hearings of the Truth and Reconciliation Commission conducted across Canada, gathered testimony from survivors of Canada's residential schools, testimony that could break the heart of any observer with a heart. It was the first knowledge I had of specific incidents of graphic abuse that the experience inflicted on Indigenous people. The Commission resulted in 94 Calls to Action on the part of Canada, very few of which have been acted upon at the time of writing. The hearings demonstrated how deliberate the destruction of family, culture and spirit was. It struck me that I was fortunate to have known and loved as many Indigenous people as I did.

My enrollment in the Bahá'í Faith as a first-year university student in Saskatoon, prior to moving back to Calgary, was my first opportunity to meet First Nations people. I had been looking for a movement which could make the world a better place. In addition, I was looking for meaning, and spiritual sustenance from some universal source. I could no longer stand the narrow, exclusionary view which had surrounded my childhood and youth, which insisted that only Christians went to heaven. I longed for something bigger, something… but I was not sure what. I saw an advertisement for a Bahá'í meeting in the university paper, so called to ask if I would be welcome. I attended and was astonished to find religious teachings that were this reasonable and inclusive. Upon hearing prayers at the end of the meeting which were written by the founder of the Faith, Bahá'u'lláh, I was flooded with a sense of recognition. I felt at home. On a deep personal level, I sensed I had found what I was looking for.

A month later, across the river at the Mendel Art Gallery, following a public information session by a group of youth, I asked if there was a way to join the Bahá'í Faith officially. A black-robed Catholic chaplain was sitting beside me, alarmed, and saying repeatedly, "You don't want to do this."

"I'm doing it," I said, signing the enrollment card. My first steps thereafter were to learn enough about the Faith to explain my decision to my parents—devout Mennonite farmers. I wanted to minimize the alarm I knew they would feel.

Enrolling as a Bahá'í was a turning point. It introduced me to a diversity of people I may otherwise never have met. The first of these was a Cree man named Thomas Asham, at a 'Feast' in Saskatoon. In time, I would encounter Persians, Africans, Asians, and Pacific Islanders.

As mentioned earlier, some of the individuals whose narratives I feature are from settler backgrounds, but many are from the Blackfoot Nations who live in the region. They were all active proponents of their Faith in the 1950s and 60s. They are the people I had the most direct knowledge of, and they inspired me to trace their footsteps into the past.

They are not a complete list of the people involved, nor do they represent a comprehensive history of the Bahá'í Faith in the province of Alberta. Many individuals from Edmonton and the northern part of the province played every bit as significant a role as those I feature. Other individuals who lived in the province played such significant roles on the national stage, that I simply could not do them justice. They each deserve a book of their own. Among them are Ed Muttart, Ted Anderson, Joanie Anderson, Ruth Eyford, Glen Eyford, and Ron Parsons.

How did this little known, and relatively young Faith, arrive in Alberta? The Bahá'í Faith was, and still is to a degree, a little-known religion which began in mid-nineteenth century Iran; teaching among other things, the fundamental oneness of the human family, the elimination of all forms of prejudice, and the principle that women and men are equals. It represented a radical departure from the commonly held beliefs and customs of the time and was viewed as a threat by Iran's clergy and government. Its founders, the Báb, and then Bahá'u'lláh, commanded that unusual power common to the Founders of all great religions, the power to inspire great love and devotion in the hearts of their followers. In a brief span of years, twenty thousand of its earliest adherents in Iran were killed by the most brutal means available to a fanatical clergy and mob.

But their Faith spread. The persecutions caught the attention of European scholars and diplomats whose travels had taken them to Iran. They were moved by the spectacles they witnessed and wrote extensively and sympathetically about them. Among these writers were the French diplomat Comte de Gobineau[1], the Cambridge orientalist Edward Granville Browne[2], and the British diplomat Lord Curzon[3]. By 1893, the teachings of the Bahá'í Faith were presented at the World Parliament of Religions in Chicago, and the first Americans became attracted to it.

It appears that the first known Bahá'í in Alberta, Esther Rennels, heard of the Faith in Chicago, and went on to live in Edmonton between 1911 and 1917[4]. Another lone Bahá'í, Mabel Pine, the first Bahá'í to live in Alberta for an extended

---

1   Gobineau, *Three Years in Asia*, 1859
2   Browne, *A Traveller's Narrative*, 1891
3   Curzon, *Persia and the Persian Question*, 1892
4   Will van den Hoonaard, *The Origins of the Bahá'í Community of Canada, 1898 – 1948*

period of time, heard of the Faith in the 1920s in British Columbia. She lived in various small Alberta towns and by 1941 settled in Edmonton where, with the help of individuals from Vancouver, began Bahá'í meetings in her home. Another Bahá'í woman from Vancouver, Doris Skinner, was the first to establish a group in Calgary beginning in 1939. Dorothy Sheets was the first local Calgarian to embrace the new Faith. Her niece and nephew, Betty Putters and Bob Burch, went on to become active, lifelong members of the Bahá'í community in the Edmonton area, and were known and loved throughout the province. Betty and Bob's mother, May Burch, and her sister, Lillian Arnette, also became Bahá'ís when they heard of it. A handful of other members of the Faith arrived in Calgary and Edmonton in the early 1940s, and the groups they established were not only maintained, but grew and continued to grow over time.

I am not an historian. I have attempted to give a fair and appreciative picture of the people I write about. I am an individual who loves stories, loves reading, and loves people. In my professional life, I was a teacher, more comfortable singing and playing piano, or organizing drama classes for young children than I was when writing research papers. I apologize for any errors that exist in my understanding of people and events, as well as for my limitations in style and delivery. The information I gathered was from a combination of interview visits with those who were still alive, interviews with their children and others who had known them, as well as published accounts about them. My own memory of people and places plays a role as well.

I am deeply grateful to the individuals who willingly shared their memories and materials with me. Bev Knowlton and Dale Lillico stand out among them. Amy Singh was also most generous in her research and sent me extensive diary notes and letters from that time.

I was gratified and confirmed in my understandings when multiple accounts coincided. There are instances where my only source of knowledge was my own memory and I recognize how faulty that can be. I have done my best to be both truthful and kindly—without distorting people's natures. They were not saints. They were abundantly human; humans with a love for the Divine and a desire to serve their fellow man.

Note about terms and changing usage regarding Indigenous people

It must be noted that terms for Indigenous people have evolved over time. Old terms have now come to sound disrespectful, sometimes to an extreme degree, depending on how they are used and who is using them. Bob Joseph from Gwawaenuk Nation, founder of Indigenous Corporate Training Inc., and a former associate professor at Royal Roads University, gives clarification. A UBC website, *https:// Indigenousfoundations.arts.ubc.ca/terminology/* gives similar clarification:

◊ The term 'Aboriginal Peoples' was used in Canada's 1982 Constitution act, so will have an on-going use in legal terms. However, individuals should not be referred to as 'an Aboriginal'.

◊ 'Indian' is also still an identifier of someone who is registered under the Indian Act but should not generally be used by non-Indigenous people to refer to them.

◊ 'Indigenous' is now the acceptable term to refer to descendants of all original inhabitants of the land—First Nations, Metis and Inuit.

◊ Most Indigenous people prefer the use of 'First Nations' if they are not Metis or Inuit. However, First Nations communities in Ontario often prefer to be referred to as 'Indigenous Peoples'.

◊ The term 'Native' is still used at times by Indigenous people themselves and in organization's names, but that doesn't give others license to use it indiscriminately. (Generally, the term 'Indigenous' is now preferrable).

I have tried to use current and respectful terminology. However, when I quote sources from decades ago, I've left the terms used then, as they were. That includes the names of places which have changed.

1   Dale Lillico

In *Geography of Blood*, Saskatchewan author, Candace Savage, looks out over the landscape from the Cypress Hills and says,

> *"Somewhere over there, in the white haze and distance, earth and heaven collide..."*

I have been driving southward, along the Porcupine Hills of southwestern Alberta, on Cowboy Trail. Like the Cypress Hills on the Saskatchewan border with Alberta, the Porcupine Hills rise above the prairie, untouched by the last Ice Age. I observe

Porcupine Hills near Highway 3. Photo source: Joan Young.

them on my left while the Livingstone Range, an unbroken
wall of mountain stretching for almost one hundred kilometers,
towers on my right. I look south, past Piikani First Nation to
the mountains beyond. Chief Mountain, sacred to the Blackfoot
People, lies on the other side of the Canada/US border. Rising
heat waves in the late summer sun make it seem entirely possible
that the souls of those who once lived in the area, are hovering
nearby. Do 'earth and heaven collide' here too? Or do they merely
blur and quiver in afternoon updrafts where eagles soar?

I'm on my way to visit Dale Lillico on her ranch which lies
in the shadow of these hills at their southern end. The hills are
their usual bleached golden brown, crowned with a sprinkling
of deep green pines near the top. Outcroppings of sedimentary
rock, remnants of an ancient sea, protrude here and there.
The more famous of these stone bluffs lie just a few miles east
at Head Smashed in Buffalo Jump,[5] where there is now an

*Southern end of the Porcupine Hills—view to the west of Lillico's ranch
house. Photo source: Joan Young.*

---

5   A UNESCO designated world heritage site, with an Interpretive Center
built into the cliff once used by the plains people to drive the buffalo
over.

                                                                 Dale Lillico

Interpretive Centre depicting the use of the cliffs in the buffalo hunts of a bygone era. The scent of sage and prairie grasses on the breeze, greet me as I get out of the car. Dale opens the door of her home and waves me in.

She has lived on this ranch, next to Piikani First Nation (formerly known as the Peigan Reserve) for sixty years, arriving in the area in 1959 to take a job at the Indian Agent's office. The way she came to hear of that job is a story of its own, which I will share in a bit. I want to ask Dale about the people on the reserve who she got to know so well in the 1950s and sixties, some of whom also became members of the Bahá'í Faith. This Faith is the strand that connects me both to Dale and people at Piikani.

I cannot remember when I first met Dale. Over the years we attended the same regional Bahá'í gatherings, but lived several hours' drive apart so we did not see one another often. When I began collecting stories about early Bahá'ís in the region, I called Dale and asked if I could visit. She was one of a handful of individuals still alive who had been part of the Bahá'í community's activities as early as the 1950s. Not only did she agree to a visit with me, she insisted I stay for a few days. It marked the beginning of a friendship which became increasingly precious to me. Over the next number of years, I made the trip down to her home many times. The crunching sound of gravel under my tires, the silhouette of a particular hill where I needed to turn left, the sight of an abandoned farmhouse near an intersection, and the position of colossal white wind turbines on the landscape became welcome and familiar landmarks on my journey.

I loved being at her home, taking walks outdoors and letting the unceasing winds that come rushing through the Crowsnest Pass from the Pacific Ocean blow over me. On occasion, the winds were so strong I would have to go back indoors. There were many things I wanted to understand, in talking to Dale. What made her, a seemingly ordinary farm girl from Saskatchewan, question the mainstream beliefs of her time and her family, and join another religion? How did she encounter that religion? Who were the people she became such good friends with on Piikani First Nation? And how was it that so many of her fellow religionists established enduring friendships across the cultural divide between First Nations and settler people?

Following breakfast on the first morning I was there, she spoke about her childhood concerns arising out of her Catholic Faith. Why, exactly, was Martin Clancy's grave conspicuously outside the cemetery fence of her community's small rural graveyard? What had he done? Would God really condemn some people throughout eternity? People who had done something perhaps only mildly wrong, or who hadn't 'accepted Jesus as their Savior'? As a young woman Dale said she was aware of the Bible verse in which Christ said, "No man cometh to the Father but through me."

In questioning Bahá'ís on the matter, she discovered that from their point of view, the 'Me' Christ was referring to was His divine nature as a Manifestation or Messenger of God. And that this same divine nature was present in other Messengers of God in other times and other places. God had not left massive parts of the planet without guidance over the millennia. It was a concept the Bahá'ís called 'progressive revelation', that God has, over the ages, progressively provided humanity with spiritual guidance in the form of 'Manifestations'—human, but divinely inspired teachers. Their guidance changed over time in terms of its social teachings—such what kind of meat should, or should, not be eaten— as humanity's needs changed and evolved. But the spiritual essentials in all the religions remained the same; acknowledgement of the Creator and the Golden Rule being at the heart of them all.

Dale's first encounter with these teachings was in Montreal, where she had gone with a friend, also from Saskatchewan, intending to become a nun. Within a short time, she realized convent life was never going to be right for her, so she left to find work. Years later, as I sat at her kitchen table with her, she opened a photo album, and flipping through the pages, she pointed to a small, square, black and white photograph of her young self in a novice nun's habit. It was hard to imagine. I had only known her as a hard-working farm wife who lived near Pincher Creek, next to Piikani First Nation for over sixty years; the mom of two boys, a school board trustee, a dear friend of the people on the reserve, a community supporter, volunteer, and a Baháʼí whose smiling face I saw at regional meetings.

From the Lillico's sunroom windows, the view to the east was unobstructed. Morning sunlight flooded the room, and I observed cattle ambling along the creek below with the occasional calf trotting to catch up to its mother. Two tall wind turbines stood just south of the house, and beyond them, a clear view of Chief Mountain was visible on the horizon.

Dale explained that one day back in the 1950s at her job in Montreal, she surprised even herself, by accepting free tickets to the 1956 Grey Cup football game in Toronto. She did not even like football much. On board the flight, she started talking to a fellow passenger, a young man named Bill Carr, who told her he was a 'pioneer' for the Baháʼí Faith in Greenland.[6] It was the first she'd heard of the Baháʼí Faith—understandably—given it was only first mentioned on the North American continent sixty years earlier.

Bill and Dale stayed in touch, and through Bill, Dale met the Baháʼís in Montreal and began attending 'firesides'[7] in

---

6   The term 'pioneer' refers to individuals who move to a location where there are typically no resident Baháʼís, hoping to introduce their Faith to people there.

7   'Firesides' are the informal meetings, usually held in Baháʼí homes, for the purpose of introducing the teachings of the Faith to inquirers.

the Maxwell home, later designated a Bahá'í Shrine[8]. She recalls washing dishes there one evening with her friend, Pam (Hutchins) Sherwin, after refreshments had been served. Pam asked her how she felt about the teachings of 'this Faith'. Dale explained her feelings of attraction to it. Pam turned to her and said, "Well, if that's how you feel, why don't you become a Bahá'í?" At the time, Pam was not yet a member either.[9]

Dale enrolled that evening, October 16th, 1957. Weeks after her decision, her brother was killed in a car accident back in Saskatchewan. Within days of his death, the Guardian of the Bahá'í Faith[10], its much loved and distinguished leader, so relied on by Bahá'í's all over the world, also passed away while visiting London in the United Kingdom. Unable to make it home for her brother's funeral and weighed down by worry and grief, she became fearful she had made a mistake in 'joining something'.

She wrote her friend, Bill Carr, expressing her concerns. He replied sending her excerpts from the Bahá'í Writings about the life of the soul after death. He also sent prayers meant especially for the progress of a loved one's soul, after death. The prayers, along with the presence and support of two kindly new room mates who were also Bahá'ís, Beaulah Proctor and Dorothy Walsch, helped her come to terms with her fears. Not long after this, she returned west to work in Calgary and was soon spending many of her Sundays visiting people at Piikani First

---

8   The Maxwell home on Pine Avenue in Montreal hosted 'Abdu'l-Bahá during His visit to North America in 1912. He was the much-loved Head of the Bahá'í Faith following the passing of its founder, Bahá'u'lláh, His father. He referred to this house, 1548 Pine Ave in Montreal, as 'my home'. It is now the only Bahá'í shrine in the western hemisphere.

9   Pam and David Sherwin were stalwart members of the Bahá'í Community of Red Deer for many years. They remained friends with Dale and her husband and David has been their frequent visitor since his wife's passing in 2012.

10 The 'Guardian', Shoghi Effendi Rabbaní, was the third and last individual head of the worldwide Bahá'í community. He was appointed by his grandfather, 'Abdu'l-Bahá, and guided the fledgling community through its formative stage in which it established its elected administrative bodies (both local and national) throughout the world and built up its World Centre in Haifa, Israel.

                                        Dale Lillico

Nation (then still known as Peigan), two hours drive to the south. Her Bahá'í friends, Arthur and Lily Ann Irwin, invited her to come along with them. Their story appears in the next chapter.

Little did Dale know at the time, how significant these visits would become in affecting the course of her life. In her handwritten account, *History of the Bahá'í Faith/ Peigan Reserve/ Years 1958- 1995*, she writes[11],

> *"In 1958 I paid my first visit to the Peigan Indian Reserve in southern Alberta… It was during one of these visits early in spring, while they were showing slides at the hall, that Alfreda Knowlton, who lived on the Reserve and was sitting with me, suggested I move to Peigan permanently. She said there was a job opening at the Agency Office so I went over to see the agent, Harold Woodsworth. After a brief discussion with him that night, I applied to Indian Affairs in Calgary the next day… In June of 1959, I moved to Peigan with my few belongings in a small U-Haul trailer."*

Dale Olivier circa 1959, Richard Stanton photo, Copyright National Spiritual Assembly of the Bahá'ís of Canada, courtesy Canadian Bahá'í Archives

11   See Appendix A

She recalls that the Indian Agent had been irritable when she
knocked on his door that evening. Alfeda had shown her the
light on his house in the distance and in a moment of faith—or
foolishness—she was not quite sure which, she walked there, a
young white woman, alone at night, in a dress and heels. "You
did?" I asked.

She replied that it really wasn't dangerous back then.
Alcohol, drugs, and gangs were not yet a problem, though
roaming dogs could be. Pauline Yellowhorn, the daughter of the
last hereditary chief at Piikani, was also asking Dale questions
during one of my visits, for her book on Piikani's history. When
she asked about Dale's arrival on the reserve, Dale answered, "I
came to the Reserve on June 22, 1959, in a big rainstorm. I got
stuck in the driveway to the steps of the clerks' residence…"

Within a few years Dale married local rancher, Bill Lillico,
and moved adjacent to the reserve, where she has lived ever
since—though at the time of writing, she and her husband, Bill,
had built a house in the nearby town of Pincher Creek for their
retirement. She has seen her many friends in the area through
births, deaths, and illness.

When I was visiting in February of 2016, a call came
informing her of the death of an adult grandson of Piikani
friends, Clarence and Alfreda Knowlton[12]. Her immediate
offers of assistance spoke of the lasting connections between
her and people on the reserve. Reflecting on some of her early
friendships, she said,

*"Back when I worked in the Indian Agent's office, I often
saw a little hand slipping me a note saying, 'Come for
lunch.' It was June David-Yellowhorn's little son*[13] *passing it*

---

12 Clarence was an accomplished country and western singer and guitar
player who had grown up on Piikani. In mid-life he also began violin
lessons in Lethbridge. He was missing parts of a couple of fingers, and
his instructor doubted he would ever be able to play, but he persisted
and played the instrument well. He and his band played for many public
occasions. Alfreda, his wife, also played guitar. The couple were central
to Bahá'í activities on the Reserve for many years.

13 David-Yellowhorn is a hyphenated last name.

                                                    Dale Lillico

Alfreda Knowlton, Clarence Knowlton, Dale Lillico. Photo source: Dale Lillico

to me. He was still too small for me to see his head over the counter. I loved getting these invitations."

She also recalled walking across the highway and down the dirt road into the Oldman River valley to the area known as Highbush, for meetings in the homes of the Bahá'ís who lived there. If the meetings were at Samson and Rosie Knowlton's, she had to pass the Holloway's whose dogs were ferocious barkers. She was grateful to see fellow Bahá'í, Guy Yellow Wings, invariably waiting for her at the top of the hill, happy to accompany her to the meeting.

I spent a sunny August day at Piikani Nation Pow Wow and Rodeo a few years ago, with Dale and my Calgary friend, Donna Coey. The two women and I were among the few white people in attendance, among possibly a thousand participants. Donna and I were amazed and delighted at the friendliness and courtesy of every person we met, even when Dale—who knew so many local people—wasn't with us. It began at the entrance gate where we were asked if we were seniors. We said we were and offered to pay the ten-dollar per person entrance fee. We were told, "We don't take money from Elders. Go on in. Have a good day."

First Peigan Local Spiritual Assembly 1961. Standing l to r: Sam Yellowface, Ben White Cow, Joyce McGuffie, Dale Olivier (Lillico), Guy Yellow Wings, Samson Knowlton. Seated: Louise White Cow, Charlie Strikes With a Gun, Rosie Knowlton. Photo source: Dale Lillico.

A slight cloud of dust was rising from the dirt road that led to the powwow and rodeo as a steady stream of vehicles drove in. Dry grass and dust mingled with the smell of impatient horses, waiting for action. Some of the horses were relay horses for the newly reintroduced 'Indian Relay Racing' events, a spectator sport more exciting than any I have witnessed. Others were rodeo horses.

Relay racing consists of five teams of four horses, each team with a jockey who races bareback around a one-kilometre track.

Dale Lillico

In front of the stands, the jockey has to leap onto the next of four mounts for another lap, while horses are still moving. The horses have brightly painted designs on their hind quarters, and the rider's uniforms identifying their team, are intensely colorful. The jockey's teammates stay in front of the crowd in the stands, hanging onto the team's remaining three horses, waiting for the changeover to the next lap. The action is almost too thrilling to bear. My heart was in my throat most of the time, and my friends and I gripped one another's hands when minor injuries occurred directly in front of us.

When we left the grandstand and made our way to the large, round pavilion with a red roof, built to accommodate crowds of spectators watching powwow dances, numerous people approached Dale to speak to her. She knew many people from Piikani, though there were also hundreds of visitors from other First Nations around the continent present. Elderly Piikani neighbors who had also been ranchers near the Lillicos, stopped for a long chat. A man she had known many years earlier, a

Piikani ranchers the McDougalls with Dale Lillio at the 2019 powwow. Photo source: Joan Young.

Bev Knowlton and Dale Lillico circa 1985. Photo source: Dale Lillico.

highly regarded local cowboy now employed by some of the
biggest cattle companies in the area, stopped to swap stories. A
key organizer of the event greeted her as a dear old friend when
she entered the pavilion and made a point of letting me know
how long the connection between them had been.

When answering more of Pauline Yellowhorn's questions
about her early relations with local people, Dale said,

> *"…there were moments when, as I think back on it, I
> believe the Agent was actively trying to discourage me
> from my personal friendship with Peigan individuals. It
> was something I had to struggle with but couldn't do much
> about—other than to maintain the relationships that I had,
> despite his apparent disapproval."*

Further to that, there were times she recalls the Agent
asking her to come along to the most impoverished homes
on the Reserve, for no other purpose that she could see, than
to discourage her from personal contact with the people.
Her respect for the inherent dignity of the people and her
appreciation of Piikani culture, is evident in her comment:

"The summer of 1959 was so exciting, as I was able to attend my first pow-wow... When I went back to my apartment, I kept my windows open to be able to hear the drumming. In 1960, my second year on the Reserve, I asked Mrs. Suzie Smith if she could make me a jacket and moccasins... and I wore these to the upcoming pow wow. Chief John Yellowhorn and Councillor Pat Bad Eagle led me to the ring for my first dance... they were very gracious and danced with me around the circle. I was so proud to have my first dance with them..."

Pat Bad Eagle, Dale Olivier (Lillico) and John Yellowhorn at circa 1960 pipe ceremony for Dale.

She concluded her comments about her life on the Reserve for Pauline saying,

"My experiences over many years with the people of Piikani, have enriched my life immensely. I am forever grateful to them for their friendship, and grateful to the Creator who brought us together in this beautiful land."

I am aware that this sense of gratitude was reciprocated by people from the reserve for the genuine friendship she showed them. Among the honours the people of Piikani bestowed on Dale were the name-giving ceremonies for each of her two sons. There were others as well.

When much-respected early Bahá'í and Band Councillor, Samson Knowlton[14] was dying in 1985, his family members noted it was Dale Lillico who came daily to check on him and offer what help she could to him and his devoted grandson, Troy (currently the elected Chief), who was staying with him and looking after him. Knowlton's youngest daughter also

Dale Lillico and Margaret Plain Eagle 2017 Bicentennial Celebration of the Birth of the Báb held in Brocket. Photo source: Joan Young.

---

14   See Chapter 3 re: Samson and Rosie Knowlton

                                          Dale Lillico

recalls being a child, and Dale arriving at the house to make tomato soup for her family members who were sick. She said it was a particularly fond memory, one that still makes her like tomato soup.

Dale's life is intimately connected with many of the people who appear in the following chapters. She has been a wealth of information about them and has corrected me on numerous misunderstandings which I had. She became a dear friend to me in the process—the kind of person I wanted to spend as much time as possible with. Her irrepressible warmth and good will, binds me to her, as it does so many people at Piikani.

2   Arthur and Lily Ann Irwin

One summer during the 1980s, I saw Arthur Irwin who was almost eighty years of age, roar up the driveway of the Sylvan Lake Baháʼí Center on his motorcycle. "That's Arthur Irwin," whispered a woman beside me, as if she were seeing a legend.

I had heard of Arthur before, his name often coming up in the context of relations with First Nations people. He and his wife, Lily Ann, were well known for being the first in the Baháʼí community in Alberta to have sustained relationships with First Nations individuals, and for gaining permission to visit reserves as Baháʼís. The friendships they formed paved the way for many others, indeed future generations including myself, to spend time with people there. It provided us the opportunity to realize that not only did we have something to share, but that we had much to learn.

What we needed to learn from the original inhabitants of the land was vast. It included a sense of wonder, a more profound connection to our Creator, a new appreciation of Nature, and—if we were humble enough—we also learned about our ingrained sense of superiority and the privileges our white skin afforded us. For that dawning awareness, we owe a profound sense of gratitude to not only our First Nations friends, but to the Irwins who introduced us to them.

Arthur and Lily Ann's openness to reaching across the cultural divide and cross social barriers that existed between settlers of European descent and First Nations people in the

1950s, was exceptional. What was it that motivated them? As
I sifted through fragments of their story left behind, I came to
believe they were inspired to act in the service of the central
principle of their Faith; the Oneness of Mankind. They were not
missionaries. They had no financial support from their Faith
community and did not live among the people who they were
teaching their faith to. Their Faith forbade proselytizing, but
encouraged respectfully sharing.

What they did was visit back and forth with regularity,
between their life in the city and the First Nations communities.
It appears they had a vision of a future in which a remarkable
transformation of society could—and would—occur. This
vision was directly informed by a statement sent to the
North American Bahá'ís during World War I by the Head of
their Faith, 'Abdu'l-Bahá. It was He who led the community
following his Father's passing in 1892. The statement said,

*"Attach great importance to the Indigenous population
of America… should they be educated and guided, there
can be no doubt that they will become so illumined as to
enlighten the whole world."*

This statement became a driving motivation for the Irwins
and focused their extraordinary expenditure of time and
energy. Their respect for the people they met was evident
in personal relationships, as well as in their participation in
traditional ceremonies which they were invited to attend.
Several Bahá'ís who knew them during the 1960s—among them
David Sherwin, Catharina Ankersmit, and Dale Lillico—have
told me about attending Sundance and other sacred ceremonies
with the Irwins, who had been invited by the people in charge.
Years later, in taped interviews with Ted Anderson, Lily Ann
referred to the ceremonies they had attended with reverence
and awe.

The message of unity that Arthur and Lily Ann wanted to
share, was rooted in the belief that Bahá'u'lláh's Revelation—so

     Arthur and Lily Ann Irwin

recent and so little known—was an instrument of such spiritual potency that it could, over time, bring mankind together in the great Age of Peace foreseen in so many of the world's religious prophecies. It recognized and respected the truths in the traditional spiritual teachings of the Indigenous people, just as it recognized the fundamental truths of other religions.

But who were Arthur and Lily Ann as individuals? What influences formed them and made them who they were? A few years ago, while going through old photos at Dale Lillico's house, I came across a picture of Arthur and Lily Ann at an apparent anniversary event. I asked what the occasion was and to my surprise, she said it was their 50th wedding anniversary. I was bewildered because I knew they had divorced at some point. Many marriages dissolve, but few last fifty years and then fail.

Arthur and Lily Ann Irwin's 50th wedding anniversary. Photo source: Dale Lillico.

I have no idea what their marital difficulties were. The fact that their marriage ended when it did, near the age of eighty, may simply speak to the fact that even people who have accomplished heroic deeds of service can also, and at the same time, possess personal difficulties. Their daughter's friend from the 1960s, related that even in her youth, the Irwin's daughter felt her parents' marriage likely would not last after she and her brother left home, though it did continue for several more decades.

It may be helpful to look at their early lives to gain a clearer view of each of them. Arthur's father was a Theosophist whom Lily Ann said she enjoyed conversing with. His mother,

a Christian Scientist, initially disapproved of Lily Ann as
Arthur's choice for a wife. According to Lily Ann, Arthur's
mother had hoped he would choose someone of her faith as
a mate. Unfortunately, Arthur does not address his personal
life to any extent in the primary source of information I have
about him; his written account of the couple's Bahá'í activities
entitled, *Early Native Teaching in Canada*[15], and most of his
contemporaries are no longer alive.

Lily Ann, on the other hand, spoke extensively about
her early life in a set of taped audio interviews made by Ted
Anderson in 1993. She said she was born in 1913 in a small
Saskatchewan community between North Battleford and Prince
Albert, the daughter of 'White Russian' immigrants. She tells
Ted that her family was desperately poor and that they lived
on a homestead. They were, according to her, kindly people
who instilled the principle of treating all people with respect,
regardless of background.

It was while speaking about her parents that first I noticed
her desire to shed the best possible light on people and events.
There were times she would share a comment that was later
contradicted in a another (larger) narrative she was giving.
A much more painful picture would emerge. For example,
after stressing how kindly and hospitable her parents were to
strangers passing through the area, she mentioned her father's
periodic drinking binges saying, "He went wild at these times,
and it affected him for another month."

By the time she was twelve and a half, first her father and
then her mother died. She was essentially left on her own,
though she had a few older siblings, one of whom gave her
a place to stay for a short time. Lily Ann then moved to
Saskatoon and began looking for work as a domestic, to get
free room and board. To her dismay, she had to Anglicize her

---

15 *Early Native Teaching in Canada* has been included in its entirety in
    Appendix B. It is Arthur's full account of the efforts they made to
    promote their Faith.

                                    Arthur and Lily Ann Irwin

Russian family name, Buzovetsky, to Busby, to get employment. In addition, the first home she worked in was a troubled one; the mother having been diagnosed with schizophrenia and the children volatile and difficult to care for. Lily Ann made great effort to continue her schooling while working there but the arrangement ended with Lily Ann being unfairly accused of threatening to kill the children when some sudden incident occurred while she was working in the kitchen, and she was seen to have been holding a knife at the time. I am struck by how traumatic these experiences must have been, and feel compassion for how they affected her throughout life.

She found the Baháí Faith in Vancouver as a young woman in her early twenties, hearing of it from Stan and Eve Kemp who were friends of her employer. She had held numerous practical nursing jobs by this time, and seemed to find that the work of caring for people like her employer, filled a deep personal need. Her comments indicated that she needed to help people and provide them with what her own life had so painfully lacked— tender affection and care. She said that reading the Bible had been a solace to her as a young person, and that she had already developed a feeling that 'Christ had returned'. In light of that feeling, she was intensely interested in what the Kemps had to say about how Bahá'u'lláh's appearance fulfilled Christian prophecy—and how it also fulfilled prophecies of other Faiths at the same time. This, she soon realized, was a profoundly symbolic fulfillment—though there were parallels in the physical realm as well[16].

She was almost thirty when she met Arthur. He was in the Canadian military at the time; about to be deployed as World War II ended in 1945. Lily Ann speaks of a brief but pleasant time following their marriage living in their first home at Cultus Lake in the Fraser Valley, before being transferred to

---

16 *Promises Fulfilled: Christianity, Islam, and the Bahá'í Faith* by Nabil Hanna (available on Amazon) is one of numerous books connecting prophecies to fulfillment.

Vernon. Arthur had enrolled as a Bahá'í shortly after their marriage, and their move to Vernon was rewarded by their association with the much-loved Austin Collin, who welcomed them and was instrumental in providing their first real experience of Bahá'í community. In fact, Lily Ann described her life as being transformed by association with him and the Bahá'ís there, saying she had long needed a sense of close and supportive community. Her statement, "I felt I needed to belong to a group. I was always alone," seems deeply reflective of her difficult youth.

From Vernon, Arthur and Lily Ann moved to Montreal to further Arthur's university studies and then to Yellowknife in 1950 where he was employed as a geologist. Arthur describes the move to Yellowknife as being made in response to a goal of the newly formed National Spiritual Assembly of the Bahá'ís of Canada, to seek out and include Indigenous Canadians in membership and institutions of the Faith. For the Irwins, it launched decades of concerted learning and effort. In his written account of their Bahá'í activity over the years Arthur says, "We focused our minds on reaching the Indians. However, we were timid and we did not seem able to communicate the teachings to the natives…"[17]

His efforts to promote the Faith in Yellowknife included a volunteer weekly radio program aimed largely at the First Nations population. That effort did not sound 'timid' to me, but his comment that they had difficulty communicating the Teachings to their intended audience is notable. He said that if anything, the program resulted in a certain amount of resentment among his white, middle-class associates. Only one individual joined the Faith while the Irwins lived in the north; Fran (Bachynski) Mclean[18], a young white woman from

---

17 These were commonly used terms for First Nations people in those years. They did not sound as disrespectful as they do now—at least to non-Indigenous observers.

18 Fran Mclean went on to become an ardent supporter of the Bahá'í Faith in Canada, spending much of her life in Nova Scotia.

                                   Arthur and Lily Ann Irwin

Winnipeg who heard of it before arriving in Yellowknife. Despite the initially discouraging results, within just a few years and two more moves, Arthur and Lily Ann would become instrumental in befriending large numbers of First Nations people and attracting them to the Bahá'í Faith in southern Alberta.

They moved to Edmonton for a few years in 1953, and spent time serving on a national Bahá'í committee compiling information about various First Nations, keeping in touch with Bahá'ís who were making efforts to befriend them, arranging translations of Bahá'í Prayers into the Blackfoot and Mohawk languages, and creating pamphlets suited to Indigenous people. The nascent Canadian Bahá'í community in the early 1950s was almost entirely white, and its less than five hundred members were scattered across the country. Among its members were only three Indigenous individuals: Jim and Melba Loft of the Tyendinaga Reserve in Ontario, and the artist, Noel Wuttunee, from the Red Pheasant Reserve in Saskatchewan—then living in Calgary. However, the make-up of the Canadian Bahá'í community was about to change dramatically.

When the Irwins moved to Calgary in 1956, Arthur began a new job managing the petroleum and mining resources of reserves in western Canada. The work involved meeting people on the reserves as well as Band Chiefs and Councillors. On one of his early trips to Piikani in south-western Alberta, Arthur met Allan Prairie Chicken, a local guide assigned to lead him to a reported petroleum seep. Allan became interested in Arthur's religion and soon introduced him to friends and relatives. In the autumn of 1956, prayer meetings which became 'firesides'[19] began at Allan's home and continued once or twice a month, which the Irwins drove down to speak at.

What was it that appealed to the people they met? The teachings of the oneness of mankind, and eliminating of all forms of prejudice, must have been part of it but perhaps

---

19 Firesides are informal gatherings often held in homes, where Bahá'ís share information on the teachings of their Faith with others.

more profoundly, it was the genuine friendliness of the Irwins. Bev Knowlton, daughter of outstanding early Piikani Bahá'ís, Samson and Rosie Knowlton, recalls her mother saying, "The white Baháís would visit in our homes. They became friends. Most white people wouldn't come to our homes. The Bahá'ís were so loving and accepted us the way we lived." This willingness to associate made a remarkable difference.

In Lily Ann's interview with Ted Anderson, she tells the story of two highly respected First Nations leaders visiting her home in Calgary in the late 1950s; a visit that sheds light on their assessment of the Irwins and on their Faith as well. She describes Pat Bad Eagle of Piikani, and Rufus Goodstriker of Kainai, as 'two tall men of striking appearance' arriving at her door asking if they could come in and sit in her house for an hour. They did not want tea or talk, just to sit. Slightly baffled, she invited them in and sat with them, fighting the urge to do something 'useful' while sitting. At the end of the hour, Pat stood up and said, "It's like this, I feel with my heart, and I think with my mind, and then I know it's true." He seemed to be affirming that the spirit animating the Bahá'ís was 'true', and that he was now assured. It should be noted that there had been complaints from the churches[20] about Bahá'í teaching activities on the reserves, and the two men had taken it upon themselves to ascertain 'truth'.

It was during the Irwins' time in Calgary that a teenage girl from Piikani was brought to their home by individuals from the reserve who Lily Ann says, "…rescued her from the attic of the Residential School where she was being kept hostage by the nuns"[21]. In Lily Ann's audio interview with Ted Anderson, she did not explain this further, but went on to express satisfaction

---

20 These were Christian churches of various denominations. The Bahá'í Faith refers to groups of believers as 'communities', not 'churches'. In some parts of the world where there are large numbers of Bahá'ís, a 'House of Worship' may be built but it is also not referred to as a 'church'.

21 I have since heard snippets of this account from people on the reserve, who did not describe her as being 'captive' in such dramatic terms.

                                    Arthur and Lily Ann Irwin

at having been able to help the girl by welcoming her into their Calgary home and helping her get into Nurse's Aide training. When she returned south, she was hired at the Pincher Creek Hospital. I asked Dale Lillico if she knew the name of the girl that Lily Ann was referring to on the tape recording. To my delight, Dale replied, "Annabelle Buffalo!"

I met Annabelle in 2018 at a gathering on the Reserve. She was a lovely person with a calm, kindly presence, the kind of woman I wanted to sit beside and feel her warmth and spirit. She is shown in a photo my daughter took that day, seated third from left. I was saddened to hear that in late 2020, she succumbed to Covid19.

L to R: Eleanora McDermott, Joan Young, Annabelle Buffalo, Nancy Big Weasel, Dayle Holloway, Antoaneta Moga. Photo source: Dermai Young.

Further to the visits of the Irwins back in the late 1950s, Arthur says,

"Starting in late 1956 and continuing through until well after the first Assembly[22] was formed at Ridván of 1961, we journeyed from Calgary to the Peigan Reserve and returned, on a Sunday, once or twice each month… Pickups at various homes on the reserve would often take two hours. Then the gatherings for prayers, readings, talks and discussions would last until late afternoon. Then we would rush home for our Sunday evening fireside in Calgary…"

The rewards for these efforts must have been, in part, the warmth of response from the people they encountered. Arthur wrote, "We are convinced that we learned more from the Peigan Indian people about spiritual matters, such as attitude toward prayer, respect for each other, the importance of silence, and the tenacity of their faith, than they learned from us. We served only as postmen—to bring the Message [of Bahá'u'lláh] to them."

I find myself marveling at the sustained effort of Arthur and Lily Ann to step out of familiar white society and spend so much time with First Nations people. There were many barriers to doing so in the 1960s. I also marvel at the courage and initiative required of Lily Ann to drive out to a reserve alone on occasion, to meet a Chief to request permission for further visits.

Arthur credits the Guardian with providing them guidance and encouragement in their efforts.

"Lily Ann and I were privileged to receive guidance from our beloved Guardian, Shoghi Effendi. Without it I doubt we would have been the instruments for achieving the teaching successes that we were…"

---

22 An 'Assembly' is the annually elected body for the administering of the affairs of a Bahá'í community in a given locality. It can be formed when there is a minimum of nine resident members over the age of 21.

                                    Arthur and Lily Ann Irwin

Indeed, Lily Ann wrote the Guardian for guidance and confirmation on all significant moves and decisions they made as a couple[23]. Despite the extraordinary demands on his time, he always replied through a secretary with encouraging and appreciative postscripts added in his own handwriting.

Arthur soon realized that most of the people he was meeting would not be able to meet the requirements for enrollment in the Baháʼí Faith in Canada at that time. The requirements included having read three Baháʼí books—which are written in beautiful but advanced English—after which an elected Assembly questioned individuals on their understanding of what they had read. The education received by Indigenous people at residential schools rarely prepared them to become skilled in reading and writing English. It was Hand of the Cause, John Robarts[24], who took the initiative with the National Spiritual Assembly to change the policy to a simplified process that merely ascertained that individuals understood the essential aspects of what they were joining.

In March 1958, Allan and Maggie Prairie Chicken enrolled as members of the Baháʼí Faith, the first to do so. Additional enrollments followed, including Samson and Rosie Knowlton, Ben and Louise White Cow, and Sam and Agnes Yellow Face. When distinguished guest, Rúhíyyih Khánum,[25] visited the Reserve in 1960, more individuals became Baháʼís, among them Elder Charlie Crow Eagle and his wife, Alice.

Rúhíyyih Khánum's 1960 visit was the first of three visits she made to Piikani. She was driven down from Calgary by the Irwins for the occasion and was honored with a name-giving ceremony by Charlie Crow Eagle, Band Councillor. The

---

23 See Appendix C for responses from the Guardian and Rúhíyyih Khánum.
24 John Robarts was the much-loved Canadian Baháʼí appointed to the station of 'Hand of the Cause of God' by the Head of the Baháʼí Faith at that time, Shoghi Effendi. The 'Hands' were appointed with responsibilities to protect and propagate the Baháí Faith.
25 See Chapter 7 for a more complete story of Rúhíyyih Khánum's visit to Peigan. She was a distinguished Baháʼí also from Canada, and was the widow of Shoghi Effendi, the Guardian of the Baháʼí Faith.

Charlie and Alice Crow Eagle (date unknown) Photo source: Dale Lillico.

Front row l to r:: Lily Ann Irwin, Agnes Yellowface, Louise White Cow, Maggie Prairie Chicken, Rosie Knowlton. Back row Dr Arthur Irwin, Ben White Cow, Dale Olivier (Lillico), Samson Knowlton, Allan Prairie Chicken (circa 1958). Photo source: Bev Knowlton.

Arthur and Lily Ann Irwin

full story of that remarkable day is told in Chapter 7. Other respected Elders who were present were Joe Crowshoe and Pat Bad Eagle. Both men remained associated with the Bahá'ís for many years though not as registered members. Joe Crowshoe, the spiritual leader and ceremonialist who performed the sacred pipe ceremony during Rúhíyyih Khánum's return visit in 1985, remained a lay preacher in the Anglican church[26]. Rúhíyyih Khánum felt a particular fondness for Joe and his wife and sent a message back through Clarence Knowlton later saying, "Again, I ask you to tell Joe Crowshoe how profoundly stirred I was by the Pipe Ceremony, and that I shall always be deeply grateful to him—and you and the other Bahá'ís who persuaded him—for that wonderful spiritual occasion. I often think of Josephine..."

By April 1960, there were nineteen adult Bahá'ís of First Nations backgrounds in Canada, nine of whom were in Alberta. Of those nine, seven lived at Piikani, and at the following Ridván (Bahá'í festival in April), they elected their first Local Spiritual Assembly.[27] In 1961, Hand of the Cause Hasan Balyuzi[28] visited Piikani and Arthur describes him as being deeply touched by the experience. Dale Lillico gave me a close-up photograph of Hasan Balyuzi and Samson Knowlton standing side by side: two distinguished looking men, one a scholar from Britain of Persian background, the other a deeply spiritual and highly respected leader among the Piikani people, the two of them clearly delighted to be together.

---

26 In *Weasel Tail*, a book of stories told by Joe Crowshoe to Michael Ross, Joe explains his comfort with practicing both his traditional religion, and with being an Anglican lay preacher, at the same time.

27 A Local Spiritual Assembly is the annually elected administrative body in a Bahá'í community, composed of the nine adults receiving the most votes in a secret ballot, with no campaigning or nominations preceding it, and conducted in an atmosphere of prayer. (There is no clergy in the Bahá'í Faith).

28 Hasan Balyuzi, the distinguished author of numerous Bahá'í history books including *Bahá'u'lláh: The King of Glory* lived much of his life in the United Kingdom and worked at the BBC. He was also appointed a 'Hand of the Cause of God' by Shoghi Effendi.

Samson Knowlton with Hasan Balyuzi at Piikani 1961. Photo source: Dale Lillico.

Young Hooper Dunbar, then an American actor and later a member of the Universal House of Justice[29], also visited. Hooper was much loved by the people there and was given a Blackfoot name as well. Dale Lillico recalls a large outdoor meeting held outside Samson and Rosie Knowlton's home, at which Hooper was invited to speak. An outdoor sound system was rigged up in the trees by Clarence, Knowlton's son, and people arrived from all around the area. Arthur expressed real pleasure at being able to introduce such visitors to the people he had come to be so fond of.

Another significant visit was made in early 1960 by National Spiritual Assembly member, Angus Cowan[30], and his friend

---

29 The supreme governing body of the Bahá'í Faith, whose nine members are elected every five years by representatives from the national communities where there exist National Spiritual Assemblies. Its Seat is in Haifa, Israel.

30 Angus Cowan was another much-loved Canadian Bahá'í who travelled extensively in his work, always visiting Bahá'ís along the way. He was elected to the National Spiritual Assembly in the sixties, and later appointed as an Auxiliary Board member, and then Counsellor for North America (appointments involving the protection and propagation of the Faith).

                    Arthur and Lily Ann Irwin

Tom Anaquod[31]. According to Arthur, a number of the Bahá'ís from Saskatchewan and Alberta had gathered for a conference in Calgary. After hearing reports of the growing community of Bahá'ís on what was then known as the Peigan Reserve, Angus and Tom decided to make a special trip to visit. They were so inspired by the people they met there, that they immediately returned to Saskatchewan and started teaching on the reserves, resulting in the message of Bahá'u'lláh spreading like a 'prairie fire' in that province. The Irwins were also called on at times, to assist the Bahá'í activities there.

John Sargent[32], of mixed Haudenosaunee and European descent, describes the scene in those days in his book, *Stumbling in the Half Light*:

"...Angus was a really sweet, pure hearted person who just loved the First Nations people, and who the First Nations really loved in return. As a result, they started becoming Bahá'ís in vast numbers. So much so that he couldn't handle the follow-up work. He wrote to the National Spiritual Assembly (NSA) of the Bahá'ís of Canada, asking them to send some reinforcements... but they were still too few. So the secretary of the Canadian NSA wrote to the NSA of the United States and said, 'Have you got any Bahá'ís experienced in working with the First Nation peoples that could come up and give us a hand?' As the NSA of the United States had heard about the work that my dad was doing on some of the reserves in the West, they asked him, 'Could you go up to Canada and help out because things are really poppin' up there?' So we went up and started working

---

31 Tom Anaquod was later also elected to the National Spiritual Assembly, it's first Indigenous member.

32 John Sargent Jr., whose mother was from the Six Nations Reserve in Ontario, was a frequent 'travel teacher' to reserves both in the US, and later in Canada, after having spent time in Africa. In the early 70s, he was appointed by the National Spiritual Assembly of the Bahá'ís of Canada to the National Indigenous Teaching Committee, with responsibilities to co-ordinate and encourage activities aimed at spreading the Bahá'í Faith among Indigenous people.

with Angus…. That was the time of mass teaching of the Bahá'í Faith on the Canadian Prairies…"

An example of Arthur's assistance to Angus in his efforts in Saskatchewan, is given by Pat Verge in her book, *Angus: From the Heart*:

"Angus had invited the Bahá'ís from Regina to Asham's Beach and told them there would be a great big meeting. When the Bahá'ís got there, there weren't any people on the beach so they began to question Angus. But pretty soon a wagon drove up, then an old car, and people began to gather after the funeral. Doug Crofford of Regina chaired the meeting and introduced the two Indian speakers, Noel Crowe and John Anaquod… they joked a lot and told stories on each other's tribe. Then they called on Arthur Irwin to speak. He spoke on the beauty of the Indian religion and its similarity to the Bahá'í Faith. Later one of the Bahá'ís from Regina questioned Arthur's approach and said to Angus, 'Wasn't it a shame, here there were all these people and Arthur had a chance to tell them about the Bahá'í Faith and he never told them?'

Angus reflected on this later: 'When Arthur spoke to the friends that day, he told them about their own faith. He built a bridge from the Indian Faith to the Bahá'í Faith. And he knew what he was doing, and the reason I know that is because pretty near all those people who were at that meeting that day have become Bahá'ís. I'd meet them many places afterwards and they'd become Bahá'ís and I'd say, 'Where did you first hear of the Faith?' And they'd say, 'At that big meeting that day down at Asham's Beach'…"

Lily Ann's contribution in all these efforts seemed more in the background compared to Arthur's, but was recognized by people who knew her. Dale Lillico said that Lily Ann was the 'driving force' in the family, initiating many of its activities.

 Arthur and Lily Ann Irwin

She made the calls, wrote the letters, got things going, and repeatedly befriended individuals they met. She developed sincere friendships with people—such as Jean Many Bears[33] of the Blackfoot Reserve (Siksika)—which had far-reaching implications for the reputation of the Faith there.

Lily Ann Irwin at the Intercontinental Bahá'í Conference, Wilmette, Illinois, 1958, Laura Davis Photo. Source: Canadian Bahá'í Archives

Lily Ann shared that when she was out visiting Jean, Jean was making tea. She kept brushing something off her skirt whenever she went into the kitchen. Lily Ann finally asked her about it and Jean replied that a 'spirit man' (a ghost) had been sitting in the doorway for some time, and that she did not know how to get him to leave. Lily Ann suggested they say prayers for him. The spirit man disappeared! This event was so significant because there had been whispers on the reserve that the Bahá'ís were bringing 'evil spirits'. Now Jean, a much respected Elder, could assure them this was clearly not true and that indeed, that the opposite was the case.

There was another occasion on which the two women were travelling to Hobbema (now Maskwacis) together, to introduce some of the people there to Dick Stanton and another Bahá'í fellow who wanted to meet First Nations people. The weather turned bad and they found themselves stuck in a snowbank, off the road and in a field, with wind howling around them. The men pushed the car out of the snow drift, but visibility was so bad they were unsure where to go. A little bird flew past the

---

33 See Chapter 6 re: Ed and Jean Many Bears

windshield and Jean said, "Follow that bird. It will show you where to go." Lily Ann did so and sure enough, the bird led them to the highway—a great relief. This appears to have been one of numerous experiences in which Lily Ann trusted and listened to her intuition and the 'spiritual realm' for guidance. She even said that was how she had approached making initial contacts on reserves. Prior to her initial trips with Arthur to Piikani for meetings, she said she was guided by a 'reverie' she had one day while washing dishes. In it, she was told (seemingly by the Guardian) that she had done the necessary preparation and should now simply arise. "Just go."

John Sargent[34] speaks of the changed conditions in First Nations communities since those remarkable early years when people were so receptive to embracing Bahá'í teachings. I was struck by his assessment:

"It is just my opinion, but I feel the First Nation peoples were more spiritually attuned then than they are now. A lot of people would say not, but I think materialism has dulled the spiritual senses of many individuals globally. We couldn't see it at first, but big changes were beginning to fuel turmoil within Indian Country. On top of the developing 'Indian Residential School Crisis', militant nationalism and particularly the increasing flow of alcohol onto the reserves, were starting to tear families and communities apart. But when we first came to Saskatchewan, in the summer of '62, the full consequences of all these things were still in the future, and the power of the Spirit was moving as a palpable force. Everywhere we went, we found the people in a state of expectation. It was almost as if they knew we were coming with a message from the Creator, and they were eager to embrace it..."

---

34 In *Stumbling in the Half-Light*

                    Arthur and Lily Ann Irwin

Diana Melting Tallow, who grew up at Siksika, met the Irwins when she was nineteen. "They were very kind to me in my young days," she said. Her association with the Bahá'í community began several years after the experience which John Sargent describes. She saw the acceptance of the Faith by First Nations and its impact on them over the years, this way:

"I think that one of the reasons for their success in reaching out to the 'natives' is due to Dr Irwin being an Indian Affairs Employee. The people of that time viewed Indian Affairs as the elite. Indian Affairs ruled their lives. Indian Affairs was their father who controlled their lives. They considered it an honour to be befriended by Dr Irwin. When the Irwins and others left the area and no longer visited the reserve, the links of the Baha'i Faith on their lives collapsed.

I commend Dr Irwin and Lily Ann for their contribution to the Faith in the early days and their desire to bring the teachings of Baha'u'llah to a people deeply entrenched in Christianity. The priests ruled the peoples' religious beliefs and wielded the power to maintain a control over the peoples' religions affiliations. The people were victims of religious indoctrination. They tried to break away from the established religions on the reserves, but most were unsuccessful.

There were some notable exceptions — individuals who had informed themselves deeply about the teachings of their newly adopted Faith and remained associated with it for the rest of their lives—either in their personal beliefs and devotions alone, or in their associations with the Bahá'í community as well. Once the Baha'is stopped reaching out to the people on the reserves with much less frequency, many went back to the Catholic Church and the Anglican Church, or Christianity as a whole."

In 1977, twenty-one years after their initial visits, Lily Ann and Arthur made a return trip, visiting people they had met in the past. Lily Ann offered the following assessment of the change in conditions:[35]

"Today what stands out clearly in our minds is that during these 21 years the Indian people have gone through great changes caused by evolutionary processes from without the reserve, and this needs to change from within. We feel that it is Baha'u'lláh's teachings that have miraculously kept the Faith alive by a few staunch believers, the extent of whose sufferings and sacrifices we will never fully know. The abuse which we heard about and some of which we observed in the few hours we were with them, is very difficult to bear... a young Bahá'í couple, although 'eager to serve the faith' on their reserve would gather their children on a Friday night or Saturday morning, about eight or ten in all, and would drive for hours somewhere, anywhere, where they could find peace, only to return late Sunday night to find their house broken into and furniture broken or stolen. Sometimes these families look for Bahá'ís in the city to put them up. Always this presents a problem or misunderstanding because Bahá'ís in the cities are not prepared for this kind of service... Life on some reserves is dangerous both in Saskatchewan and Alberta, where Bahá'ís are opposed and ostracized by their own people... Many old believers have passed on, only a few are left, however the few left, are holding onto the Faith. Communications between Bahá'ís on reserves and those off reserves are not too good, mainly because they do not understand each other's ways and thinking. Both try and wonder why they are not doing better..."

Despite the waning of the visible community of First Nations believers in the years that followed, it must be remembered

---

35 See Appendix for Lily Ann's complete 1977 report.

                                    Arthur and Lily Ann Irwin

that in the 1950s and 60s, it was the Irwins who led the way in crossing barriers of prejudice and suspicion to build bridges of friendship. There is much that can be learned from their unflinching willingness to associate—lessons which can now be brought to bear in establishing trust in an era of Truth and Reconciliation, an era in which there has begun to be significant learning on the part of the dominant society, and remarkable growth in First Nations confidence and self-determination.

In the 1960s, it was primarily the Irwins who led the way for Bahá'ís in Alberta to cross barriers of prejudice and suspicion, and build bridges of friendship between people of the two cultures. Arthur passed away in 1994. The tribute received from the Bahá'í World Center at the time of his passing said,

> *"The Universal House of Justice has received your email messages . . . and was saddened to learn of the death of dear Arthur Irwin. His services, particularly in the field of native teaching, have won him an enduring place in the annals of the Cause in Canada. Kindly assure the members of his family of the loving prayers of the House of Justice in the Holy Shrines for the progress of his soul.*
> *Department of the Secretariat June 23, 1994"*

When Lily Ann died in 2002, the following message was received:

> *"The Universal House of Justice has received your email... and was grieved to learn of the passing of distinguished and devoted maidservant of the Cause, Lily Ann Irwin, whose selfless and unflagging contribution to the teaching work among the First Nations Peoples of Canada was deeply appreciated by the beloved Guardian and inspired many others to follow in her footsteps. Her many years of dedicated service as a member of your community are well remembered by the House of Justice which will offer loving prayers in the Holy Shrines for the progress of her soul throughout the Divine realms."*

I add my own humble prayers for the progress of their souls
as well, as I view the examples of their lives in light of 'Abdu'l-
Bahá's admonition,

*"Love ye all religions and all races with a love that is true
and sincere and show that love through deeds and not
through the tongue…"*
*'Abdu'l-Bahá, Selections from the Writings of 'Abdu'l-Bahá,
p. 69*

                              Arthur and Lily Ann Irwin

3   Samson and Rosie Knowlton

Samson and Rosie Knowlton will be remembered as the bedrock of the Baháʼí community that emerged on Piikani First Nation. They were individuals of remarkable character. They were trusted, respected, and relied on by others. Service to their community and to their Faith was central to their lives. What always struck me about Samson and Rosie was the generosity of spirit with which they reached out to settlers like me. I was one of the many white people they treated with remarkable hospitality.

Their daughter, Bev, said that when Allan Prairie Chicken introduced her parents to the first Baháʼí they encountered—Arthur Irwin—they had been considering joining one of the various Christian religions which were active on the reserve. Samson had stopped drinking and the two of them were searching for a faith that would suit them both. The Anglican church did not 'move' either of them, and her father disliked the Catholic Church. These were the main choices on the Reserve, though it turns out

Samson and Rosie Knowlton in front of their home. Photo credit: Bev Knowlton

Rosie was also familiar with the Full Gospel Church but was not comfortable with 'all that jumping up and down'.

The two of them enrolled as Bahá'ís in 1958 during a fireside meeting when well-known Bahá'í, John Robarts[36], visited the reserve with Arthur Irwin. The meeting was in their home down in the river valley below the townsite of Brocket, in the area known as Highbush where many meetings took place over the years. This spot on the earth seems blessed for numerous reasons, but nature blessed it with stands of chokecherries and saskatoons. Further from the hillside, between it and the townsite, grew an abundance of sages and grasses used in smudging to fill the senses and soul with their purifying and fragrant smoke. Over the years, I have come to notice that when I smell this smoke—even from a distance—my spirit knows to slow down and let my troubles go.

Samson told the story of enrolling in the Bahá'í Faith, this way. "As I got up to sign my [enrollment] card, I was thinking to myself, I have found what I have been searching for and I really feel good about it." He finished signing and turned

Early Bahá'í meeting at Piikani. Hand of the Cause, John Robarts seated in front row, the second adult from right. Photo source: Dale Lillico.

36 Well-known and much loved Canadian Bahá'í and 'Hand of the Cause'

   Samson and Rosie Knowlton

around to see the others in the room, including his wife, standing behind him waiting to sign enrollment cards as well. It was a heartwarming moment filled with possibility. They then had enough members to elect a Spiritual Assembly, the basic administrative body in a Bahá'í community, made up of nine adult members elected to conduct the affairs of the community.

I first met the Knowltons as a young mother in the late 1970s when I attended one of their annual summer picnics. They invited Bahá'ís from the region, as well as local friends, to the gathering by their house in the Old Man River valley. The event featured an outdoor concert of country music provided by their son, Clarence, and his band. As I arrived that day, music reverberated from the temporary stage, across the river, and up the hill towards the townsite of Brocket. Cars were parked along the narrow roadway and any available patch of grass. People brought lawn chairs and contributions of food, and the happy greetings of delighted friends who had not seen one another in ages, abounded.

Samson and Rosie Knowlton and friends. Photo source: Eleanora McDermott.

I had driven down from Carstairs, north of Calgary, with my infant son. As I scan my memory, I recall that my car did not have air conditioning, and that the drive took three hours. I have no memory of stopping to change diapers, feed the baby, or find a bathroom. But I certainly got there in one piece which led to that moment in Rosie's living room when she invited me to change my baby's diaper in her bedroom. I felt welcomed and comforted by her kindness, the kindness of one generation of mother to another.

In one of my early conversations with her, she asked me if I had ever met a lady called Bessie Eckstrand who lived on a farm near Carstairs—the town I had lived in for much of my life. Though I did not really know Bessie, as a child I had been a classmate of her nephew, Rod. Rosie said she hoped I would meet Bessie one day and pass along her love and greetings. I made a point of doing so the following year. I recall being surprised that Rosie, who had lived at Piikani all her life, had a white friend in Carstairs. It almost didn't add up in my limited experience. I had not grown up near a reserve, so I had almost no contact with Indigenous people as a child. I had heard racist and pejorative comments about 'Indians' at hockey games when my town's team played against the team from Morley. But I had not actually met an Indigenous person until I was a young adult.

Rosie told me the story of how she met Bessie. As I recall—though her daughter tells it somewhat differently—she met Bessie one summer when the kids were young. Bessie's husband worked for the highways department and was stationed on the stretch of highway near Brocket. The Eckstrands were looking for a spot where they could set up their holiday trailer for the summer months so Bessie and the children could be nearby. They approached the Knowltons about setting up near their house and were welcomed. The two women became life-long friends, writing letters or calling each other from time to time until Rosie's passing in 1981. I am grateful to have met this pair of big-hearted friends, one Indigenous and one White.

   Samson and Rosie Knowlton

When I asked the Knowltons' youngest daughter about the friendship, she smiled, and with a far-away look in her eyes said, "Did you know Bessie had a daughter named Beverley? That's how I got my name."

Samson and Rosie's friendships with white people extended to allowing Bev to live with the Wrate family in Lethbridge for a year, giving their daughter the opportunity to attend what they hoped would be a better high school. Enid Wrate was an enthusiastic and active Bahá'í who they had met

Bev Knowlton. Photo source: Bev Knowlton.

through various activities. Cindy, her daughter, was the same age as Bev and on weekends, often went along to stay at the Knowltons on the reserve. Bev's memory of the high school experience in Lethbridge was that it was an unhappy experience of racism from many of the students. The hurtful instance she shared was a comment that had been flung her way, "If you put flour on your face, you could looks like us." She returned to her old high school the following year.

She also provided an insight into her mom's early years. Rosie went to the Victoria Jubilee Home (a residential school) just west of the reserve which had opened in 1897[37]. Rosie was an exceptionally good student who excelled at English, completing her schooling early. She wanted to be a nurse so requested permission from the Indian Agent to attend nursing

---

37 Victoria Jubilee Home later became known as the Anglican St. Cyprian's School.

school. Her request was denied. It seems all such decisions, those affecting every aspect of a First Nations person's life, were in the hands of the Indian Agent. He told Rosie, "You go back to the reserve and get married and have babies. Indian women can't be nurses."

Rosie kept learning what she could about medicine and got a job at the Indian Hospital on the reserve for a while. I find it hard to imagine that this bright young woman's desire to get advanced education required the consent of a government official. Sure, that was the 1920s but an inner voice shouts: *"What kind of government would authorize this kind of control of a whole segment of its population?"*

I am evidently just beginning to comprehend how profoundly unjust and racist the policies and practices of my country's government were, and how little I knew about the Indian Act. The Act controlled all aspects of life and held that Indigenous individuals were wards of the state, had no voting rights until 1960 (unless they relinquished their Indian status) and could not leave their reserves without a 'pass'[38]. They were not even allowed to get a lawyer without government permission. As late as 1972, when Bev's young husband died tragically, she found she still had to get consent from the Department of Indian Affairs[39] to get a lawyer to handle his estate.

Samson's residential school education was limited to approximately fifth grade, though he was there much longer.

---

38 A Canadian Encyclopedia article by Rob Nestor states the 'Pass System' was "…a process by which Indigenous people had to present a travel document authorized by an Indian agent in order to leave and return to their reserves." He also states, "Though some Indigenous people living under the pass system made attempts to resist their oppression, it was a difficult undertaking with potentially serious consequences. Indian agents held a lot of power over Indigenous communities, and many Indigenous people were therefore afraid of challenging the agents' authority. Indigenous people also had little relative political power at the time; they were only able to become full citizens in 1960—the same year Status Indian people could vote federally." *https://www. thecanadianencyclopedia.ca/en/article/pass-system-in-canada*

39 According to the Canadian Encyclopedia, the appointment of Indian Agents began to be phased out in 1960, but the Department of Indian Affairs maintained control over vital aspects of an individual's life.

Samson and Rosie Knowlton

According to his daughter Bev, so much labour was required of the children, that they did not have much time for proper classroom instruction. The school was set up as a working farm, and the labour to maintain it—both inside the school and outside on the farm—was done entirely by the children.

In a 2015 documentary film[40] made by Dr. Eldon Yellowhorn, a Simon Fraser University professor who grew up at Piikani, the archeologist, Sandie Dielissen, also says that though the children received a rudimentary education, they spent much more of their time keeping the school running. Among all the objects found in the archeological dig, not a single toy—or remnant of a toy—was found, only domestic objects.

But Samson had a keen and discerning mind. When he decided to investigate the truth of the Bahá'í Writings as an adult, he spent hours having Rosie read them aloud to him, her dictionary close at hand. Seeing the two of them sitting together this way, is a precious memory for family members who saw them.

Eleanora McDermott, Photo source: Joan Young.

Knowlton's eldest daughter, Eleanora, who had left home by the time her parents became Bahá'ís, shared insights about her upbringing. She said that when picking saskatoon berries with her mother as a child, she had been told, "The first berry you pick, don't eat it. Hold it in your hand. We are going to thank God for the abundance of

40 *Digging up the Rez*: Piikani Historical Archeology

berries. Then we will bury this first one in the ground so that we will have an abundance of berries next year."

Further to her childhood, she said,

"We were taught to share. I didn't know we were poor. It was only after I left and went to the big city, that I realized we were poor in material possessions. I never felt poor living on the Reserve. Through osmosis, I learned you share your best with visitors. In the old days, people travelled by foot or in wagons, so when they stopped at your home, it was an honour for the homeowners. The homeowners would feed them and the travelers were given food, blankets, and other goods to assist them as they continued on their journey...

Mom belonged to a quilting bee and a cooking club. The club worked at the school preparing lunches for the children. She was also on the Ways and Means Committee which got water pumps for the homes...

At a young, age, just before bedtime, I remember Mom telling me to pray. I asked her what I should say to God. She replied, 'You had food to eat and you were not sick. Think of the things that happened to you and you can thank God for that'."

Prayer seems to have become a significant part of Eleanora's life from a young age. She said that when she was still very young, an old man would walk past their house in the mornings on his way to the creek. He would stand in the water, wash his face, and pray. The kids asked why he did that, and he replied he was 'talking to God'. According to Eleanora,

"We wanted to do it too, so we imitated him. We'd all stand in the water washing our faces and repeat after him, saying the prayer. Mom used to tell us in the mornings, 'Don't eat so fast. You'll choke.' But if he happened to come by before we finished our breakfast, we would just leave telling Mom, 'We're going to talk to God.' This went on most of the

summer. Then one day he disappeared. I think the adults knew where he went and that he'd only been visiting for the summer."

Eleanora also recalled times when leaders on the reserve met to discuss issues in their home with Samson. Eleanora was allowed to listen in on the meetings but was told not to interrupt with unnecessary questions. Her brothers would say, "Don't ask baby questions." She chuckled at the memory—with feigned indignation. When she was a young teenager, Samson reportedly gave her a copy of the Indian Act and said, "Here, you study this because you're gonna get an education and come back and help the people."

Of the many Bahá'í meetings hosted in the Knowlton home, some included distinguished guest speakers: among them were Rúhíyyih Khánum[41], John Robarts, Hasan Balyuzi, Hooper Dunbar, Peggy Ross, Angus Cowan, and members of the

Eleanora McDermott, David Sherwin, Jean Hedley. Photo source: Joan Young.

---

41 See Chapter 7 on Rúhíyyih Khánum's 1960 visit

National Spiritual Assembly of the Baháʼís of Canada. To each and all, the couple extended warm hospitality. People remember Samson calling out from the door as they left, "Come back soon…"

Jean Hedley, a long time Baháʼí from High River, was one of those who recalled Samson's booming, bass voice calling people to "Come back soon." Even more vivid in her memory was the sound of his deep voice calling out in prayer, often saying the Baháʼí prayer that begins, "All praise, O my God, be to Thee Who art the Source of glory and majesty…" She said she still thinks of Samson when she hears someone read that prayer.

What I recall, when he and others said prayers in the Blackfoot language, was the word Áʼpistotooki. I heard it so often enough that finally, in 2019, I asked Nancy Big Weasel, a Piikani woman whose home we were guests in, what it meant. She explained it is a name for the Creator, or God. I have since learned another Blackfoot name for the source of all life— Iihtsipaitapiiyoʼpa.

Rosie Knowlton kept a meticulous guestbook during the 1960s. Bev brought it to show me over a restaurant lunch one day. She had it wrapped in a beautiful soft scarf, like a precious relic, which it had indeed become. As I looked inside, I saw familiar names, some with comments and the dates written at the top in Rosie's meticulous handwriting. One of the entries was a little longer than most. It was from Noel Wuttunee, the first Indigenous person to enroll in the Baháʼí Faith in Canada.[42] Mr. Wuttunee would have been living in Calgary at the time. He was a Cree artist who studied at the Alberta College of Art in Calgary, and six years later would be one of the Indigenous artists who painted the murals that graced the 1967 *Indians of Canada* Expo pavilion in Montreal. Dale Lillico remembers him as a good-looking young man, dressed notably smartly. His January 23, 1961 entry in Rosie's guest book reads:

---

42 Another Indigenous Canadian, Melba Loft, had enrolled six months earlier but was living in the US at the time.

                                    Samson and Rosie Knowlton

"This is the first Indian Bahá'í fireside I've been in, and I'm happy to see the Indians take to the sky once again with the strength and power of Eagle wings. How far we will fly with the winds of Bahá'u'lláh's teachings, once again we can cry out with the Eagle's voice and be heard and live with a purpose!"

Ed and Jean Many Bears, highly respected leaders among their people and the first from Siksika to enroll as Bahá'ís,[43] also travelled down to visit the Knowltons and attend meetings in their home. Jean's signature appears in Rosie's guestbook several times. She and her husband had also been introduced to the Bahá'í Faith by Arthur Irwin.

Some of the Knowlton's visitors stayed longer than for just a daytime visit. Frank and Judy Royal[44] along with Frank's mother, Alfreda Bearhat, arrived one summer when their kids were young, for the annual summer picnic, after which it began to rain. The road down the hill from the highway was made of dirt, which became slippery when wet. The Royals found themselves stuck, unable to get up the hill for a week. However, in the hospitable company of the Knowltons, it became a week of shared meals, stories, and as Frank described it years later, "One of the best weeks of my life."

Jean Hedley with Frank Royal at Siksika. Photo source Jean Hedley.

Their hospitality also extended to youth, and they supported various activities that

---

43 See Chapter 6 on Ed and Jean Many Bears.

44 Frank and Judy Royal were Bahá'ís from Siksika First Nation east of Calgary.

Samson Knowlton, visitor from Alaska, Rosie Knowlton and daughter Beverley. Photo source: Eleanora McDermott.

their daughter participated in. Amy (Woodward) Singh of Cutknife, Saskatchewan, recalls staying in their home in the sixties:

"Once when I was just a new Bahá'í, 1966 probably, some Edmonton youth (Virginia Evans who had a VW beetle, and maybe Morine Fraser and I) drove down on a weekend to support the Bahá'í youth at Piikani. They were having a non-alcoholic dance. Clarence Knowlton and his musical friends… were involved. We hadn't made any arrangements for where to stay but had thought we could roll out our sleeping bags in the hall and stay there… Beverley must have told her folks, because Samson and Rosie invited us to stay overnight at their house. It was so delightful! It reminded me of my grandma's house—cozy and colorful with knickknacks on the shelves—and they were so good to us, so kind. I remember having bacon and eggs in the morning, something my poor university student budget didn't allow…"

                                          Samson and Rosie Knowlton

After Samson's passing in 1985, *The Bahá'í World*, a yearbook of international Bahá'í activities and accomplishments, included an 'In Memoriam' about him and mentioned his travels and connections to Canada's first Indigenous Senator, James Gladstone:

"In 1960, Samson accompanied Canada's first native Senator, James Gladstone, a Blood Indian, to Ottawa to present to the federal government a proposal urging it to extend to native people the right to vote in federal elections. He was also instrumental in having eliminated the 'permit system' which prevented Indians from leaving the Reserve…"

Both Bev and Dale Lillico questioned aspects of this account during a visit I had with them in Dale's home in February of 2020. While there is no doubt Samson was a much respected Band Councillor—appointed for life in those days—and a leader in the community who would have been concerned about these issues, when the women heard the above quote, both expressed misgivings about Samson's direct role in getting the vote for Indigenous people and in eliminating the pass system. They recalled both Samson and Rosie feeling particularly grateful to John Diefenbaker, whom they heartily credited with getting the vote for them. Dale was working at the Indian Agent's office on the reserve at that point in time and would have had knowledge of significant trips and events. Given she was such a close, personal friend of the Knowltons as well, it seems she would have remembered something of such significance. This conversation got me to question aspects of some of the original reports on Indigenous Bahá'í events on which early articles in publications were based. Could it have been that at times, a non-Indigenous secretary of a Bahá'í committee with no personal knowledge of the events and little understanding of the culture—who lived elsewhere in the region—was asked to write a report and did their best? I thtink it likely.

I was struck by how closely Bev and Dale's memories coincided with the other's. Naturally, there were specific incidents of which only one of them had knowledge, but their understanding of how the government and the reserve interacted and functioned over the years was the same; as was their memory of people who lived there. Bev said that while she did not recall her father making trips for Senator Gladstone per se, she was aware they had worked together on issues such as getting better housing on Reserves. She recalled the Senator stopping at their house to speak with her father when she was seven or so years old. She answered the knock at the door but did not recognize the man standing there, and thought he looked like a 'white man'. Speaking in Blackfoot, she shouted to her father, "There's a white man here to see you." To her astonishment, the 'white man' proceeded to speak to her in fluent Blackfoot. She was so surprised she turned and ran back into the house.

Eleanora said she recalled her father telling her that when he had made two of his Bahá'í trips across the country, Senator Gladstone had asked him if he could check on housing conditions on the various Reserves at which he stopped, and report back. According to her, on his first trip across Canada, Samson was shown the nicer homes that existed. He came home and told Rosie, "We are the poorest reserve in Canada!" On his second trip, Eleanora said he decided to travel unannounced and saw how poor living conditions really were for so many people, including the dirt floors in their homes.

A 1961 article in *The Canadian Bahá'í News* refers to Samson as 'Chief Samson Knowlton' which his daughter Bev says is incorrect. As mentioned earlier, he was a lifetime Band Councillor. His good friend, John Yellowhorn, was 'Chief' in those years, the last of the hereditary Chiefs before the position became an elected one. It's possible the striking photo of Samson as a handsome young man wearing full regalia with a feathered head dress left the impression with a white writer that

     Samson and Rosie Knowlton

this meant he was 'Chief'. It didn't. It meant he had earned the honour of wearing it by his deeds and character.

Both daughters recall a major 'teaching trip' for the purpose of introducing the Bahá'í Faith to people on other reserves, made by their father. That trip had an extended itinerary that included numerous stops across Canada. *The Canadian Bahá'í News* in July of 1961 reported:

Samson Knowlton in regalia. Photo source: Nancy Big Weasel.

"Chief Samson Knowlton, then chairman of the first Peigan Reserve Assembly, 1961, and an elected member of the Band Council for the Peigan Band of the Blackfoot Confederacy, along with John Hellson, originally from Cornwall, England, were part of a teaching team that visited many Reserves. Over 61 First Nations [people] became Bahá'ís in 1960 to 1962. The team carried letters of introduction to the Chiefs of all the Six Nations Reserves in Ontario and Québec, and were welcomed with a special ceremony on some of the Reserves. Their itinerary included the following reserves: the Nanaimo Reserve in BC, the Squamish Reserve in Capilano BC, the Mohawk Reserve in Ohsweken Ontario, the Chippewa Reserve in Kettle Point Ontario, the Mississauga Reserve in Curve Lake, and the Mohawk Reserves in Caughnawaga, Québec. The teaching team gave copies of the small prayer book, Communion with God, *which has meant much to the new Indian Bahá'ís on the reserves in Saskatchewan and Alberta."*

In searching for other news of his travels, I was also able to find accounts of trips he made to Browning, Montana, where a Bahá'í who'd moved from Washington, DC, George Miller, relied on Samson to make contact with Blackfeet[45] people in order to share the Faith with them. In *Montana Bahá'í History*, Betty J. Bennett[46] tells of George Miller inviting Samson down in 1961, and the two of them staying in a motel for two weeks, spending their days 'teaching' and showing slides in various homes. Samson was related to several of the Blackfeet families in Browning. The creation of an international border by Europeans had not altered their close connection to the Blackfoot in Canada. There had always been visiting and familial connections between the two groups. Samson made follow-up trips for Bahá'í purposes and Betty Bennett describes one of these as a meeting where they had rented a hall in Browning and numerous people arrived under the influence of alcohol. They were perturbed by the thought that white people had rented their hall. Samson and a fellow Bahá'í from Piikani, Guy Yellow Wings[47], slowly calmed them down, speaking in Blackfoot. Guy went on to explain the connections behind all Faiths and great spiritual traditions in the Blackfoot language. The few white Bahá'ís present must have heaved a sigh of relief.

Samson made further 'travel teaching' trips in Alberta, according to an article in *The Canadian Bahá'í News*, which describes him as being a member of a teaching team which also included Chester Kahn of New Mexico (Navajo) and Baptiste

---

45 The Blackfoot people in Canada (the North Peigans) were separated from the 'South Peigans' by the creation of the international border along the 49th parallel. Those on the American side of the border became known as Blackfeet, while those on the Canadian side were known as Blackfoot. Among the Blackfoot Confederacy in Canada were the Siksika, Kainai, and North Peigan (Piikani) people.

46 available at *https://Bahá'í-libarary.com*

47 Guy Yellow Wings was a member of the first Local Spiritual Assembly at Piikani, as were Samson and Rosie Knowlton and Dale Lillico. Dale recalls that Guy was the fellow who would wait at the top of the hill to escort her past barking dogs on their way to Assembly meetings at Knowltons.

                                   Samson and Rosie Knowlton

Shortneck of the Louis Bull Band (Cree). He was also actively farming at this time, so travels for his Faith were no small service.

He also attended National Bahá'í Conventions held every April, as an elected delegate from southern Alberta. He is listed as being among the six delegates elected from the region to attend the 1968 National Convention[48], and appears to have been a delegate on several other occasions as well. John Raynor[49] sent

Rosie Knowlton (in dark coat) at Sylvan Lake Bahá'í Summer School 1967. Photo source: Joanie Anderson collection.

a striking photo (next page) of Samson dressed in a suit and tie, sitting beside Harvey Iron Eagle from Saskatchewan, both wearing 'delegate' ribbons on their suit jacket lapels. In the photo, taken at the 1966 Convention, they are sitting at a table with folders of printed material in front of them. There are heavy brocade curtains of the conference wall, visible behind them. They are handsome and smartly dressed. But I cannot help wondering if they feel comfortable sitting for long hours listening to mostly white people talking. I am a white person and I sometimes feel like fleeing meetings where fellow white people talk so long. I cannot know their sentiments, but I feel gratitude for their patience and courtesy to the rest of the people.

---

48 The National Convention is held yearly for the purpose of electing the nine-member National Spiritual Assembly and consulting on the affairs of the national community.

49 John Raynor is one of Alan and Evelyn Raynor's children, a well-known Bahá'í family from Toronto. Alan may be best known for his extensive efforts and travels to educate the Canadian Bahá'í Community in the centrality of the concept of 'the Covenant' to their Faith.

Samson Knowlton and Harvey Iron Eagle at 1966 National Bahá'í Convention. Photo source: John Raynor.

Alan Raynor, Harvey Iron Eagle, Samson Knowlton, Alex Poorman, Evelyn Raynor. Photo source: John Raynor.

    Samson and Rosie Knowlton

Bev told me a story of one particularly disappointing journey Samson made with hopes of attending a Bahá'í Conference in New Mexico. He had forgotten the paper at home that gave the address, so searched for the venue in vain. He finally gave up and returned home—disappointed and broke. Something about his dedication and the expense he went to to get there, is particularly poignant to me, sixty years later.

In the context of the Truth and Reconciliation Commission's follow-up work, I attended a United Church service in Waterton Park, in July of 2016 with Dale Lillico. Numerous individuals from Piikani Nation were there and I recognized the name one of their speakers, Daryl Crowshoe. I thought he might be related to Joe and Josephine Crowshoe, the couple who were such good friends of the Knowltons. Daryl confirmed he was indeed related to Joe and Josephine and wondered how I knew them. I told him I used to come visit Samson and Rosie. He broke into a big smile and said, "Samson once told us he got to be the first Indian ever, to get on a jet plane and go far away, to a meeting, with the Bahá'ís." Daryl may well have heard Samson's story at one of the occasions Bev described as the community coming together to hear Samson tell of his travels. She said people were so rarely able to travel in those days, that when they did, everyone wanted to hear about it.

Piikani group photo of 2017 Bicentennial Celebration of the Birth of the Báb. Photo source: unknown.

I would have loved to have been there myself, to listen to Samson tell his stories and sit with his dear wife, Rosie. Writing about him and Rosie has filled me with a degree of tenderness I did not expect to feel. Others, who have shared memories of the couple, have added to my feeling that these were among the dearest of people who have passed on to the spirit world. I hope I have come close to a fitting account of their lives, and that future writers will be able to give a much fuller view.

Rosie left this world in 1981, and Samson followed her in 1985. The words of a Bahá'í prayer written by 'Abdu'l-Bahá for the departed, come to mind as I wish them well on their heavenly journey. "…Make these precious souls, companions of the inmates of Heaven… and immerse them in the sea of lights…" [50]

---

50 'Abdu'l-Bahá, *Twenty-six Prayers revealed by 'Abdu'l-Bahá*

  Samson and Rosie Knowlton

4   Joyce McGuffie

In 1959, shortly after Dale Lillico (then Olivier) moved to Brocket on Piikani First Nation, a teacher from Zimbabwe, then known as Rhodesia, also arrived. Her name was Joyce McGuffie. New to Canada, she had been walking down the street in Calgary one day when she noticed a sign advertising a teaching position on an 'Indian Reserve'. She applied and was hired at Saint Cyprian's Residential School at Piikani. It did not take long for her innate sense of justice to notice how badly students were being treated by staff. In great discomfort, she resigned and switched to a position at the day school.

Some of the local people knew that Dale was a Bahá'í and thought Joyce might be interested in her beliefs. They suggested to Joyce that she go meet her. Joyce had never heard of the Bahá'í Faith before, but upon meeting Dale, became interested. The two women went on to became dear friends. Their relations with local people left an enduring impression on people at Piikani. Years later, one of them[51] who was then a child on the Reserve, recalled that the two women were a vital and much-loved part of her growing up. "I couldn't hate white people because I grew up with Dale and Joyce, as part of my life…"

She is one of numerous people—some Indigenous, some settlers—who have expressed deep respect and affection for Joyce. When I mentioned her name to Brian Berteig of Swift Current, Saskatchewan, he immediately brightened and wanted

---

51   Bev Knowlton

to read what I had been able to learn about her. He knew her in her later years, when she lived at Fort Qu'Appelle.

When I think of Joyce, I see her in a landscape of sun, wind-blown grasses, and wide-open spaces. In my vision of her in Canada, her beloved Rocky Mountains are at her back but she is out on the plain, scanning the horizon. When I 'see' her where she grew up on the African continent, she is on the high 'veld', another inland plateau, which is remarkably similar to the terrain in southern Alberta. There are farms with livestock and crops at an elevation of 1000 metres or more. However, the Chimanimani Mountains in Zimbabwe are to the east of the open plain, on the border with Mozambique. These mountains are where she saw the sun rise, while in Treaty Seven Territory the sun sets along a similar, craggy line on the western horizon.

Dale was still a new Bahá'í when she met Joyce, and despite Joyce's clearly expressed interest in Bahá'í teachings, Dale was uncertain of her ability to explain them very well. She called on 'Hand of the Cause of God', John Robarts, to help her when he visited the area. She invited John and Joyce to dinner together in her apartment. Joyce's initial questions on spiritual matters related to the Bahá'í teachings on life after death. "What about people who have never heard of Jesus Christ, or follow some other Faith?" Joyce asked. Like others who found their way to the Bahá'í Faith during those years, Joyce did not harbour notions that her white, Christian background assured her – and only people like her—of a place in heaven. She had a deep love and respect for people of other races and religions, whom she met as equals, with keen interest.

Pat Verge in her book, *Angus From the Heart*, speaks about how Joyce's decision to become a Bahá'í was influenced by Angus Cowan's[52] story of his own life:

"...He was talking to the collection of people who were mostly Indian people there. And he was telling them how he had been an alcoholic and how joining the Faith had been his salvation, and how, as a result of this, he had got spiritual background which had helped him so tremendously. This impressed me so much, I couldn't believe it."

Angus recalled that Joyce told Peggy Ross[53] that she did not think she wouldd be 'much of a decoration for the Faith' so she had not enrolled. Peggy assured her she had felt that way too at one time, and to Joyce's amusement Peggy said, "It's like jumping into a swimming bath in the deep end and you can't swim. You just flap and flap and flap..."

To her friends' delight, Joyce overcame her hesitation and enrolled. "That was the one thing about Angus, he made you feel that you were important. He made you feel that you were necessary to the Faith," said Joyce.

The year was 1960. When she decided to become a member of the new Faith, she was determined to do whatever she could to advance its interests. In practical terms, that meant working to assist people to improve conditions in their community. She took her Faith's teachings to heart which said, "To be a Bahá'í simply means to love all the world; to love humanity

---

52 Angus Cowan was the Canadian Bahá'í who, perhaps more than any other, devoted his entire life to sharing his Faith, love, and personal resources with First Nations people across the prairies. His work in Saskatchewan was the impetus for much of the expansion of the Bahá'í Faith on reserves there. He was elected as a member of the National Spiritual Assembly and later appointed an Auxiliary Board member. Still later, he was appointed a member of the Continental Board of Counsellors—which meant even more extensive travel.

53 Peggy Ross was a much-loved Canadian Auxiliary Board member who travelled the country extensively. She also spent much time with First Nations Bahá'ís in Saskatchewan and was a frequent collaborator with Angus Cowan.

and try to serve it; to work for universal peace and universal brotherhood."[54]

At Pikkani, she put great effort into befriending people and encouraging them to gain confidence and show their successes to the world. With her help and encouragement, the first handicrafts outlet was set up by Madeline Good Rider and her family and friends. Dale felt the success of their business could be credited to the fact that they had encouragement, were good leaders, and made much of the craft work themselves. Their beading featured traditional Blackfoot designs—beautiful geometric forms differing from the floral motifs of the Cree people to the north. "It kept a lot of people busy and feeling good about themselves," said Dale. The business continued to flourish for many years, standing on the north side of Highway 3, just east of the village of Brocket.

Joyce also encouraged people to try gardening though the results of that were less than rewarding. "Local dogs dug up much of the work that had gone into it," explained Dale. I had to smile when I heard this. My own dog, a Labrador retriever, is a keen digger in my back garden, especially when she sees me digging.

Introducing Alcoholics Anonymous on the Reserve, arranging meetings and bringing in speakers were other activities Joyce initiated. According to Dale, "It was a small healing for a rampant disease."

Joyce's teaching assignment in Brocket was grades four to nine. Her approach and regard for the people, the students and families of those she was teaching, is reflected in her comment to *The Regina Leader Post's* Ben Cashman, who interviewed her about her life in 1985 when she was living in Fort Qu'Appelle:

"It was quite a different situation from any I had been in before. I did not understand the Indian culture and it became a major problem. I went to the chief and asked for his help, and he was actually taken aback. He said I was the

---

54 'Abdu'l-Bahá, *Star of the West*, 28 April 1912

 Joyce McGuffie

first one that had ever asked help of himself or his Council. The first question I put to him was 'How do you punish your children when they misbehave?' Well, that started a whole new world for me…"

Bev Knowlton said that Joyce was her teacher in grade four at the Day School. She said that she and her fellow students loved all the folk dancing activity breaks Joyce would give them, a welcome change from reading, writing, and arithmetic. No other teacher had given them such a frequent, joyful activity.

Joyce also eagerly participated in the social and cultural life of the community on the reserve. Early in her time at Brocket there was a severe drought. She and Dale were invited by Samson Knowlton to attend a prayer ceremony for rain on a hill south of Brocket. The ceremony was conducted by spiritual leader and healer, Pat Bad Eagle. Afterwards, the attendees went down to Samson and Rosie Knowlton's house by the Old Man River for lunch. When it was over, the two women, privately still somewhat skeptical about the powers of native spirituality, continued visiting. Samson suggested they get going home before it started to rain. Given there was scarcely a cloud in the sky, Dale remembers being surprised at the suggestion. But they left, and walked up the hill to their respective apartments. They had scarcely closed their doors behind them when the clouds opened in a downpour. "That taught me not to doubt the power of native ceremony," mused Dale, sixty years later.

Upon retiring from teaching in Brocket in the late sixties, Joyce moved to Cardston, a town that borders the Blood Reserve, now known as Kainai. She joined a number of Bahá'í friends who were living in the town with the hope of establishing a Local Spiritual Assembly there. Among them were John Hellson, Diana Melting Tallow (Hellson), Eva Statz (Tranter), Morgan Gadd, and Meredith McLean (Gadd). Living just outside of town was Carolla Black Rabbit, who became a dear friend to Joyce. More than fifty years later, Diana took me to visit Carolla, who had remarried and was living in Airdrie, near Calgary. We met her husband and a grandson she had raised, and sat at her kitchen table sharing precious memories and prayers. Her husband graciously served us refreshments, saving his dear wife the labour of carrying things following a heart attack she had recently suffered.

"Joyce was like part of our family," Carolla said.

Her daughter, Janice, was a child when they lived near Cardston, and she became especially devoted to Joyce. Janice, along with the Hellson children and Dylan Gadd participated in the Bahá'í childrens' classes Joyce taught. At times, Janice would also travel with Joyce. Like a young duckling, she would follow along behind Joyce, seemingly becoming imprinted on Joyce's mannerisms. Carolla's other children recall a very particular move, unique to Joyce, which they observed Janice begin to duplicate. When she was especially excited over something, she would jump up in the air and click her heels together. Then she would laugh and slap her thighs.

That delightful gesture became a vivid and treasured memory of Joyce. Janice, passed away in her fifties—far too early—having become an accomplished teacher and educator, another way in which she followed in Joyce's footsteps. Carolla noted that Janice graduated from University with a Bachelor of Arts in 1998 and her Bachelor of Education degree in 2003.

Diana recalled enrolling as a Bahá'í herself during the years she lived in Cardston. Joyce and Eva became close friends of hers during that time, even living in the same large home together for a while, a house which Diana and her husband at that time, John Hellson, had purchased. The house had several suites in it and Joyce and Eva each rented one. Joyce would frequently babysit the Hellson children when the parents had to travel, and the children came to call her Nanny. According to Diana, Joyce was firm but fair and the kids loved her. "She wouldn't let them get away with things—which was good," she said.

As Diana and Carolla shared memories, both of them began to chuckle as they recalled the extent to which Joyce was determined that their small group help establish a Spiritual Assembly on the Blood Reserve next door. Assemblies were to be formed in April on the first day of the Bahá'í festival of Ridván if there were nine or more adults living in a community. Joyce would send someone out to collect people who needed a ride to bring them to a meeting called for the purpose of an election. In one case, Diana arrived at the home of a woman who was sleeping on her couch. Diana returned to town without her. When Joyce heard Diana's explanation she replied, "Well, go wake her up then." The woman did indeed vote that day.

Another fond memory Carolla had of Joyce was the time she went to the Sylvan Lake Bahá'í Summer School with Joyce and another woman. The three of them tented together for the week and attended classes during the day. One morning they decided to say morning prayers out on the lake in one of the camp canoes. Upon returning to shore Carolla jumped out first and the canoe tipped, dunking the other two in the water. Joyce climbed on shore saying, "I thought native people were supposed to know all about canoeing." They came out laughing, having also had a morning bath.

Diana shared that Joyce was instrumental in deepening her understanding of the Faith. She said that Joyce often sent her and Mary Ann Crow from the Blood Reserve to various conferences and training sessions. Many of these training sessions were held at the Bahá'í Centre near Fort Qu'Appelle in Saskatchewan. In speaking about the experience Diana said,

"She [Joyce] lived in a suite below us in Cardston, Alberta, a Mormon town. The Mormon Temple loomed large in the background. I'm grateful to Joyce because we met Hands of the Cause, Counsellors, and other learned Baha'is through her. She made sure that we attended a World Conference in Iceland by sponsoring Mary Ann and looking after her

eighteen-month-old daughter. She also assigned travel teaching trips to us at Siksika and Browning, Montana. We attended meetings in Edmonton and other parts of Alberta at her behest. (Mary Ann and I became skilled drivers in icy road conditions and on snow-covered highways).

I had a child during the time she was with us. She would come up to my suite after I gave birth to perform calisthenics with me, to help me regain my strength and shape. I still exercise to this day.

She organized the event, including the menu, for Hand of The Cause Enoch Olinga's visit. It was to be a turkey dinner. We bought fresh turkeys from a nearby farm. We each took one turkey to cook. Carolla cooked her turkey at our place. All of a sudden Joyce came in telling us that the turkey she had, was not 'developed' and that she couldn't stuff it. We ran back to her suite to examine the bird. Carolla burst out laughing and showed us the problem. Joyce had been trying to stuff the bird's neck pouch."

Diana and Carolla's comments reveal how rich the experience of living near Joyce was, and how deeply committed she was to helping others.

The stories that remain about Joyce's life in Africa before she came to Canada, feature strength and resilience. In one, she is thrown from a horse fifty miles from home and cracks a hip but manages to walk the entire way home[55]. The stories also tell of her physical fitness, and that she had studied calisthenics in Denmark for three years after teacher's college. She taught fitness to the Africans living nearby, and vigorously pursued her own fitness throughout life. My memory of her physical presence later in life, is of a vigorous woman of medium height, striding purposefully along the pathway from the dining hall at Sylvan Lake Bahá'í Centre to the meeting hall, short gray curls framing her face, a twinkle in her eye, and a ready smile on her face.

---

55 Michael and Judie Bopp recalled Joyce telling this story when they still lived in Pincher Creek, just west of Piikani.

                    Joyce McGuffie

In *Angus: From the Heart*, Pat Verge mentions that Joyce took one of her Christmas vacations to visit the reserves in Saskatchewan where Bahá'í activities were occurring:

"Angus went to Calgary to attend a youth meeting, picked Joyce up and brought her back. She spent a week on the Poorman reserve. The Poorman Assembly made all the decisions where Joyce would stay and who she would visit. 'They took her for a ride in a sleigh and they just treated her like a queen,' said Angus. While Joyce was there, a big meeting, with over 100 Bahá'ís from Pasqua, Cote, Muscowpetung, and Poorman was held in the home of Mike Kay. One man had walked 10 miles through snow in the freezing temperatures to be there..."

Ben Cashman's interview with Joyce examines a range of her lifetime accomplishments:

"When you see Joyce McGuffie out for a walk, she looks and acts like any other member of the community. There is a friendly spring to her step and she projects an open, friendly attitude. You would never guess she has taught gymnastics to African tribes, operated an experimental farm in Rhodesia, taught African adults to read and write, taught school in a small English village, taught on an Alberta reserve, and launched what is believed to be the first kindergarten on a Canadian reserve."

Joyce McGuffie at Sylvan Lake Bahá'í Summer School. Photo source: Joanie Anderson collection

As a child on the farm in South Africa, droughts had been so severe that in the mid 1930s, her family moved to Swaziland. When she married, she moved to Zimbabwe with her husband. Recalling her childhood Joyce said, "… we had difficult times on the farms in those days. We had no electricity and were always short of water. I can remember, as a youngster, my two brothers and I would put our names in a hat to find out who could wash first, in the little water we had."

Dale recalls Joyce telling her about the extraordinary moment during her husband's military deployment to Libya in World War II, that their African farm foreman came in from the fields and said to her, "The master is dead…" Joyce assured him that her husband was fine. She had just heard from him a few days before. Days later, official news came confirming her husband's death in fighting in Tobruk at the time the foreman had come in to tell her so. In relaying this to me, Dale became quiet, then said, "Do you know what the Writings say about the African people? They were "…compared by Bahá'u'lláh to 'the black pupil of the eye' through which 'the light of the spirit shineth forth'…"[56]

According to Ben Cashman, when Joyce's husband was sent to the front in North Africa, she was appointed as acting director of the 22,000 acre experimental farm they lived on, in his place. It was a job she no doubt carried out with efficiency and vigor. In 1972, she returned to southern Africa, to Lesotho, as a Bahá'í pioneer with her friend, Eva (Statz) Tranter. According to Canadian Bahá'í archivist, Ailsa Leftwich, they spent eight months there, from October 1972 to May, 1973, in a part of Africa which was undoubtedly a happily familiar landscape for Joyce.

Upon returning to Canada in 1973, Joyce lived at Fort Qu'Appelle, Saskatchewan, for nine years, working with local First Nations Bahá'ís holding classes for children and

---

56 Letter to National Spiritual Assemblies in Africa, from the Universal House of Justice, 8 February 1970.

                                    Joyce McGuffie

volunteering at the 'San' hospital nearby. After that, she returned to Piikani for a period of time, working as the custodian of the Bahá'í Center which opened there in 1986. She contributed $4000 to its renovation, clear evidence of her love for the people it was to serve, and her willingness to translate love into material means.

In her eighties, when someone in a group of Bahá'ís who had gathered in Ft. Qu'Appelle suggested she was 'getting on in years', Michael Bopp said he saw her get down on the floor, stand on her head, and say, "But I can still do this…"

The film maker, Bev Bliss, who interviewed Joyce for Vision TV near the end of her life, noted Joyce's independence of spirit as her outstanding quality. She said of Joyce,

> *"She was truly a breathlessly independent woman. There were a clutch of women both in the [Bahá'í] faith and society during the first half of the 20th century who broke (or possibly simply ignored) the constraints of society's expectation and followed their own path in life on their own terms. They were independent in thought, passion and deed. I was often struck by how independent women were portrayed in film as 'paying a price'… In Joyce's case she did marry. She was poor, confined to a wheelchair, and in the care of her daughter when my team interviewed her. It could not have been an easy situation for her, given her pleasure in fitness and independent nature. It made me appreciate her sacrifices so much more."*

Joyce had been a Bahá'í for forty years, when she passed away in 2002 at the age of ninety-seven in a Calgary nursing home. Those who knew her, miss her immensely, and when her name comes up in conversation, they smile hugely, and vie to be the first to tell their story of a moment they spent with her.

5   Beatrice Ashton and Louise White Cow

A circa 1959 color photograph shows Beatrice Ashton and Louise White Cow standing at the Brocket train station on Piikani First Nation. There is still passenger service on the CPR's southern line through the Crowsnest Pass to the west, and Beatrice is waiting to catch the train back to her home in Lethbridge, 80 km east. There is no station master at a stop as small as Brocket, so she has to flag the train herself and is holding up the flag to do so. Beatrice and Louise have been at a Bahá'í meeting together in a home on the Reserve. Both women are smartly dressed and smiling. They are enjoying one another's company and peering into the afternoon sun.

Beatrice, a white society lady from Cleveland, Ohio, is sophisticated, educated, and has travelled abroad. She has received a first-class education from the prestigious Vassar College for women in New York State. Louise, a Blackfoot woman from Piikani First Nation, lives where she grew up, on the reserve by the Old Man River, with a full view of the Rockies near the Montana border. From the age of six, she had attended one of the now notorious residential schools that Indigenous children in

Louise White Cow and Beatrice Ashton, circa 1960, Photo source: Dale Lillico.

Canada were forced to attend. She was a student at the Victoria Jubilee Home—later known as St. Cyprian's—along with her sister, Rosie Knowlton. She would not have been allowed higher education if she wanted it.

Dale Lillico gave me the photograph I have described, one of the many she took during the years she lived on, and then near, the reserve. Looking back through the decades into the photo, I reflect on how unusual it was for these two women to be together. The question could be asked, "What on earth is Beatrice Ashton doing in Brocket?" Or "What is Louise White Cow doing with an American society lady?"

Beatrice made her initial acquaintance with Canadian Bahá'ís through courses she taught at the Bahá'í Summer Schools held in Banff in the early 1950s. The subject of many of her courses was the emerging Administrative Order[57] of the world-wide community which was being guided by the Guardian, Shoghi Effendi, along the lines laid out in the Sacred Writings of the Faith.

In 1958, she moved to Lethbridge as part of the 'Ten Year Crusade', an international Bahá'í plan to spread its members to more locations throughout North America and the world. Bahá'ís referred to such moves as 'pioneering'. The November 1958 issue of The Canadian Bahá'í News notes, "Beatrice Ashton, Waukegan, Illinois, who was formerly secretary of *The 'Bahá'í World* [58] Committee and has frequently taught at summer conferences in Canada, has pioneered to Lethbridge. This makes five believers in Lethbridge, the goal to be reached in 1959."

Beatrice, being deeply versed in the Administrative Order of the Bahá'í Faith, hoped to teach the Bahá'ís nearby about it as

---

57 The 'Administrative Order' of the Bahá'í Community refers to the elected institutions established by the Founder of the Faith, for the administration of its affairs. There is no clergy in the Bahá'í Faith, though there are individuals appointed to an institution referred to as the 'Institution of the Learned' whose function is to encourage and inspire the achievement of the goals and plans of the worldwide community, for set periods of time.

58 A yearbook of the accomplishments and development in the Bahá'í world community.

                    Beatrice Ashton and Louise White Cow

well, when she arrived. Years later, Dale Lillico recalled being one of the people, along with the Bahá'ís at Piikani, whom Beatrice intended to educate on this subject. According to Dale, it was Beatrice who was the quick learner. She soon realized that some things—perhaps administrative functioning in particular—had to be allowed to develop gradually, and with cultural sensitivity. "She may have learned more from us than we were able to learn from her," mused Dale.

Beatrice Ashton, Laura Davis photo. Source: Canadian Bahá'í Archives, copyright National Spiritual Assembly of the Bahá'ís of Canada

Beatrice describes her experience in letters she wrote, excerpts of which were published in *Bahá'í Canada* in October of 2001 when a retrospective of Canadian accomplishments was undertaken. I had to smile at her initial impressions of the white residents of Southern Alberta—among which were my own family and neighbours. We must have seemed a very odd and narrow-minded bunch:

> *"On October 22, 1958, I entered this goal to increase the Group and to assist with Indian Teaching. I left Waukegan, Illinois… and was assisted in choosing my goal by the Canadian National Spiritual Assembly. The first impression of Lethbridge was of bright sunshine, wide open blue skies, a small clean town and friendly people. Western Canada is separated by great distances from the more settled, sophisticated Eastern Canada, and seems like a different country, not only in physical terrain but even more so in the outlook of the people. Western Canada, in my experience, is*

Beatrice also joined whole-heartedly in Baháʼí activities in
the region. She must have made occasional trips to Calgary
because Catharina Ankersmit, who had recently arrived in
Canada from the Netherlands, recalls meeting Beatrice at
firesides in Calgary in the late 1950s, and being struck by both
the sincerity of Mrs. Ashton's devotion as well as the dignity of
her bearing. "She was a real lady…", Catharina said. When Dale
Lillico heard Catharina's comment about Beatrice, she smiled
and said, "We were country bumpkins compared to her."

In her report to the Pioneer Committee, Beatrice refers to
joining a Writers workshop. Cindy Newkirk, now of Lumsden,
Saskatchewan, shared the following experience of meeting her.
"When I was nine, we moved to Lethbridge… my grandmother
moved from Pincher Creek to Lethbridge too, joining a writers'
workshop… She met Beatrice Ashton there and when my
grandmother failed to attend a meeting, Mrs. Ashton followed
up and learned that my grandmother's cancer had come back…
she was in hospital to stay…"

Beatrice visited Cindy's grandmother, Beatrice Ankill,
in hospital and willingly conversed with her about life after

                    Beatrice Ashton and Louise White Cow

death—something most people were reluctant to do. She also brought Bahá'í books for her to read. As her disease progressed, Mrs. Ankill got her daughter, Enid Wrate—an avowed atheist at the time—to read aloud to her. The books affected Enid profoundly. She would come home saying, "Cindy, listen to what we read today!"

Both twelve-year-old Cindy and her mom began attending Bahá'í meetings, and Beatrice organized a children's class especially for Cindy. They studied the early heroes of the Faith from *The Dawnbreakers*[59], and Cindy came to adore the kind attention and fascinating material Beatrice provided. Beatrice also invited Cindy and her mom to get seasons tickets to the Lethbridge Symphony Association with her. "So, the three of us, dressed to the nines once a month took in opera, piano, violin, symphony or ballet. We found our horizons greatly expanded!"

In another photo (next page), Beatrice and Louise White Cow are standing together, flanked by several others. The two women's arms are companionably linked. Ben White Cow is standing behind Louise. Louise's sister, Rosie Knowlton, and her husband, Samson, are at left. Dale Lillico is at right. The photo is taken down the hill from Brocket in 'Highbush', where Louise lived much of her life.

At the time of the photo, Louise had several children from an abusive former marriage and was hoping to marry Ben White Cow, a kindly man. But she was prevented from marrying again because the Catholic church would not sanction a divorce from her previous husband. She had learned of the Bahá'í Faith along with her sister, Rosie, and her brother-in-law, Samson Knowlton. Alan Prairie Chicken introduced them to Arthur Irwin, the Calgary Bahá'í who was travelling back and forth with his work as a geologist for the federal government.

---

59 An authoritative history of the Bábi Faith covering the few short years before most of its followers became known as Bahá'ís. It was written by Nabil-i-Azam, a historian by training, and eye-witness to the astonishing events occurring in Iran in the mid 19th century.

Samson Knowlton, Rosie Knowlton, Beatrice Ashton, Louise White Cow, Ben White Cow, Dale Olivier (Lillico). Photo source: Dale Lillico.

Though the photo does not tell me this, I have learned that Louise was about to get legal help with her divorce from The Needy Litigants Society in Calgary, which she succeeded in getting. The Bahá'ís had just obtained legal recognition of their status as an independent Faith that could authorize its own marriages[60]. Louise and Ben were married in July of 1960. The ceremony was conducted in Calgary, and Louise's young niece[61], recalls being somewhat baffled by all the fuss over Louise's hair and clothing in Dale Lillico's apartment in preparation for the wedding. The young cousins, among whom

---

60 Arthur Irwin refers to Louise White Cow's situation in *Early Native Teaching in Canada*, Appendix B.

61 Bev Knowlton

                         Beatrice Ashton and Louise White Cow

were Louise's daughters from her previous marriage, sat on the stairs leading up to Dale's second storey apartment and waited.

According to *The Canadian Bahá'í News* in 1961, and cited in Glenn Cameron's online *Bahá'í Chronology*[62], Ben White Cow and Louise were married in the first legally recognized Bahá'í marriage ceremony in Canada, in a service authorized by the Spiritual Assembly of the Bahá'ís of Calgary. The article noted the significance that it was a First Nations couple who had the honour of this unique event. "Thirty people attended from Edmonton, Lethbridge, Regina, Peigan Indian Reserve, and Calgary…"

In Dale Lillico's unpublished account of those days[63], she describes the home the White Cows went on to create and their hospitable spirit:

"Ben and Louise White Cow were very active Bahá'ís with a large family. They lived between Frank and Cecile Holloway's and the Knowlton's. Despite their poverty, the White Cows doors were always open to everyone who came. Louise had a way of making a meal out of very little and always found a place for the weary to sleep. Their large family gathered many friends, and these remained friends until their death. One year, a son of theirs passed away and the White Cows wanted to have a Bahá'í funeral. We all put our resources together and the service was held from their humble home, for a packed crowd. There was country music played on a record player and Dale Lillico conducted the service for them."

I received a beautiful photograph of Ben and Louise standing in front of their house with two of their young children. It was a photograph taken by Richard (Dick) Stanton, part of the National Spiritual Assembly's collection, and sent by the archivist, Ailsa Leftwich. It shows their whitewashed log home

---

62 *https://Bahá'í-library.com/chronology*
63 See Appendix A

Louise and Ben White Cow with two of their children, circa 1960, Richard Stanton photo, Copyright National Spiritual Assembly of the Bahá'ís of Canada, Courtesy Canadian Bahá'í Archives

in the river valley. The family's smiling faces are illumined by the particularly clear light of a late autumn morning. The leaves have fallen from the trees but the air must still be warm because Louise is not wearing a coat. If all was quiet, they may have been able to hear the sound of the river flowing nearby. In 1995, this entire area in the flood plain of the Old Man River Valley was devasted by a terrible flood and forever altered. Now, not a house remains.

Returning to Beatrice Ashton and her time in Lethbridge, it appears she continued delivering courses, researching, editing, and compiling reports for the Bahá'í World Centre. An example of Beatrice's own fine writing is the account she wrote of the 1963 Bahá'í World Congress held in London, found in *The Bahá'í World 1963-1968*. She went back to the United States before moving to Haifa, Israel, in 1970 to work in the Research Department for the Universal House of Justice[64], cataloguing and indexing the letters of the Guardian.

Millie Collins, a Hand of the Cause of God from America, who lived for many years at the Bahá'í World Center, was one

---

64 The supreme governing body of the Bahá'í Faith, first elected in 1963.

  Beatrice Ashton and Louise White Cow

of Beatrice's closest personal friends.[65] Scans of handwritten letters between the two women, courtesy of the US Bahá'í Archives, show the tenderness Millie felt for Beatrice. She signed off a January 1953 letter saying, "… Oh Beatrice dear, how I long for one more visit in our 'hide out' room – maybe – God willing… all my heart, deepest love, Millie."

Earlier in the letter, Millie admitted coming down with a cold on top of almost unceasing arthritic pain. She had been away for meetings, and when she returned to Haifa she found all her belongings moved from her own poorly heated rooms to the Guardian's house at his request. To her even greater surprise, she found herself moved into the very room that the Master, 'Abdu'l-Bahá, had occupied during his lifetime. Her letter to Beatrice, written hurriedly in sentence fragments, says "… only other person in it was May Maxwell – now I'm here – great bounty." She also asked Beatrice to send her six pounds of powdered milk, twelve jars of canned chicken, and a bottle of vitamins. She closes the letter saying, "Sorry dearest to trouble you so soon…"

---

65 Millie (Amelia) Collins was appointed a 'Hand of the Cause of God' by the Guardian. She lived for some time in Haifa, assisting the Guardian with his many responsibilities, providing solace to his widow after his passing, and aiding in the transition that resulted in the election of the Universal House of Justice. Millie was a woman of significant financial means who chose to live modestly. When she offered to pay for a period of rest for the Guardian in Europe, he accepted the money but spent it on the beautiful 'Collins Gate' which now leads to the Shrine of Bahá'u'lláh at Bahjí, near 'Akká. Many of the Bahá'í properties on Mount Carmel, including the Temple site, were purchased through her generosity. The International Archives Building was also completed and furnished with significant financial contributions from her. Regarding her move to the Guardian's home, Donna Seyed-Mahmoud, in her course on Millie Collins, said the Guardian's home was considerably warmer than the place where Millie had been staying, and he insisted she move in with him and his wife, Rúhíyyih Khánum, a sign of his deep personal concern and affection for Millie.

Louise and Ben White Cow were remembered after their passing by the family and friends from both near and far who loved them dearly, as indicated in the following note:[66]

"In June 1991, a special gathering was held at the Peigan Bahá'í Center,[67] organized by the White Cow's daughter, Jocelyn, and her husband Eddie James Bad Eagle Jr, to commemorate the lives of Ben and Louise. Special guests included Counsellor Don Rogers of the International Teaching Centre in Haifa, Israel, his wife Barbara, Continental Board of Counsellors member Jacqueline Left Hand Bull-Delahunt, National Spiritual Assembly Member Louise Profeit-Leblanc, Auxiliary Board Member Ruth Eyford, National Teaching Committee members John Sargent and Paul Bujold. Many friends from Alberta also attended the memorial gathering."

By now, Beatrice Ashton and Louise White Cow have both been in the 'next world' for many years. So have all their friends. I like to think of the two of them as smiling at the sight of one another, perhaps strolling through one of the spiritual 'gardens'[68] together, waving to their friend Millie, and basking in each other's company. Louise's sister, Rosie Knowlton, will surely be near-by and join them at times. This scenario is of course, the product of my own flight of imagination, but it is not entirely divorced from Bahá'í teachings on life after death.

---

66 Note in Pat Verge's document of background information on the story of the Bahá'í Faith at Piikani, written for Band Council's deliberations on the fate of the Bahá'í Center.

67 The Bahá'í Center at Peigan, 1985–1995, was called the Naat Owá Pii Bahá'í Centre.

68 Bahá'ís believe in life after death as a spiritual and conscious reality, not a physical state or place.

6   Edmund and Jean Many Bears

In 1961, Edmund and Jean Many Bears became the first Bahá'ís at Siksika. Siksika is one of the nations of the Blackfoot Confederacy and is located an hour's drive east of the city of Calgary along the Bow River. In their later years, the Many Bears would spend significant time in Calgary (Mohkinstsis) working to better conditions in the city for their people. Their souls left this world before I was able to meet them, so my knowledge of them comes to me entirely from other sources to whom I am grateful.

Two things aroused my immediate interest when people spoke of them. One was a story told by Allison Healy[69] about what had appealed to Jean in the new religion she had joined. The other was a 1950s era, black and white photograph of Ed and Jean standing in front of a canvas tent, sent to me by someone who had known them as a fellow traveller on the summer pow wow circuit of the 1960s. In it, their faces appear to welcome a conversation—to come sit with them awhile; to listen to a teaching story.

Roger White, the noted Canadian poet and much-loved member of the Bahá'í Community, writes the following 'In Memoriam' in *The Bahá'í World Volume XIV*:

"Edmund was a recognized leader among the Blackfoot people, as his father had been before him... The Many Bears learned of the Faith from Dr. Arthur Irwin and his

---

69 Much loved southern Alberta Bahá'í from Kainai (Blood Reserve) featured in chapter 12.

wife, Lily Ann, and accepted it in October 1961... They immediately became active in carrying the Faith to others of the Blackfoot tribe and their determination and enthusiasm contributed greatly to the formation, at Ridván 1962, of the Spiritual Assembly of the Blackfoot Reserve..."

Other members of that first Spiritual Assembly[70] included Nellie Little Light, Martha Medicine Traveller, Barbara Chief, Frank Turning Robe, Theodore Chief, Timothy Breaker, and Arthur Little Light. I have only a fleeting memory of meeting one of these individuals—Martha Medicine Traveller. I am led to understand that Martha was a woman of ceremonial standing in her culture, and I too, could sense her deep spiritual mien. The image of her that I recall is of her walking toward her house across the dusty, dry grass of the Bow River flood plain—known as 'The Flats'—in late summer. The year may have been 1973. She had been at an afternoon prayer meeting which I also attended, and slight puffs of dust were rising from beneath her moccasins as she walked. Something about the sight of the sun warming her back, the warm orange color of the cotton print dress she was wearing, the heat waves rising beyond her, the cottonwoods along the nearby Bow River, and the smell of sage in the air, stayed with me. It reminds me that true veneration of what is holy, may be most accessible in the wide-open cathedral of the Great Plains. The plains were also the spiritual and temporal home of Ed and Jean Many Bears.

Arthur Irwin, in *Early Native teaching in Canada*, describes the introduction of the Bahá'í Faith to the people at Siksika in the early 1960s:

"The Blackfoot teaching was assisted by two teachers from distant places. Jim Walton, a Tlingit Indian from Alaska came to southern Alberta and remained for a month or two in 1962... By Ridván, 1962 when the first Assembly

---

70 The nine-member, annually elected body, administering the affairs of a Bahá'í community. (There is no clergy in the Bahá'í Faith).

                                    Edmund and Jean Many Bears

was formed, there were some 15 or more adult believers. By Ridván, 1963 there were many dozens of Bahá'ís on the reserve… it was the summer of 1962 when Mabel Robinson pioneered to the town of Gleichen near the reserve boundary, where she rented a tiny, abandoned storefront on the main street… From here she carried out much of her teaching of the adults and children on the reserve, occasionally trudging on foot to the reserve homes."

Roger White's *In Memoriam* notes that Edmund had served actively on the Band Council, as well as in the traditional Blackfoot organization, the Brave Dog Society. One of its functions was to provide security to the community. A 1968 interview[71] with George First Rider, an elderly Kainai man, explains that the Brave Dogs are a traditional Blackfoot society—one of numerous societies to which men could be initiated—given they had somehow earned the privilege. Belonging to a sacred society still carries certain privileges and responsibilities, and specific songs and ceremonies are attached.

In Memoriam gives further information about Edmund:

"By occupation he was a farmer and although he had a little formal education, he had a thirst for knowledge and a deep desire to improve the condition of his people. In the Bahá'í teachings he found a solution to the depressed state of his people and a heightened understanding of the spiritual capacity and noble station of man."

The Many Bears saw the needs of less fortunate people from their community who had gone to the city, a place where they were met with less than hospitable responses from most people they encountered. They were instrumental in forming the Native Friendship Club in the 1950s, along with the Arthur

---

71 *https://ourspace.uregina.ca.* This website gives the origin story of this society in an interview with George First Rider. Interviewed in 1968 by John Hellson and Dave Melting Tallow (translator). Copyright belongs to Diana Melting Tallow who actually made the recording.

and Lily Ann Irwin, and Dorothy and Joe Francis (First Nations Bahá'ís with experience in this area in Regina). The purpose of the club was to foster friendship and understanding between Indigenous people and the white population, and provide a safe and friendly place in the city for such interaction. It was in this context that the Many Bears first encountered the Irwins and the Bahá'í Faith. The club developed into the Calgary Indian Friendship Centre in 1964, with Edmund serving as its director. Arthur wrote, "Meetings were held in Calgary, or on one of the three nearby reserves—Sarcee, Blackfoot and Stoney. Through this club we became friends with many lovely Indian people…"

John Sargent, a Bahá'í who grew up on the Six Nations Reserve in Ontario, sent me a photo of the Many Bears in front of their tent at a powwow. John spent significant time on the prairies in his youth, and recalled seeing the Many Bears at powwows in the 1960s. When I sent him a draft of some of my work to comment on, he replied saying, "I noted with some pleasure mention of Ed and Jean Many Bears… I also greatly admired them. They used to follow the powwow circuit, set up

Jean and Edmund Many Bears. Photo source: John Sargent.

                              Edmund and Jean Many Bears

their camp, hang the Greatest Name[72] in their tent and begin holding firesides. Good, exciting times!"

The scene John paints of Ed and Jean enjoying the powwow circuit in summer, is lovely to imagine. Based on my own experience of these events, I can 'see' them inhaling the freshness of the morning upon waking, fixing breakfast, and visiting friends. In time, drummers will begin their steady beat. To think of them using their canvas tent as a venue for teaching others about their newly adopted Faith, somehow surprises me. This ready sharing of their Faith with others, demonstrates what seems to be a certain sense of urgency on their part. They seemed to wholeheartedly believe that this new Faith held within it the seeds of a renewed and transformed society; that it would inspire the longed-for Age of the Brotherhood of Man, the 'Kingdom of God on earth'; something their people and an ailing world desperately needed.

John Hellson was an ethnologist from Cornwall, with deep early ties to the Many Bears and the Blackfoot people. He had married a young Blackfoot woman, Diana Melting Tallow, without whom he would not have had the access to the people and culture, that he was given. In the last weeks of his life, I encountered him in a palliative care unit, and asked what he remembered about Ed and Jean. I showed him John Sargent's photo of the couple in front of their tent and he exclaimed, "I've been in that tent!" He pointed out that they were the 'cream' of Blackfoot society; looked up to and highly respected; having the prerogatives that the traditions of their culture afforded them.

Among other things, they were tipi owners. The design painted on their tipi had to have been ceremonially transferred to them by someone who had the cultural right to do so. This is still the case in Blackfoot culture. The original owner would have acquired the design in a vision, and the prayer songs

---

72 'The Greatest Name' is a Bahá'í symbol, often depicted in Arabic script and framed, which can be translated as "O Thou Glory of the Most Glorious".

accompanying it would have been memorized and passed on with the design. John said that when you entered a tipi, you entered 'another world'. He recalled the Many Bears tipi as being fully furnished, with willow beds and 'pillows' of thin willow strips to lean on.

The Many Bears signatures occur several times in Rosie Knowlton's meticulously kept guest book from the early 1960s, indicating the travel and friendship between them. Jean's comments reflect a relationship of loving support and a willingness to drive long distances to be together.

I found traces of other trips the Many Bears made in the early 1960s in a set of photographs sent to me by Cindy Newkirk. The photographs belonged to her mother, Enid Wrate, and featured a group of twenty or so Siksika Bahá'ís among whom were the Many Bears, posing for the camera in the outdoor amphitheatre of the Banff Centre for the Arts. Cascade Mountain is clearly visible behind them in one of the photos. The Banff Centre for the Arts was the venue for Bahá'í Summer Schools for western Canada and parts of the northwestern States during the 1950s and sixties until 1967 when the school was offered the use of Ed Muttart's Sylvan Lake property. It was the Many Bears who were no doubt instrumental in bringing the group of their friends and neighbors along to the Banff school.

I asked Diana Melting Tallow if she knew the names of the individuals in the photographs at Banff. She had grown up with them and listed the names of the adults, all of whom have now passed away. Only those who were children are still alive. Among the individuals were some whose memory she found particularly poignant. She said,

"I was impressed with Florence Calf Child's image. Her love for the Faith shone through her face and eyes … She had her arm around Lorna Cat Face who seemed to be in a state of wonder with what she probably heard at the Bahá'í gathering. Florence seemed to know Lorna's feelings and seemed happy

  Edmund and Jean Many Bears

for her. She had her arm around her as if to help her enter the Faith. Ed and Jean looked happy and proud of being Bahá'ís. Jean was beautiful. She exuded calmness and safety. I loved being with her. Edmund loved her."

It is lovely to hear Diana's personal memory of these individuals and her recollection of the tenderness in their relationships. "Edmund loved her…" is particularly illustrative of their relationship. Diana also recalled Jean's Blackfoot name, Iitspai'kanna, meaning 'Sparkling in the Mist'.

A remarkable story Allison Healy told—as passed on to me—was that she had been riding in the back of the Many Bears' car as a teenager, and that she had asked Jean what attracted her to the Bahá'í Faith. Jean had replied that she could "smell God" when she heard Bahá'í prayers. Perhaps the fragrance she was inhaling was that of roses; whether there were any actual roses around or not. At moments of heightened spiritual potency, early believers in Persia were inclined to smell roses, and it should be noted that the western plains of Turtle Island where Jean lived, had their own particular abundance of highly fragrant wild roses in summer.

Ed and Jean's service to their newly adopted Faith, in addition to serving their community of origin, is all the more remarkable because it occurred during the last years of their lives when their health was failing. Cindy Newkirk provided me with group photos (following pages) of people from Siksika who attended the 1966 Bahá'í Summer School in Banff at the invitation of the Many Bears. The 'pioneer' to nearby Gleichen, Mabel Robinson—who would have been in close association with the Many Bears—is shown with several women from Siksika, her light-colored hair clearly visible.

They had only been Bahá'ís for a brief seven years before both of them passed away. Roger White explains, "Although dogged from the beginning of their Bahá'í lives by ill health and the need of frequent medical care, the Many Bears and

Ed Many Bears and friends from Siksika at circa 1964 Banff Bahá'í Summer School. Photo source: Cindy Newkirk.

Siksika Bahá'ís at circa 1964 Banff Bahá'í Summer School. Photo source: Cindy Newkirk.

  Edmund and Jean Many Bears

Siksika Bahá'ís with Mabel Robinson. Photo source: Cindy Newkirk.

their white Bahá'í friends made many teaching trips throughout the Canadian west, winning friends among the people of the Peigan, Blood and Cree Indian tribes." He goes on to explain,

"They also visited other Indian tribes from the states of Montana and Washington. Jean had a compelling and quiet manner and was a very effective teacher. On many occasions she confirmed people in the Faith. Edmund was an especially effective teacher in the Blackfoot tongue and frequently at Bahá'í gatherings was asked to intone prayers in that language. He possessed a gentleness, strength and

assurance which marked him as a leader. One could feel a spiritual strength emanating from him during periods of prayer."

Arthur Irwin describes some of their Baháʼí travels in the United States and the resulting 'fallout' with administrative bodies in the Baháʼí community who were trying to keep track of membership:

"…On another occasion, Ed and Jean Many Bears made one of their frequent trips into the United States to visit Indian relatives and friends. They didn't hesitate to enroll ready souls using Canadian cards[73]. Our teaching committee had its knuckles rapped via the United States NSA and the Canadian NSA, for failing to train our Indian believers in the proper procedure for contacting the American Teaching Committee. The Indian Baháʼís disregarded the [international] border and were not concerned about administration when there was teaching to be done amongst their tribesmen across the line… Lily Ann and Jean Many Bears made several teaching trips together—sometimes it was a foursome including Ed Many Bears and me. We helped with teaching visits to the Louis Bull, Samson, and Pigeon Lake reserves."

Roger White quotes a friend of the Many Bears speaking of their wonderful personal natures.

"They were very genuine, loving Baháʼís, inflamed with the spirit of the Cause. Due to ill health and the many pressures put upon those who moved between two cultures, it was often with great personal sacrifice that they continued their service to the Cause… They each had a profound understanding of and respect for Baháʼuʼlláh and His teachings. One felt a certain peace and tranquility in their

---

73 'Canadian cards' refers to the Baháʼí enrollment cards which were filled in and sent to the National Office to register new members.

            Edmund and Jean Many Bears

company - quite assuredly a combination of their Indian heritage and the influence of their newly found but well-beloved Faith. Their teaching efforts and the example of their lives created a bridge of friendship between the Indian and white communities, and their influence assuredly will direct in some measure many whose lives they touched."

Some of Jean's 'teaching trips' with Lily Ann Irwin are referred to in Chapter 2 about the Irwins. Her intuitive knowledge and closeness to the spiritual realm were evident in these experiences, and deeply respected by Lily Ann.

Referring to the end of their lives, Roger White says, "Succumbing at last to the physical frailties which had plagued them, they died but several weeks apart. Even in death they taught—those attending the memorial service held by the Bahá'ís of Calgary described it as an outstanding demonstration of love and brotherhood."

I regret how little I was able to uncover about this remarkable couple fifty years after their passing. Their luminous souls left this world in 1968. I would have loved to have spent even a moment in their presence.

7 Rúhíyyih Khánum's 1960 Visit to Piikani

There are stories which happen to people that become 'seed' stories. They germinate, take root, and new generations of people continue to pass them on. That is how I see the stories of Rúhíyyih Khánum's visits to Treaty Seven Territory. This remarkable woman's first visit in 1960 is legendary in my mind; as well as in many other people's estimation. I thought it was the first of two visits, but over lunch one day in Calgary, a friend[74] who grew up at Piikani said, "Did you know she made three trips to Piikani?" I was surprised but grateful to learn there was a third, however short it might have been.

In 1960, two years after the first individuals on Piikani embraced the Bahá'í Faith, Rúhíyyih Khánum, the distinguished widow of the Guardian, Shoghi Effendi, requested a meeting with the people there. Who was this woman?

She was born Mary Maxwell of Montreal, in 1910. Amatu'l-Bahá, the title bestowed on her by the Guardian, can be translated as 'Maidservant of God'. Her family is esteemed by Bahá'ís the world over; her mother being considered the founder of both the Canadian and the European communities. On the back cover of a biography of her family, *The Maxwells of Montreal*, written by her dear friend and travelling companion, Violette Nakhjavani, is a lovely tribute:

"One family, bonded in their love for the Bahá'i Faith and for each other, committed through decades of uninterrupted

---

74 Bev Knowlton

service to the promotion and establishment of that Faith worldwide. Of the mother, 'Abdu'l-Bahá wrote that "her company uplifts and develops the soul". The father, a noble, cultured and saintly man, was an outstanding architect not only of the Shrine of the Báb but as a partner in the most preeminent architectural firm in Canada during the first quarter of the 20th century. And the daughter grew up to play a unique role in history as the wife of the Guardian of the Bahá'í Faith. They were the Maxwells of Montreal."

Rúhíyyih Khánum speaking to a group in the 1960s. Photo source: Canadian Bahá'í Archives.

Rúhíyyih Khánum made her home in Haifa, Israel, following her 1937 marriage to Shoghi Effendi. When she visited Canada in 1960, her meeting with the Chief and Council at Piikani, then still known as Peigan, was part of a larger trip across the country. An October 1960 *The Canadian Bahá'í News* article describes the visit this way:

"On the morning of May 21, Rúhíyyih Khánum, Mrs. Jean Chute, Arthur Irwin, Lily Ann Irwin, and John Hellson drove from Calgary to the Peigan Reserve, and were met at the Knowlton home by members of the Peigan Bahá'í group and two of the (Band) Councillors, Walter Bastien and Charlie Crow Eagle, the latter of whom, although elderly and in poor health, had walked three miles to attend the meeting."

     Rúhíyyih Khánum's 1960 Visit to Piikani

The moving image of the elderly Charlie Crow Eagle walking three miles to attend, lingers. Ḅev Knowlton, at whose childhood home this event occurred, clarified the positions of various people who attended, including the Chief and Council. She said in those days, Band Councillors were lifetime positions, as was Chief. This is in contrast to today, when Councillors are elected for four-year terms, so the respect accorded these individuals at that time was significant. Lifetime Councillors Joe Crowshoe, Walter Bastien and Samson Knowlton were present at the event, as was their traditional lifetime Chief, John Yellowhorn. Traditional healer, Pat Bad Eagle was also there, though he is referred to as a 'Councillor' in the article. It goes on to say,

> *"When Rúhíyyih Khánum was seated, Head Chief John Yellowhorn, Councillor Pat Bad Eagle, and Councillor Joe Crowshoe entered and were introduced... Other guests continued to arrive until there were 30 adults and about 12 children present...*
>
> *Rúhíyyih Khánum in addressing the gathering, spoke of her early and continued interest in the Indian people and of her recent visit to the Hopi Indians in the United States. She told them that the Indians have a great destiny and indicated the need of civilization for the qualities that the Indian people could bring to it.*
>
> *She then said, 'When I knew I was coming here... I wanted to offer to your chief for the people, not for the Bahá'ís or for any particular person, but for the people, a gift from me—something that is made in Persia, because I thought it would interest you... And this (pointing to the Greatest Name in the center of the rug) is a prayer. It says, 'O Glory of the most Glorious'...*
>
> *Chief Yellowhorn received the gift graciously on behalf of the Band Council... Then Councillor Crow Eagle asked that all go outside so that they might give a special name*

The images of passing clouds, the sun coming out the moment the Great Spirit is called upon, the quiet of the setting in the Old Man River Valley, the chill in the spring air as wind blew over them from the snow-capped mountains to the west, and the immense dignity of Charlie Crow Eagle as he prayed, are truly moving.

A report in *The Canadian Bahá'í News* the following summer, describes Charlie Crow Eagle and his wife picking berries in Washington State with friends. It referred to him as Chief Crow Eagle, (though it must be noted again that he was a Councillor,

At 1960 Name-giving ceremony in front of the Knowlton home. (l to r:) unknown, Samson Knowlton, John Yellowhorn, Rúhiyyih Khánum, Charlie Crow Eagle, Joe Crowshoe, Pat Bad Eagle. Photo source: Dale Lillico.

                    Rúhíyyih Khánum's 1960 Visit to Piikani

Rúhíyyih Khánum being greeted by Councillor Joe Crowshoe 1960. Photo source: Dale Lillico.

not a 'Chief') and it said he spoke to the people there of the visit of Amatu'l-Bahá Rúhíyyih Khánum, in the most reverent and loving manner.

Her visit on that day in 1960 is still spoken of at Piikani, by those who were there. Samson Knowlton, in sharing his memories with visitors to his home over the years, said he considered Rúhíyyih Khánum's visit the most significant part of his life as a Bahá'í. Her presence, reverence, and respect, as well as her repeated follow-up letters and messages to the people thereafter[75], made an unforgettable impact.

Her appreciation of the sacredness and validity of traditional First Nations spirituality was notable. Following her third visit in 1986, she wrote back to the National Spiritual Assembly of the Bahá'ís of Canada[76], saying, "I need not tell you what a profound experience the pipe ceremony on the Peigan Reservation was. It was probably the most moving thing that

---

75 See Appendix D for messages Rúhíyyih Khánum sent back to individuals at Piikani.

76 See Appendix E for her letter to the National Spiritual Assembly with her thoughts on relations with First Nations people.

Rúhíyyih Khánum (standing) at 1986 opening of the Baháí Centre in Brocket, Joe Crowshoe (seated) performing ceremony. Photo source: Dale Lillico

happened to me in my whole trip, and one of the most moving things that has happened to me in my whole life…"

One of the visitors attending the 1960 meeting said, "This has been one of the most memorable days… to hear her address the Chief and Councillors as if they were kings." Sixty years later, Bev Knowlton said, "I got to be the girl who gave Rúhíyyih Khánum a bouquet of flowers." She also described the preparations her parents and relatives went to for the day. The men cut grass and tidied up outdoors. Everything was taken out of the small, two room home to make space for seating. Her mother, Rosie, and her aunt, Louise White Cow, scrubbed every available surface to be so clean that she laughingly explained, "You know, they both went to Residential School and cleaned to the extreme. They even scrubbed the outhouse down. They wouldn't let us kids use the outhouse the morning before, so we wouldn't mess it up. We had to go in the bush."

Rúhíyyih Khánum's deep affection for the people she met there is reflected in personal letters and cards she sent back. In

1981, upon hearing of the passing of Rosie Knowlton, Rúhíyyih Khánum sent a hand-written card of condolence to Rosie's husband, Samson. She not only sympathized with his loss but referred back to the day she met him in 1960, with tenderness and regard. I was shown the original card by Knowlton's eldest daughter, Eleanora McDermott. The message inside read:

Haifa, Israel
June 25, 1981
Dear Samson,

Through Jamie Bond, I heard of the death of dear Rosie and want to write to express my loving sympathy. When we have been together for a lifetime, separation is very hard—as I well know from my own life. My visit in your home in Peigan so long ago, and the giving of my name, Natu Okcist, is always fresh in my memory and one of the great events in my life. So many times I have spoken of it, in many countries of the world. If there is anyone who still remembers me, please give them my warm greetings.

To them and your family my love,
Rúhíyyih

Following her 1986 visit to Piikani for the dedication of a Bahá'í Center, at which a sacred pipe ceremony was conducted by Joe Crowshoe, she wrote to the Knowlton's son, Clarence, saying,

…Again, I ask you to tell Joe Crowshoe how profoundly stirred I was by the Pipe Ceremony, and that I shall always be deeply grateful to him—and you and the other Bahá'ís who persuaded him—for that wonderful spiritual occasion… Please give my love to all the dear friends there – Bahá'í and not Bahá'í, especially your own family—and tell them I remember them in my prayers at the Holy Shrines.

With warm Bahá'í love,
Ruhyyih

She recognized the spiritual capacity of Indigenous people as extraordinary and viewed it as something the world desperately needed. On numerous occasions, she referred to the 1916 statement of 'Abdu'l-Bahá that said, "Attach great importance to the Indigenous population of America... should they be educated and guided, there can be no doubt that they will become so illumined as to enlighten the whole world."

On December 31st, 1963, three years after Rúhíyyih Khánum's first visit, a special ceremony was again held at Piikani. It was a blessing of the vial of soil which she had brought from the inner Shrine of Bahá'u'lláh in 1960. It was conducted by Pat Bad Eagle, one of the Elders referred to in Chapter 2, who had visited the Irwins' home in Calgary in the late '50s to assess for himself, the spiritual nature of their Faith. An old colour photograph shows him kneeling in the bleached, dry grass of a hilltop. Thin winter sun envelops the participants, among them, Pat's wife, Susie, with a blanket around her shoulders. There must have been a chinook wind blowing as

Soil blessing ceremony on hill near Brocket; Pat Bad Eagle kneeling in center, his wife Susie Bad Eagle is behind him, Chief John Yellowhorn (the taller man) and Councillor Samson Knowlton are at right. Photo source: Bev Knowlton.

 Rúhíyyih Khánum's 1960 Visit to Piikani

two of the men are not wearing jackets. This ceremony is still remembered with reverence by those who knew of it. Some of the sacred soil was mixed with the soil on a hilltop south of the townsite of Brocket, and some was placed at the four corners of the Knowlton home where the meeting with Rúhíyyih Khánum had been held.[77]

In September of 1960, Charlie Crow Eagle expressed the hope that Rúhíyyih Khánum would someday make a return visit to the reserve. According to a report in *The Canadian Bahá'í News* in October 1960:

"The meeting was opened with revealed prayers and our good friend Charlie Crow Eagle prayed in Blackfoot. He prayed that the Great Spirit would bring to realization Rúhíyyih Khánum's desire to one day visit every reserve in America. He prayed that she would come back to Peigan and that this [Bahá'í] Faith would spread quickly and bring light and hope to his people, and he thanked the Great Spirit for sending the Bahá'ís to his reserve."

Charlie Crow Eagle's hopes for her to return were fulfilled, twice. On the most well-known occasion in 1986 when she opened the Bahá'í Centre on the reserve in Brocket, she arrived in a small private plane with her friend and travel companion, Violette Nakhjavani, much to the delight and excitement of a waiting crowd.

The visit I had not known about was a brief one, occurring in 1982 when a Native Council was being held at nearby Kainai (the Blood Reserve) where she was an honored guest. Councils like this were events for Indigenous Bahá'ís from all over the continent to come together to share hopes, aspirations, concerns, and celebrate their cultures. While at the Council, she expressed the hope that someone would be able to drive her over to Piikani again for a brief visit. It was Earl Healy, a member of Kainai Nation, who took her there. Earl had a nice

---

77 Bev Knowlton's account.

Rúhiyyih Khánum arriving on a small plane at 1986 Bahá'í Centre opening. Photo source: Bev Knowlton.

big sedan at the time and had cleaned it meticulously, setting beautiful blankets of Indigenous design on the seats. He waited for her after the meeting. Time dragged on. He started to wonder if her plans had changed. Finally, she emerged from the hall and got in the car.

He took the back road to Piikani, thinking it had more beautiful views than the longer highway route via Fort Macleod. He pulled over at a certain spot, pointing out sacred Chief Mountain in the distance. She got out to take a picture of the mountain, despite a few trees partially obscuring her view. Earl suggested he pull ahead to get a clearer view of the mountain. "No," she said. "This is absolutely perfect. The Guardian taught me how to take good pictures. And as you know, he was an expert photographer."

Her appreciation of the landscape, and her deep love and regard for the people, form a significant part of the enduring impact of her presence at Piikani. I believe Rúhíyyih Khánum and the people she met at Piikani will be associating with love and affection in the world to come as well. Perhaps they will

Rúhíyyih Khánum's 1960 Visit to Piikani

1986 ribbon cutting for new Peigan Bahá'í Centre. Photo source: Dale Lillico.

sing and chant prayers while inhaling the fragrance of roses and sweet grass. Surely, they will smudge[78] with tobacco, sage and sweetgrass as they recall the times they had together in the shadow of the mountains, near the Old Man River.

It should be noted that the Bahá'í teachings on life after death say, "Know thou of a certainty, that in the divine worlds, the spiritual beloved ones will recognize each other, and will seek union, but a spiritual union. Likewise, the love that one may have entertained for anyone will not be forgotten in the world of the Kingdom. Likewise, thou wilt not forget the life thou hast had in the material world."[79]

---

78 The practice of smudging (purifying from negativity and distraction with the smoke of plants such as sage and sweetgrass) is often done by First Nations in preparation for prayer. I know many people raise a brow at the thought of tobacco after generations of cigarette addiction in the larger culture. However, it has an honorable place in Indigenous culture and the next life is a spiritual reality, not a physical one, but physical images can give a feeling for a spiritual reality. And if Indigenous people consider these plants sacred, including tobacco, I'm all for it in that context.

79 'Abdu'l-Bahá, Bahá'í Scriptures, p. 483

8 The 1966 Calgary Youth Conference

In the midst of continuing Bahá'í activity in smaller centers within Treaty Seven territory during the 1960s, a major Youth Conference took place in the thoroughly urban setting of the University of Calgary. In 1966, the university campus had only a handful of buildings set between groves of young trees, on a large tract of land in northwest Calgary. It had just been granted autonomy from the University of Alberta, and there were big hopes for its future.

During Christmas break of that year, young Bahá'ís from western Canada, the far north, and the western United States came together to learn more about their Faith and consider ways of advancing its aims. A striking diversity of race and background existed among them, and the event would have effects on its participants well into the future. We get a glimpse of the enthusiasm it engendered, from a letter written at the time, by participant, Amy Woodward (Singh), to her parents:

"Dear Mom and Dad… the conference was really terrific… around 40, probably more, but we came from all over… So, we had Indian, Eskimo, Negro, Dutch, Chinese, and a lady from Malta, a man from Israel, the kids from the US and us, and the guy from the West Indies. And out of all that mixture there wasn't one kid that didn't seem especially nice! I just hated to leave…"

Amy was a new Bahá'í at the time and had found herself a member of the organizing committee putting the Conference together. She was a student from Cutknife, Saskatchewan, studying Occupational Therapy at the University of Alberta in Edmonton. In her unpublished memoir she gives a glimpse of how the conference came together:

> *"I don't remember just how this began, but somehow the University Club and the Edmonton Youth Club joined forces to work on a ground-breaking project... to be held at University of Calgary over the Christmas break... As I recall, I just tried to do whatever the others told me to do. I was astonished at young Morine Fraser's capacity... she knew a lot of people who could be speakers, and had astonishing secretarial skills... It wasn't a local project, and in the end proved to be an international one... It could be that the NSA was trying to empower the few youth there were, to take an active role."*

The chairman of the administrative committee was Ed Muttart of Calgary, a relatively new Bahá'í himself. He had first encountered the Faith just a year and a half earlier while attending a teachers' conference at the Banff Center for the Arts. Despite being so new to the Teachings of the Faith, he also gave several of the conference keynote talks. Ed would go on to make significant contributions to the Canadian Bahá'í community throughout his life as a member of the National Spiritual Assembly (NSA), but also as an individual with—among other things—his gift of the beautiful

Ed Muttart on a swing at Sylvan Lake Bahá'í Centre. Photo source: Ed Muttart.

The 1966 Calgary Youth Conference

lakefront property at Sylvan Lake for a Summer School and retreat facility. He spent many years nurturing and developing the facility and its educational programs.

His co-chairman was Dr. Soheil Bushrui, a professor at the University of Calgary at the time, who went on to hold numerous significant posts in academia thereafter. According to a 2015 *news.Bahá'í.org* article written after his passing, Dr. Bushrui went on to teach at universities in Africa, Europe, the Middle East and America, "…one of the world's foremost scholars of Arabic and English literature." The lectures he gave at the Calgary Youth Conference in 1966 were on topics related to Islam and its significance. Other presenters at the conference were Lily Ann Irwin speaking on *Pilgrimage to the Holy Land* and Alex Frame on *Youth and the Modern World: Choosing a Career.*

Amy forwarded a brochure she had saved from the conference, which gave an outline of topics to be covered, and listed some reference books participants were asked to bring. It appeared they were in for some serious study. Though organizers acknowledged participants may need to 'pack light', they suggested bringing the *Quran* (preferably the Rodwell translation), *Bahá'í Administration, Bahá'í Prayers,* and *The Book of Certitude.* Amy can't remember owning all these books, so there must have been some latitude, or availability of books for lending. Lectures were given daily at 10 am and 11:30 am, and the afternoons consisted of either another lecture or a workshop. Cindy Wrate (Newkirk) recalls being on the social committee in charge of evening activities. Amy further described the diversity of conference participants, and their challenges in getting there, in a letter to her parents:

"They [the Americans] wonderfully represented both the black and white races and included Carol Adams, Carol Brooks, Reggie Newkirk, and Jim Wonders. Two of them, Ann and Charlie Hook, were a young couple with a small toddler. There was a kid who came from the eastern NWT,

*David Tagoogna (who also used the last name Kabloona),
and from Yellowknife in the western NWT was Will van
den Hoonaard, [originally from Holland] ... Virginia
[Evans] and Alex [Frame]... kids from the Reserves in
southern Alberta, as well as Mary Okemow from Samson
Reserve near Edmonton (who shared a motel room with
us). It was a wonderfully diverse and happy bunch..."*

Two of the Americans who attended were Reggie Newkirk
and Jim Wonders[80], servicemen stationed in Colorado who
brought others along with them from New Mexico, Colorado,
Wyoming, and Montana. Amy mentions that they travelled
through a blizzard to get there. The roads through Montana
on the eastern slopes of the Rockies get many metres of snow
each winter, and prevailing winds tend to push the snow up and
over the continental divide. One of the roads through the area,
known as 'Going-to-the Sun Road', is not even open in winter,
the top of it frequently lying under 24 metres of snow[81]. Though
the conference participants would not have taken this road,
other roads through the area would also have been treacherous
during a blizzard. I can only image the trepidation experienced
by the drivers.

The spirit of the 1966 conference was such that it had an
influence on other students who were on campus, studying
during their Christmas break. They began to be attracted to its
sessions. Amy Woodward explains.

*"There were some (Calgary) university kids that had come
up to study and they got interested and sat in on the lectures
and discussions. They came to all the activities after that,
and we found out a day or two later that they'd been staying*

---

80 See chapter on Reggie Newkirk for more about Reggie and Jim's lifelong
friendship. A photo of the conference (next page) shows Jim Wonders
seated in the middle of the back row and Reggie Newkirk seated in the
second row, second from right. Amy Woodward (Singh) is sitting in the
back row beside Jim Wonders, 5th from left.
81 This road is a thrilling switched-backed climb over the Logan Pass,
often featured in *Most Dangerous Roads* articles.

1966 Youth Conference at University of Calgary. Photo source: Cindy Newkirk

up all night to study so they'd be able to come! They were nice people too… We were in bed by 1:30 or so for the first two nights but not after that, because that and mealtime were the only chance we had to get to know each other. So it was more like 3:30 or 4 AM for me for the rest of the week, and anywhere from there to 7 AM for some hardier individuals. I'm not sure how they managed to survive, but they were still going strong when I saw them last!"

The image of late-night socializing marathons becomes vivid as she goes on to say that she had never experienced such a joyful spirit of unity before. It must be remembered that the spirit she describes existed between young people of completely different backgrounds. She says she had been completely skeptical that such an atmosphere existed, prior to this experience. "I'd heard about having a spirit of happiness and love and unity etc. between people before—and thought it was a bunch of nonsense, but now I know…"

For her, the Conference had the effect of focusing her attention on 'living the Bahá'í life', not merely enrolling as a Bahá'í. Reflecting on her ensuing learning over the years, she said,

"What I didn't fully grasp, was that becoming a Bahá'í doesn't suddenly make you perfect. Certainly, I was aware of that in my own case, but apparently I had high expectations of others. Anyone who believes Bahá'u'lláh has brought a new message from God and is willing to try to align his or her life with His teachings, can enroll as a Bahá'í. That point is just the beginning of a lifelong process of transformation... Belief in something is easy, but practising it takes time and effort, and probably failure, which is followed by more effort... The true test of a Bahá'í is whether their deeds reflect a sincere effort to practice the Bahá'í teachings..."

She also described follow-up events to the conference involving youth from both sides of the international border. American youth invited the Canadians down to a conference in Albuquerque, New Mexico for a return engagement in the spring of 1967. She recalls one 'carload' coming from Canada that she was part of:

"Virginia Evans took her VW beetle. She and I traveled from Edmonton to Lethbridge where we picked up Cindy and Bevan Wrate. We took turns driving (Virginia, Cindy, and I) and sleeping. Bevan was too young to have his driver's license. From Browning, Montana, we traveled with some American Bahá'ís... and had adventures! But that's another story..."

The First Nations youth who attended were also immersed in the spirit of the Calgary Conference. Like the others, they were affected by the sense of excitement and spirit among the participants. As mentioned, Amy's First Nations friend, Mary

Okemow, from Samson Cree Nation was there and shared
a motel room with Amy and other girls. Wilton Knowlton,
Blandine Bastien, Lewis Strikes With a Gun, Dayle White Cow,
and Bev Knowlton, all from Piikani, arrived with Cindy Wrate
of nearby Lethbridge. Bev said it was a 'big deal' for them to get
away from home for something like that. I asked her if she had
felt nervous about going, but she recalled that given they were
travelling with their long-time friend, Cindy, she primarily felt
excitement at the opportunity. Once there, meeting other young
people, they were standing in a group as Reggie Newkirk,
the young African American who had come from Colorado
approached them. He introduced himself and asked each one
where they were from. By the time he got to dark-eyed, dark-
haired Cindy Wrate, he asked, "And which tribe are you from?"
After only the briefest hesitation, she replied, "The Lethbridge
Tribe," much to her First Nations friends' amusement. That
meeting led to the couple's marriage two years later.

The participants at the conference went on to study,
work and serve their communities in a variety of ways.
Reggie Newkirk became a recognized expert in the field of
human rights and race relations, working for Human Rights
Commissions and related agencies in numerous Canadian
provinces and territories. Will van den Hoonaard said it
focused him on the need to pursue an education, which he
clearly did as he went on to become a professor and researcher,
publishing significant works on themes such as research ethics.
Bev Knowlton became a skilled counsellor working in the field
of child protection. Lewis Strikes With a Gun became a nursing
orderly. Amy became an occupational therapist, and Alex
Frame went on to become a media expert and producer. Wilton
Knowlton was an accomplished musician and worked as an
addictions counsellor as well as a police officer. Dayle Whitecow
became a fine seamstress. These are the achievements of just a
handful of the of those who attended.

There were further interactions between the conference participants the following year, including a July meeting in Waterton National Park at the Belly River Campsite for youth of the two countries. Hand of the Cause of God, John Robarts and his wife, Audrey, joined them there. Then, in the late fall of 1967, Jim Wonders organized a group of American youth to attend another Youth Conference near Fort Qu'Appelle in Saskatchewan.

These are the few examples that I was able to find of the fruits of this Conference—no doubt a mere fraction of what actually resulted.

9 Reggie and Cindy Newkirk

◇◇◇◇◇◇◇◇◇◇◇◇◇◇◇◇◇◇◇◇◇◇◇

"Cindy, listen to what we read today!" Enid Wrate's animated comment to her daughter, Cindy, shared many years later in Cindy's handwritten account, gives an indication of the enthusiasm her mother was feeling for the teachings she was encountering in the late 1950s in Lethbridge. Enid had come home from the hospital where she had been reading a Bahá'í book aloud to her dying mother.

Enid's mother, Beatrice Ankill, had recently met and become friendly with the American Bahá'í 'pioneer' to the city, Beatrice Ashton. Mrs. Ashton had joined the same writers' workshop as Mrs. Ankill, so when Mrs. Ankill stopped attending sessions, Mrs. Ashton inquired. She began to visit Mrs. Ankill in hospital, and willingly engage in conversations about life after death, something most visitors were uncomfortable doing. She brought her Bahá'í books to read, and as the illness progressed, Mrs. Ankill began asking her daughter, Enid, to read them aloud to her. Enid, formerly an avowed atheist, was developing a growing interest despite herself. Cindy, then a twelve year-old child, observed the effect the books were having on both her mother and her grandmother.

"Beatrice [Ashton] brought Grandma Paris Talks[82]*, containing a message that she felt she had searched for all her life. 'Oh Enid,' she said to my mom. 'This is exactly the thing my students really needed to know to prepare them*

---

82 *Paris Talks* is a compilation of talks given by 'Abdu'l‑Bahá in Paris during His western travels in 1912.

*for meaningful lives.' ... Mom would spend every afternoon
with her, working through another Bahá'í book, with special
attention to the journey of the soul and life after death.
My mom came home from these visits to the hospital and
gradually changed from angry, bitter, and confused to
joyful, hopeful, patient, and in wonder."*

Enid began attending 'firesides' to learn more. Cindy
describes the experience of being included with the adults:

*"One Friday she took me with her to one of these in Mary
Burroughs' basement suite. Down the staircase we went to
a cheerful, bright kitchen. A group of people greeted us both
as if we were long lost friends. It really affected me, the fuss
they made over meeting me—a child—whom they spoke
to with complete respect as if I were an equal. I couldn't get
enough of it."*

Soon, to Cindy's delight, Beatrice Ashton organized a class
especially for her to learn about the early history of the Faith.

"Once a week we read from The Dawnbreakers[83]. *Midway
through the class we stopped for cookies and Tropical
Punch. One day while Mrs. Ashton poured the juice and
set out the cookies, I flipped ahead in* The Dawnbreakers...
*I was so engrossed in what I saw that I did not respond to
the invitation to come to the table... Mrs. Ashton hurried in
and closed the book..."*

Cindy had stumbled across illustrations of martyrdoms
occurring in Iran during the 1840s and 50s. Thousands of
early Bábis[84] were killed by fanatical mobs in grizzly incidents
incited by the clergy. The Báb was teaching that a new age had

---

83 The authoritative and exquisitely detailed account of the extraordinary
    exploits of the early heroes and martyrs of the Bábi Faith (precursor to
    Bahá'í Faith) in Iran in the 1840s. It was written by Nabil who was not
    only an eyewitness to much of what happened, but a brilliant historian
    by training as well.
84 Followers of the Báb.

                                      Reggie and Cindy Newkirk

come and that another Messenger of God, greater than Himself, was at hand. Beatrice was concerned that without adequate context and preparation, the graphic illustrations might be the stuff of nightmares for Cindy. Cindy, however, had quite another response.

"I tried to remember the amazing pictures of martyrs I had briefly seen. They seemed to be illumined with a kind of holiness that made me think of the bravery of early Christians who faced lions. The following week I brought eight dollars of my babysitting money to Mrs. Ashton… 'I would like to buy my mom The Dawnbreakers *for her birthday. She only has a couple of books,' I said, hoping she would not see through my ulterior motive. When Mom's* The Dawnbreakers *finally arrived, I skipped ahead many times… When we were married, Reggie would read from* The Dawnbreakers *some nights, or I would read aloud to him. We both love to be read to…"*

Cindy said that on the evening her grandmother died, her mother did not get to the hospital before she passed away, but the doctor told her that the last thing her mother said was, "Tell Enid, Bahá'í." Both Cindy and Enid believe she was telling them that she wholeheartedly believed in Bahá'u'lláh too, as she knew they now did.

Reggie grew up in the Bedford Stuyvesant section of Brooklyn, New York, in the 1950s. Decades later, he said he had never been in a white home until he was well into his twenties. I was shocked. Then it dawned on me that I had never been inside the home of anyone of a different race either, till I was about the same

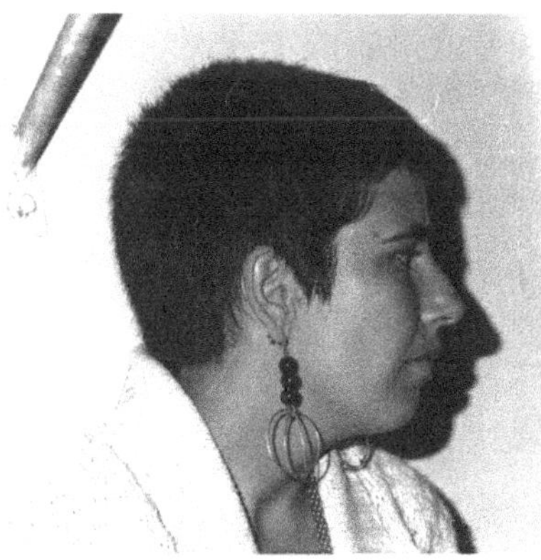

Cindy (Wrate) Newkirk. Photo source: Joanie Anderson, Sylvan Lake collection.

age. Reggie also described growing up surrounded by gang culture. The violence in the neighborhood where he grew up left such an impression that it was still with him, to a degree, when my friend, Donna Coey and I visited in 2015. As he and Cindy were seating us at their supper table, he explained he was still uncomfortable sitting with his back to the door. His growing up years had taught him he needed to be ready to run—or fight—so he needed to face the door to see who was coming.

He was first introduced to the Bahá'í Faith in Colorado in 1961 by Archie Evans, a fellow American serviceman who had just recently heard of it himself. Both were stationed at Lowry Air Force Base in Denver, members of the 451st Strategic Missile Wing, part of Strategic Air Command. The two became great friends. Both were from New York City—Reggie from Brooklyn and Archie from Harlem. Archie started up a discussion group on the base, on a variety of subjects including religion, philosophy, civil rights and the war in Vietnam. Reggie joined the group. In an unpublished account Reggie wrote in 2016, he recalls inviting Archie for lunch at the Mess Hall next to their barracks one day. After the first few mouthfuls Archie made an announcement. "Today I've made a wonderful discovery and if it is true, it is the most wonderful thing that has happened in the world!"

In a booming voice, Archie went on to say, "Christ has returned!" Alarmed, Reggie looked around. Seeing the expressions on people's faces, he suggested Archie speak in a lower voice. Reggie admitted that while he was no expert on Christianity, he did recall that when Christ returned, the heavens would be cleft asunder, angels would appear singing Hosanna, and similar miraculous events would occur. He had not seen any such things, nor had he heard the voices of angels singing recently—except for Aretha Franklin's.

Archie lowered his voice and began to share what he had been told about the Bahá'í Faith by a new fellow he had been assigned to work with. After some delay, Archie arranged for

   Reggie and Cindy Newkirk

Reggie to meet the man who turned out to be Lynn King, an Alaskan Bahá'í living in Denver. Lynn invited Reggie to spend a weekend with him and his family. Reggie said he was initially quite suspicious of the invitation. Why would a white guy want to have a black guy in his home for the weekend? But he accepted and relaxed when he was introduced to Lynn's wife, Loretta[85] and their four small children. "Any white dude married to a Native American can't be all bad!" he thought.

The year was 1961. At the King's house, intense discussion went on all weekend. Over the following months, there were regular conversations. They studied Bahá'í books together and in September, Lynn invited Reggie to a fireside in Denver where the speaker was the actress, Julie Sader, Robert Mitchum's sister. Reggie was a fan of Mitchum's work, and eager to go. It took place in the motel room where Julie and her husband, Elliot, were staying:

> *"During the latter part of Julie's talk, I became aware of what I can only describe as a 'manifest presence' that seemed to envelop the entire room and all of us within it. I leaned over to Lynn and whispered, 'Can you feel it?' Lynn, wide-eyed, said, 'Yes.' Everybody else in the room felt it too—each person was smiling, and their eyes reflected a soulful kind of joy."*

Reggie said he felt protected, accepted, and strengthened. After only a brief hesitation, he asked how to join the Faith, and was offered an enrollment card. He later said he felt he had three 'teachers': Archie who introduced him to the Faith, Lynn who studied with him and whose family life exemplified the principles of the Cause, and Julie Sader whose love for him at that fireside and since "…continues to resonate in my heart."

---

85 Loretta King was known in the Bahá'í community as an Auxiliary Board member and was later appointed to the International Teaching Centre at the Bahá'í World Centre in Haifa, Israel. She was a niece of Jim Walton's, the Alaskan Bahá'í who spent time teaching the Faith at Siksika in southern Alberta.

Some weeks after his decision to enroll, Reggie experienced doubt. Walking back to the base one night, he felt 'odd about signing up'. It was the height of the Cold War and as a member of the Air Police (Combat Defense Force) he had security clearance to guard American missile silos. He wondered if the Bahá'í Faith could be a communist front organization:

"It was a moment of crisis in my new Faith. I phoned Lynn from a public telephone booth saying I was concerned about signing the enrolment card because the only organizations I knew that required people to sign up were communist front organizations in the U.S.A. I asked him what I had do to resign. He said, 'Just tear up your identification card'. After a few weeks of reflection, my anxiety resolved, and I decided not to resign."

In 1962 another Bahá'í, Jim Wonders III, was also stationed at Lowry Air Force Base. He and Reggie became fast friends. In fact, their friendship was so 'tight' that Reggie said they thought of each other as 'brothers from a different mother'. They stayed in touch throughout life, and when Jim passed away in 2015, Reggie flew to Corpus Christi in Texas, to attend his funeral. To Reggie's surprise, Jim left him money in his will, so Reggie used to it to make a financial contribution to the Bahá'í Fund in Canada[86], contributing it in Jim's name. He wrote the Canadian National Spiritual Assembly explaining Jim's services over the years, including his facilitation of cross-border youth activities in the 1960s. He said, "I'd like this amount to be earmarked… for the Framework for Action in Saskatchewan and Alberta to facilitate efforts to reach Canadian Indigenous youth and junior youth."

Reggie's association with, and affection for, First Nations people began in his early days as a Bahá'í. He travelled with Bahá'í friends such as Nelson Lee, Bob and Carol Manuelito, John Sargent Sr. and his son, John Sargent Jr. to the Navajo Reservation, the Hopi Community, and Taos Pueblo, making

---

86 See Reggie's letter regarding this in Appendix F.

                                              Reggie and Cindy Newkirk

friends there. They also made trips to the Wind River
Reservation, the home of the Eastern Shoshone and Northern
Arapaho. Cindy also developed close friendships as a teenager
with First Nations youth, especially the young Bahá'ís from
Piikani. She often stayed the weekend at the Knowlton's home
on the reserve, and travelled to conferences, such as the 1966
Youth Conference in Calgary with youth from the reserve.

As mentioned in Chapter 8, Reggie and Cindy met at the
Calgary Youth Conference. They were married in 1968 in
Lethbridge, where they were both enrolled in programs at
the University; Reggie in history and philosophy, and Cindy
in English literature. Excerpts from an article about their
wedding in the *Lethbridge Herald* at the time give a picture of
their unusual ceremony. Indeed, theirs may have been the first
inter-racial wedding in the city. The decorations and choice
of clothing alone give a glimpse of the era. Bahá'ís who have
lived in the area for some time may recognize the names of
individuals the article mentions as contributing to the ceremony:

*"The first wedding of the Bahá'í Faith to be held in
Lethbridge was performed when Cynthia Wrate, daughter*

The marriage of Cindy Wrate and Reggie Newkirk. Photo source: unknown.

*of Mr. and Mrs. Jack Wrate, Lethbridge, was married to
Mr. Reginald Newkirk, son of Marion Sands and Leroy
Fields of New York City. The wedding was held Saturday in
the art gallery… of the Yates Memorial Center. Mrs. Helen
Marshall, chairman of the Calgary Spiritual Assembly,
officiated.*

*The Bahá'í Faith is a relatively new religion announced in
1863… In His writing, Bahá'u'lláh said, 'The fundamental
purpose animating the faith of God and his religion is to
safeguard the interests and promote the unity of the human
race, and to foster the spirit of love and fellowship amongst
men'…*

*For the ceremony, the bride wore a white sari, the
traditional dress of the Indian woman, and gold slippers…
She wore yellow and pink gladiolas in her hair. The groom
wore a gray Nehru suit, with a white turtleneck sweater.
A wooden medallion around his neck carried the Bahá'í
symbol…*

*When the guests were seated, the bride and groom sat
facing them. They were surrounded by baskets of yellow,
pink, and orange gladiolas… There were no attendants.
After an introduction and a short prayer by Mrs. Helen
Marshall, Mr. Ed Muttart read an excerpt from the Bahá'í
revelation. Mrs. Anna Gangur then read a prayer. Martin
Dixon read poetry from* The Prophet *by Kahil Gibran…
Mrs. Kay Muttart then read excerpts about love from all
the major religions… Mrs. Jack Wrate [Enid] then read the
Marriage Tablet from the Bahá'í Sacred Writings…. They
exchanged rings and the vow, 'We will all verily abide by the
will of God'."*

When I visited the Newkirks in the fall of 2016 in their
Lumsden, Saskatchewan home, we were chatting at the
breakfast table with the aroma of warm buttered toast filling the
kitchen. Hot oatmeal was being served and tasty preserves were

　　　　　　　　　　　　　　　Reggie and Cindy Newkirk

Reg and Cindy at breakfast 2016. Photo source: Joan Young.

set out in front of us. Conversation turned to that long ago time in Lethbridge and Cindy showed me a book they had received as a wedding gift in the mail from Beatrice Ashton at that time. "*The Priceless Pearl*[87], hot off the press from Haifa for a wedding gift," she explained. Wistfully she added, "I am forever grateful that she had the courage and wisdom to teach a woman on her deathbed. It bore many fruits!" After breakfast, Reggie took me walking in the surrounding Qu' Appelle River valley, the chill, crisp fall air filling our lungs and the sharp smell of decomposing leaves filling our nostrils.

---

87 *The Priceless Pearl* is Rúhíyyih Khánum's book about the life of Guardian of the Bahá'í Faith, Shoghi Effendi, whom she had married. It is a touching and beautifully written portrait of the remarkable man who passed away in 1957.

Following their university years in Lethbridge, the Newkirks moved to Calgary which is where I first got to know them. They remained for several years before moving to Vancouver when Reggie was hired to work at the British Columbia Human Rights Commission. I recall my first impressions of Reggie. We had both been elected as members of the Local Spiritual Assembly in Calgary, and I was struck by his unusually sharp and discerning mind. He had a critical mind in the best sense of the word. He examined situations for their true nature and for their under-lying principles. I felt he made us all a little 'sharper' in our analysis and consultation. He did not have the cultural or temperamental cloak over his comments that most of us white Canadians seem to have. Where we frequently apologized for our opinions and 'beat around the bush', Reggie spoke directly, and his comments were often a challenge to what I now see as 'fuzzy thinking'. However, he made his points without becoming personal or oppositional. It was instructive.

On my first visit to their home in Lumsden in 2010, I found Cindy had become an artist of delightfully original imagery. Her paintings hung about the house. In later visits, I observed Cindy to be an early riser who would already be at work at her desk when I woke in the mornings, meticulously illustrating

Cindy Newkirk, Reggie Newkirk, and Cindy's mother, Enid Wrate at Sylvan Lake. Photo source: Joanie Anderson, Sylvan Lake collection.

                                   Reggie and Cindy Newkirk

tiny books into which she had copied extracts from Bahá'í Writings. The quotations were embellished with miniature pen and water-color drawings. On one of my visits, Donna Coey came with me, and the two of us marvelled at how beautiful common objects had become once painted with Cindy's whimsical designs. There were riots of happy color in her home and garden. I was also struck by the depth to which both she and Reggie delved into the Bahá'í Writings. It seemed a regular part of their day, and they did so together. I also observed their participation in the town; inviting people to their home for meals, socializing with groups who had common interests, Reggie serving on the Town Council, and Cindy participating actively in Arts clubs and women's groups.

Over the earlier years of their marriage, their Bahá'í activity was varied and extensive. In 1974, they went 'travel teaching'[88] to the Bahamas for several weeks and visited Reggie's old friend, Jim Wonders and his family who were pioneering[89] on Eleuthera Island. "We had a terrific time meeting local residents," said Reggie. The June 1975 issue of *The Canadian Bahá'í News* reported the couple also travel teaching in Europe and Ireland, following a pilgrimage they made to the Holy Land.

Thereafter, in the early 1980s, Reggie's served as an Auxiliary Board member[90] under Counsellor Angus Cowan. By 1989, he was elected to serve on the National Spiritual Assembly of the Bahá'ís of Canada. According to Ailsa Leftwich, the Canadian Bahá'í archivist, Reggie continued to serve on that body until

---

88 Travel teaching refers to visiting other areas where the local Bahá'ís have most often set up a meeting for them to speak about their Faith.

89 Pioneering is a term for Bahá'ís moving to an area where there are few Bahá'ís, in an effort to interest members of the local population in the Faith. It is different than being a missionary, in that the pioneers are expected to become self-supporting members of the community that they move to.

90 Auxiliary Board Members are individuals appointed to this Board by Continental Boards of Counsellors. Their responsibilities are the protection and propagation of the Faith, and they frequently travel and meet with Bahá'ís to both educate and inspire them in accomplishing the community's goals and plans.

1999. Beginning in 1993, he was elected yearly to serve as its Secretary, and moved to Toronto to be able to do fulfil this role. Ed Muttart, upon reading an early draft of this chapter exclaimed, "We served together on the NSA. When it met in other cities, we were roommates." It was evident he held fond memories in his heart of time spent with Reggie.

I am aware that the time in Toronto was not easy for either Reggie or Cindy. Not only did working at the National Center and serving on the national body pose its own unique challenges, the couple's vastly different temperaments—and possibly their differing backgrounds—resulted in marriage difficulties and a long period of separation. I was amazed and pleased to see, that after many years of being apart, Reggie's faithful and devoted determination to repair the marriage, as well as Cindy's own development of personal strengths, allowed them to reunite.

In his later working years, after serving as the Secretary of the National Spiritual Assembly, Reggie's concern for Indigenous people and their struggle for justice was intensified. Having worked for the Human Rights Commissions of Alberta, BC, Nova Scotia, and Saskatchewan over his long career, it was at his last post in Saskatchewan before retirement, that he became increasingly involved in the spiritual and cultural traditions of First Nations people, and his friendships with First Nations individuals deepened profoundly. His close friendship with Bev Knowlton's son, Malsum Cabaiosai, an accomplished Men's Fancy Dancer, culminated in Malsum driving out to Saskatchewan from Calgary where he lived, to support Reggie and conduct and co-ordinate a Traditional Dance Initiation. Malsum explained,

> *"In the 'Old' ways it was about acknowledging the spirit of that lodge and committing to it. Today it is seen as giving back to the powwow community by making an offering to the powwow in the form of a 'give away' and/or a 'Dance*

                          Reggie and Cindy Newkirk

Special' to be recognized by the powwow community. Often there is a mentor that is guiding the dancer through teachings regarding the dance style, regalia, and the songs associated with the different dances."

In 2018, Reggie commented on the origins of his interest in traditional dancing, in an email.

"Some years ago now I had a brief conversation with Earl Healy during which he encouraged me to consider learning to take up Men's Indigenous powwow dancing. Though I had (and still have interest in that dance style) it was many years later that l started learning to dance in that style. As I found some traditional male dancers, l began to learn more about how to perform various dance steps… It also took some time for me to learn how to dance to the drumbeats… Sneak Up and other dance styles. I've spent a lot of time

Reggie Newkirk (centre) at his initiation into traditional Indigenous powwow dancing. His mentor, Malsum Cabaiosai, in background. Photo source: Bev Knowlton.

Given their love for him, I am sure he was no burden. Malsum's on-going support and mentorship was a gift from the heart. Following the 2015 National Bahá'í Convention which Reggie attended in Calgary, Malsum and his children, along with his mother, Bev, took Reggie with them to the largest powwow in North America—the Gathering of the Nations in Albuqerque, New Mexico. It must have been a remarkable experience watching three thousand dancers in full regalia, entering the giant arena from four directions. Apparently Malsum's children did not let Reggie out of their sight, such was their love and concern for him.

Within a few years of his initiation into traditional dancing, Reggie and Cindy spoke to me about the onset of age-related, cognitive decline that Reggie was experiencing. Though the experience was undoubtedly more difficult than what they shared, the measure of humility and grace it must have taken to say what they did, is striking. Reggie explained much of his own condition saying it was often the seemingly simple processes that eluded him, while the more profound concepts enshrined in religion and philosophy were still comfortable areas to have discussions in. Cindy seemed to have informed herself extensively about his condition, and stepped in to assist where possible.

I found it alarming at first, that the man who, in a very real sense, had 'taught me to think' in those early days on the Calgary Spiritual Assembly, was now having difficulty thinking himself. It made me pray to find half the grace and dignity with which to accept the same, should it become my condition in years to come. I was glad to hear that their youngest son, Amoz, had moved in with them to help, and no doubt their other two

　　　　　　　　　　　　　Reggie and Cindy Newkirk

remarkable children, Tallis and Sitarih, are doing what they can. I am grateful to have spent the time that I did in the presence of this dear couple. Perhaps there will be a bit more time together—even in this lifetime.

10 Pam and David Sherwin

Pamela Rosemary Sherwin, nee Hutchins, came to Canada from England, looking for one of the many nursing jobs that had been advertised. She worked first in Alberta, then travelled to Montreal in the late 1950s for an upgrading course in psychiatric nursing. Montreal was where she first heard of the Bahá'í Faith.

In those days, nurses lived in accommodation provided by the hospital. Not long after she arrived, she was assigned a new roommate who soon became her dear friend, Ruth Monk (Eyford)[91]. Pam was intrigued by Ruth's active social life—she seemed to go out most evenings. Pam had found it difficult to make friends in a new city where most people spoke French, so she asked Ruth about her activities. Ruth revealed that she was a Bahá'í, and that most often she was going to Bahá'í meetings at the Maxwell home[92] in Mount Royal. She invited Pam to join her.

Pam soon found herself deeply interested in the teachings of this new Faith. At an evening 'fireside', the speaker, John Robarts, who was giving the talk, asked those who were not

---

91 Ruth Eyford became a much loved and respected member of the National Spiritual Assembly of the Bahá'í's of Canada. She was later appointed to serve as an Auxiliary Board member. She was known as a woman of exceptional insight and organizational ability.

92 The Maxwell home was the home of accomplished Canadian architect, William Sutherland Maxwell, and his wife, May Bolles Maxwell. This home at 1548 Pine Avenue West was the center of Bahá'í activity in Montreal for many years, hosting 'Abdu'l-Bahá during his visit to North America in 1912. He referred to it as his 'home' and it was later designated a Bahá'í Shrine, the only one on the continent.

members of the Bahá'í Faith why they were not. He had a genuinely curious and open manner, and he asked this question of people on other occasions as well. Pam left the room to think by herself. Upon finishing his remarks that evening, John found her standing on the stairway, gazing at a painting of 'Abdu'l-Bahá. He proceeded to ask her the question directly.

"I believe in Bahá'u'lláh and His teachings, but I want to talk to the Anglican priest before I declare[93]", she replied. "Oh, he will only put you off." But Pam insisted, "Oh he won't put me off…"

"Well then you believe. Then you are a Bahá'í. You can sign your card[94] now," John said.

She turned around and said, "I will."

What John, nor anyone else observing her on the stairs that evening would not have known, is something her husband, David, shared with a group of friends gathered for prayers at Dale Lillico's home in Pincher Creek, many years later. The conversation turned to souls whom individuals had known, who were no longer in this world. Pam had passed away some years before this gathering.

"You know Pam had an unusual capacity to see 'other realms' at times," he said. He went on to share that as a child, Pam had an illness which could easily have killed her. While she was critically ill, she dreamed of a place with lush, green grass and daffodils. In that bucolic place, she became aware of the kindly, reassuring presence of an older gentleman in a long cloak, wearing a turban. He assured her that while the place she had gotten a glimpse of was indeed beautiful, there were important

---

93 Bahá'í have used the term 'declared' or 'sign your card' to refer to the decision of an individual to enroll in the Bahá'í Faith as a member. Becoming a member involves the privileges of voting for its elected representatives, serving on its elected bodies, and contributing to its funds. 'It involves a request (usually written) to one of its elected bodies to be registered as a member and implies a belief in the station of its Founder, Bahá'u'lláh, as the latest Messenger of God. No ceremonial rites are involved.

94 Membership enrollment card

                                          Pam and David Sherwin

things that she still needed to do in the physical world. It was not yet time for her to make her transition to heavenly realms. Her memory of the man's face in her dream was intact fifteen years later, when she recognized it as the face of 'Abdu'l-Bahá, whose portrait was hanging in the stairwell.

Another example of Pam's 'unusual capacity' was on display during their 1963 trip to England. Though they were no doubt happy to revisit the places where they had grown up, the specific purpose of this trip was to attend the Bahá'í World Congress[95] which was taking place at the Royal Albert Hall in London. It was the first time Bahá'í communities around the world were sufficiently established to be able to elect their supreme governing body, the Universal House of Justice, whose functions and powers had been laid out in the sacred texts of the Founder. It was at this occasion that David and Pam seated themselves up in one of the grand balconies.

Pam looked out over the audience on the main floor below and exclaimed, "Look! Do you see?" David wondered what she was looking at.

"There's Bahá'u'lláh, 'Abdu'l-Bahá, and Shoghi Effendi sitting in the front row!" Though he could not 'see' them himself —and knew they had all passed on—her comment struck him to the core. In sharing the anecdote David explained, "I did look, but I did not share her vision—her insight. I was happy though, to be in that grand arena with over six thousand Bahá'ís from all over the world."

---

95 A review of that Congress written by Beatrice Ashton in *The Bahá'í World 1963-1968*, says the occasion was referred to as 'The Most Great Jubilee', the one hundredth anniversary of Bahá'u'lláh's declaration of His mission. Beatrice referred to the significance of the fact that the Guardian had set the time and given the objectives for this historic gathering before he passed away, a mere five and a half years earlier, while in London. The first election of the Universal House of Justice had just occurred in the Holy Land, and its members were introduced to the 6000 people present. Its election marked a significant milestone and achievement. Also introduced and applauded, were the many 'Knights of Bahá'u'lláh'— individuals who had arisen to be the first to move to a country or territory where there had previously been no Bahá'í; in fulfillment of 'Abdu'l-Bahá's *Tablets of the Divine Plan*.

In 1960, prior to meeting David and while Pam was still working in Montreal, the National Spiritual Assembly of the Bahá'ís of Canada had drawn attention to 'Abdu'l-Bahá's words written during World War I, about the great spiritual potential of the Indigenous peoples of North America: "Attach great importance to the Indigenous population of America… should they be educated and guided, there can be no doubt that they will become so illumined as to enlighten the whole world."

Pam resolved to see where she could make efforts to meet Indigenous people. She applied to the Charles Camsell Hospital in Edmonton, a hospital for Indigenous patients with tuberculosis who required long term hospitalization. While working there between the years 1960 to 1964, she made friends with much of the staff and many of the patients. Also living in the Edmonton area, was her friend, Ruth Eyford who was by then married to Glen. She often babysat their children, Helgi and Thora, when the two of them attended meetings. She also participated in the Bahá'í community of Edmonton—particularly in its efforts to reach out to people on nearby Reserves.

It was at one of the Bahá'í firesides in the city, that Pam met David. He had recently come to Canada from England as well, also looking for better economic opportunities. He had come with his brother-in-law and recalls that his pregnant sister stayed behind in England until her child was born. She had, however, connected the two men with Canadian friends to stay with when they arrived, and David said he found his Canadian hosts unexpectedly delightful. They helped get the young men settled and took them sightseeing to places such as Jasper. "They even allowed us to take a turn at the wheel of their 1957 Plymouth, the kind with the big fins and a 4-barrel carb," said David, smiling and demonstrating with his hands the movement of the long, heavy cars; the great length of which slowly rocked as they glided down the road.

I could not help but smile as David shared the graphic image. The two of us were, at that moment, driving towards Pincher

                    Pam and David Sherwin

Creek in a very different vehicle, a small SUV from the year 2014. I am old enough to recall a 1957 Plymouth myself, and was a child when my neighbors bought the first one in the community—a pink and gray two-tone beauty. Actually, it could more appropriately have been called a 'two-tone floozy', given the attention it seemed designed to attract. None of us had ever seen anything like it; flaring wings at the back, curvaceous mounts on the lights, and embellishments along the sides.

Back to Pam and David's Canadian story: David had been working at *Aero Caterers* in Edmonton when he met a Caribbean fellow named Newell Hudson. Newell was a Bahá'í and informed David of his religious beliefs. Soon David was attending firesides at Darryl Sturrock's[96] home, and it was Darryl who first introduced him to Pam. David's friendship with Darryl, the Putters, the Kidds, and especially with Maxine Fraser, brought him into association with First Nations people as well. It was in that context that he and Pam began to travel to reserves together, most often to Hobbema (now Maskwacis) and to the Paul Band at Wabamum.

Around this time, David moved to Sherwood Park, a residential area close to Edmonton, to increase the number of adult Bahá'ís to nine so they could form a Local Spiritual Assembly. The election of this body—which administers the affairs of the community—required that at least nine adult Bahá'ís reside there. David lived with the Kidd family first, then moved in with Betty and John Putters and their family. He recalls early travels for Bahá'í purposes, with a match-making attempt on the side.

"As a new Bahá'í, I was living with well-known Bahá'ís, Betty and John Putters, in Sherwood Park. The Bahá'ís throughout the province were closely connected and the Putters felt that Dale Olivier (Lillico) who'd just moved to Brocket on the Peigan Reserve near Pincher Creek, needed

---

96 Well-known Edmonton Bahá'í

a car. They asked me to drive down a Studebaker car they'd purchased for her use. It was probably a matchmaking setup, but although I gave it some thought, a relationship did not bloom... Getting back to the delivery of the Studebaker, there was a Bahá'í gathering one evening and I was asked to say a few words about the unity of mankind. I'm afraid my talk did not go well, but Dale covered for me, and I don't think that any permanent damage was done...

David recalls being invited to attend a Sundance as well, along with Arthur Irwin, who knew people at Peigan well.

"It was a privilege to attend the Sundance, though as we could see, no effort was made to exclude anyone who was interested. The costumes[97] were very colourful, the dances evocative of native history and tradition, and the drum music almost hypnotic at times. There were many dances that featured a number of elaborately costumed individuals that told stories, and other quieter ones where everyone was invited to join the circle. I was impressed with it all, perhaps particularly with the inclusion of young children in the special dances as they embraced their traditions..."

David Sherwin and Pam Hutchins were married in February of 1962, with Glen Eyford officiating for the Spiritual Assembly of the Bahá'ís of Edmonton. It was the first official Bahá'í marriage in the city; the first time a Bahá'í couple did not have to go through another legally sanctioned ceremony conducted by a church or Justice of the Peace on the same day. The three couples, the Sherwins, Lillicos and the Eyfords went on to become lifelong friends.

The Sherwins left Sherwood Park in 1964 when David was hired to a teaching position in a Red Deer Vocational High School, teaching Food Preparation. Once settled, they applied

---

97 First Nations refer to their elaborate and astonishingly beautiful traditional outfits, as 'regalia'.

to adopt a child, requesting a child of Indigenous or mixed-race parents. Pam secured a part-time nursing position in a nursing home while they were waiting, and would have taken full-time employment, but it was not acceptable for women applicants to work fulltime in those years. In December of 1964, they welcomed their daughter, Farah Mea, into their home, and two years later, Robb Stuart joined their family.

During their time in Red Deer, they continued to visit individuals they had met on trips to reserves, including Sam and Victoria Currie on the Montana Reserve. They were also part of the formation of the first Spiritual Assembly of the Bahá'ís of Red Deer. I recall travelling to the Sherwin's home in Red Deer with a group of Bahá'í youth from Calgary in 1971, in order to spend an entire night praying for the establishment of a Spiritual Assembly in that city—where there were not yet enough resident Bahá'ís to form one. The Sherwins hosted the lot of us with grace and good humor, and within months, an Assembly was indeed established. It seems that us youth had a very innocent,

Pam Sherwin with children at Sylvan Lake Bahá'í Centre. Photo source: Joanie Anderson, Sylvan Lake collection.

David Sherwin and daughter, Farah, eating watermelon at the lakefront. Photo source: Joanie Anderson Sylvan Lake collection.

yet profound faith at the time, something life and its challenges would season with experience, but not take away.

During the ensuing years, the Sherwin family volunteered a tremendous amount of time to Bahá'í Summer Schools conducted at nearby Sylvan Lake Bahá'í Centre. Pam was usually camp nurse and David, camp chef. His meals featured fresh and nutritious ingredients in tasty combinations, and his patient smile from within the kitchen at mealtimes was a welcome sight. Jean Hedley of High River, recalls attending a Manitoba Summer School in later years at which David was also the cook. On a drive that the three of us (Jean, David, and myself) took together to visit Dale in Pincher Creek in 2019, Jean made a point of expressing her gratitude to David for helping accommodate her dietary restrictions, which were new to her at the time.

Mavis Edey[98] of Red Deer recalled how much the Sherwins' kindness and hospitality affected her in the years after she met them:

"I became a Bahá'í through a book I read in 1980 in Provost, and when we moved to Red Deer that year, my first

---

98 Mavis Edey's own life became an example of service for her years of membership on the Alberta Bahá'í Council, extensive local outreach to children and junior youth, and care and responsibility for the programs and property at Sylvan Lake Bahá'í Center.

 Pam and David Sherwin

Feast[99] was at their home. I had three small children under four, and another on the way. Munkholms who had just moved here, had four youngsters. So this wonderful, quiet, welcoming community suddenly had seven very active young children to contend with overnight! Pam just took over and went downstairs to play with them after devotions! I was so impressed at how welcome the Sherwin's made us feel—complete strangers in their home!! After that Pam helped develop a children's program for each Feast, compiled a song book, and encouraged Eleanor and I to start weekly children's classes, which we did for years. It set a pattern for my coming service to the Faith, putting Bahá'í things first on our calendar, and working everything else around them."

Looking back over the years, David remembered one occasion in Red Deer with special fondness; the 1970 Alberta Regional Convention held in the cafeteria of the school where he taught. The event became memorable with the presence of the African 'Hand of the Cause of God', Enoch Olinga, who was on a North American speaking tour at the request of the Universal House of Justice. Mr. Olinga was from Uganda. His devotion to the Bahá'í Faith and his initiative and joyfulness in sharing it with his fellow Africans, earned him the title 'Father of Victories' from the Guardian, Shoghi Effendi. He was known for his 'great, joyous, consuming and contagious laugh'. In 1979, he was assassinated in his home during the civil strife following Idi Amin's rule, along with members of his family. According to Mr. Peter Vuyiya who arrived in Kampala a few days later, "Staying in the middle of the town, I had the full effect of the state of anarchy in Kampala at night… it was impossible to tell the police Kombis from any other that might have been

---

99 'Feasts' are the bedrock of Bahá'í community life, occurring once every nineteen days. "This Feast," states 'Abdu'l-Bahá, "is held to foster comradeship and love, to call God to mind and supplicate Him with contrite hearts, and to encourage benevolent pursuits... It rejoiceth mind and heart..."

responsible for murders in the city and its environs. Every night, however, brought with it the murder of yet another family."

David's recollection of Mr. Olinga's attendance in Red Deer was:

"Hand of the Cause Enoch Olinga was a quiet, unassuming individual who had the ability to easily command an audience both with his physical presence, and the magnetism of his oratory. But in the circumstance of this Regional Convention, his quiet side was evident as he allowed the Bahá'ís to conduct their business, speaking only when asked. He made a special effort to be inclusive of the Indian friends who were in attendance, including Victoria Currie,[100] who treasured his memory and the photo that they shared.[101]"

Pam and David continued serving their Faith and the community in Red Deer for thirty more years before moving to Vancouver Island. The list of their services is long: raising children, working full time, serving on the Local Spiritual Assembly and its committees, participating in teaching campaigns, serving at Sylvan Lake Bahá'í Center, initiating firesides, and hosting countless meetings and events in their home. Their move to Shawnigan Lake on Vancouver Island in 2000, was to volunteer at Maxwell International Bahá'í School. Pam assisted in the nursing office and David worked with building maintenance. They served in this capacity until 2010

---

100 An Indigenous Bahá'í from a nearby Reserve who'd become friends with the Sherwins.

101 I also recall attending this convention in Red Deer. I arrived with friends from Calgary. The vehicle we arrived in was Angus Cowan's, and he was to take Mr. Olinga back to the airport in Calgary afterwards. We stopped for supper in a Red Deer restaurant along 'Gasoline Alley' before leaving. I recall feeling tongue-tied in Mr. Olinga's presence; perhaps mesmerized by his smile and dimly aware of the awesome gap between my own spiritual condition, and that of the giant sitting across from me. My main memory of the conversation is that Angus kindly made efforts to include us all in the conversation, but we mainly sat staring at the beaming Mr. Olinga. He may be the only person I have ever asked for an autograph; to which he graciously responded with a note written in my prayer book, a note which became particularly precious after his assassination.

                                        Pam and David Sherwin

David Sherwin and Ted Anderson at Sylvan Lake. Photo source: Joanie Anderson, Sylvan Lake collection.

Inuit musician, David Sherwin, Farah Sherwin, Catharina Ankersmit (aka Kathy Poulsen) and John Poulsen. Photo source: Joanie Anderson, Sylvan Lake collection.

when they moved back to Red Deer. While still on Vancouver Island, Pam received news that her dear friend, Ruth Eyford, was dying of cancer back in Alberta. Ruth reached out to Pam and without hesitation, Pam packed up and spent the last three months of Ruth's life with her, as caregiver and friend. That act, more than any other I am aware of, tells the story of Pam Sherwin.

Pam passed away on October 12, 2012, and is buried in the Alto Reste Cemetery in Red Deer, close to her son, Rob Stuart Sherwin. Rob suffered from severe diabetes from the age of twelve and succumbed to a heart attack at forty.

David's loving note of remembrance, when asked about missing his wife was, "Pam lived a life of sacrifice; her artistic and creative talents were subjugated to the needs of her family and to those of her Faith. I miss her greatly and wish that we had a few more years together, during which her wishes could have flourished."

Upon hearing David say that in her Pincher Creek home, I heard Dale Lillico add, "Remembering Pam brings back recollections of her with a camera around her neck, taking such exquisite photos of flowers, trees etc. Despite vision difficulties later in life, her camera and her subject were always very clear. I still have several which she left with me in an album."

I also wish David could have had those extra years with Pam that he longed for. At the time of writing, he is still an active man near the age of ninety, involved in Bahá'í community activities, still cooking on occasion for groups at the Sylvan Lake Bahá'í Center, and sharing his wealth of knowledge about the Bahá'í Faith in group settings. I became very fond of him as he shared his memories with me. It was at a time when the two of us were participating in the same conference calls for prayer and study circles[102], during the Covid 19 pandemic. Staying in touch with one another became a valuable antidote

---

102 Study circles have become an integral part of the community's activities, designed to develop individual capacity.

                                    Pam and David Sherwin

to the isolation of the time. David's deep knowledge and rich understanding of Bahá'í teachings, often left me in surprise and with admiration.

11   Helen Marshall

◇◇◇◇◇◇◇◇◇◇◇◇◇◇◇◇◇◇◇◇◇

Helen Marshall was a beacon of happy hospitality for 1970s students and flower children in Calgary. She had numerous friends among the First Nations people coming into the city as well. I saw her as a grand lady in her long dresses, pure white hair swept into a tasteful French twist, and her welcoming smile. She hosted almost nightly gatherings in her home at 921 - 18 Avenue SW which, with the support of the Local Spiritual Assembly, she had opened as a Bahá'í Centre. The house contained three suites, and she rented out the other two to students, of whom I was one.

She made her visitors tea and coffee, answered their questions about the Bahá'í Faith which they were newly discovering, and hosted innumerable discussion evenings and Feasts[103]. Her warmth was palpable and kept us coming back. Who was this woman, and how did she end up in Calgary, a founding member of its Bahá'í community?

I can only give an incomplete answer. She passed away before I thought to ask specific questions about her early life. However, living in her home's second floor suite as a student, and later in her main floor suite when I got married, gave me the opportunity to spend significant time with her, getting to know her well. We had many afternoon cups of coffee together. When Helen made you coffee, it was a simple affair of putting on the

---

103 Feasts are the regularly occurring occasions (once in 19 days) for the community to gather for devotions, consultation and socializing with refreshments.

kettle and dropping a teaspoon of instant coffee granules into a mug. Funny how tastes change over the years—now, I might reluctantly accept a cup of instant coffee—but at Helen's house in those years, it was a fragrant beginning to a nice long chat.

Helen Margaret Fairbairn Marshall was born in 1904 in Borden, Manitoba. She told me that as a young woman she came west from Manitoba on the train, and while still east of Calgary caught her first glimpse of the snow-covered Rockies. "I was awe-struck," she said.

She loved beauty in any form, and the awe she felt for the grandeur of the mountains extended to a passionate love of classical music, art, animals, and poetry. She also had an unusual capacity for devotion, a reverence and tenderness for the Central Figures of her Faith. It may be significant that one of the frequently used titles referring to the Founder, Bahá'u'lláh, is *The Blessed Beauty*. She read every available book about Him, His son, 'Abdu'l-Bahá, and His great-grandson Shoghi Effendi. She made notes about their lives on index cards and told stories about them in tones of wonder.

Her capacity for devotion was evident in the way she looked at the large framed photograph of 'Abdu'l-Bahá taken in New Hampshire in 1912; the one that shows Him smiling and seated against the background of tropical plants. The photograph hung in her Calgary home when I first met her, and it was hanging above her bed in the nursing home where she lived at the end of her life, a devastating stroke having left her immobile and speechless. I commented on the photograph during what turned out to be my last visit to see her. Given the effects of the stroke, I was uncertain if she could hear me, or if she knew who I was. But at the moment I pointed to the photograph, she turned to look at it and became animated, trying to speak. I could not understand what she was saying but in that heart-breaking moment, squeezed her hand and fought back tears. As I walked away, down the hall, I thought I heard her call, "Joan!" Clear as a bell.

"It's impossible, Helen can't speak," I said to myself. But I have wondered ever since if she did indeed call out to me. And I have regretted not going back to check. She passed away not long after that, on March 12, 2003, at the age of 98.

What else do I know about this remarkable woman? And how did she make her way in the world? She was single all the years I knew her. But while I still lived in her home, she showed me a letter she had received from the lawyer of a Vancouver man who was still—evidently—her husband. It informed her that he had passed away. She smiled ruefully, saying she had not really expected to be informed. As I recall, the man was her second husband; the first, the father of her daughter, was killed in the war.

She raised her daughter, Margo, first in Vancouver, then in Calgary. I remember her telling me about having taken Margo to Calgary's grand old hotel, the Palliser, designed by William Sutherland Maxwell[104] of Montreal, and built during the early years of the century. Her daughter was still a teenager and wanted to see the debutants descend the grand staircase at their coming-out ball. Among them were her daughter's high school friends. "I knew she would have liked to be among them," said Helen with a tinge of regret, "But it simply wasn't within my means."

Helen's 'means' were modest when I knew her, coming largely from renting out suites in her home. Prior to that, she had been an executive secretary in numerous places including Vancouver, Calgary, Montreal, Red Deer, and Banff. Most of these were 'pioneering' posts to which she had moved with the goal of assisting a fledgling Bahá'í community. For a period of time, she was also a partner with an Indigenous friend in a Calgary gift store that sold authentic Indigenous handicrafts, called *The Loon's Necklace*.

---

104 William Sutherland Maxwell, one of Canada's foremost architects in the early twentieth century, was Rúhíyyih Khánum's father and a 'Hand of the Cause of God'.

Her Calgary home was in the area known as Lower Mount Royal. Up the hill from her house—in Mount Royal proper—were the grandest homes in the city, set along tree lined streets and overlooking the city. The front of her two-story Edwardian home had a veranda on the right hand side of the door, framed with pillars. As you entered the foyer, the faint smell of carnauba wax greeted you emanating from the hardwood floors. Her office/library was on the right, and to your left through a set of French doors, was the living room. At the end of the living room was a large, cased opening to the dining room and combined, the two rooms served as a large, pleasant meeting space. It was decorated with simple but tasteful furnishings. Cranberry-red area rugs protected the hardwood floors. There were a couple of potted ferns, a gas fireplace, coffee tables, numerous comfortable chairs, and a solidly built forest green couch, which was only slightly marred by the vigorous attentions of her two cats. There was a distinct absence of the common figurines and doilies of the era, such as so many houses contained.

Her two rescue cats, Tammy and Zirin-Taj were a mother/son pair. Tammy was the rather overweight mother—mainly white with soft orange patches. Zirin-Taj was her stately, long-legged son whose distinct patch of gold between his ears had earned him his name which means 'Crown of Gold' in Persian.

According to her friend, Del Craig[105], Helen had rescued the cats from under a car where they were huddled in evident distress, and soaked in oil. She coaxed them into her house, cleaned them up, and the two of them never left her tender care again.

Sometimes, when I was invited down, or had invited myself down, she would play classical music on the cabinet record player. Mahler, Mozart, and Verdi were among her favorites. She would talk about the music and the choirs she had sung in, stroking all the while, one of her cats. At times, she would close her eyes and sway slightly; a thing I also saw her do when Bahá'í prayers were being chanted or read.

105 See Chapter 14 on Del Craig

                                          Helen Marshall

She had a strong desire to share the knowledge she had acquired over years of reading and study. The index cards she made of key Bahá'í references were used for course outlines on various topics. I would hear her clicking away at her manual typewriter when I came home from University classes. I do not know when and where Helen first heard of the Bahá'í Faith—I never thought to ask her about it. As I probe my memory for conversations about her earliest Bahá'í experience, the name of a Montreal Bahá'í, Raymond Flournoy, comes to mind. She talked about him more than once, and it seems they had attended meetings together in Montreal. She certainly lived in Montreal before her various moves in Alberta and BC. Perhaps she attended his famous Friday evening firesides. I am unable to find anyone who knows for certain. She was clearly very fond of Raymond Flournoy, and I recognized his name when I met him at National Conventions in the late 1970s—a dignified, gentle man with a melodious voice.

Catharina Ankersmit of Canmore[106] told me that when she arrived in Calgary from the Netherlands in 1955, Helen was already a Bahá'í and holding 'fireside' meetings for people to learn about the Faith. Dale Lillico recalls moving to Calgary in 1957 and becoming a member of the first incorporated Local Spiritual Assembly in the city, along with Helen Marshall.

Helen was, at times, the chairperson of the Calgary Spiritual Assembly, which evidently had close ties with other Bahá'ís throughout the region; as indicated by newspaper reports of the 1968 Bahá'í marriage of Reggie and Cindy Newkirk in Lethbridge where Helen officiated on the Calgary Assembly's behalf.

My brother-in-law, Glenn Cameron, the creator of *A Basic Bahá'í Chronology* and the subsequent website, *https://Bahá'í-library.com/chronology*, mentions Helen serving as a delegate to National Bahá'í Conventions and serving on committees with people of other Faiths in the city:

---

106 See Chapter 15 on Catharina Ankersmit, aka Cathy Poulsen

Spiritual Assembly of the Bahá'ís of Calgary 1957. Standing: Sylvia Demers, Arthur Irwin, Mel Harrison, Gordon Scott, Nora Harrison. Seated: Lily Ann Irwin, Helen Marshall, Barbara Scott, Dale Olivier (Lillico). Photo source: Canadian Bahá'í Archives.

"The first mention of Helen Marshall is in The Canadian Bahá'í News *#98 March, 1958 p.1 where it was announced that she was one of nineteen delegates to the 11th National Convention, the lone delegate from Alberta. The month before (February 1958) contains an account of her participation in the wider Calgary community. 'The [Bahá'í] community was asked to the meetings of the Calgary Brotherhood Council and to appoint a member to the Religious Commission Committee. Helen Marshall is becoming an active member of this committee serving with representatives of the Jewish, Anglican, Catholic, Mormon, United and Unitarian Faiths.'"*

I recall her telling me that she and her friend, Sylvia Demers, were friendly with various prominent Indigenous people in the city, including the well-known Cree lawyer, Bill Wuttunee. There seemed to be social ties between them. She also knew Bill's brother Noel. Noel was an acclaimed artist and the first Indigenous person to enroll in the Bahá'í Faith in Canada. It seems he had been introduced to it by his wife at that time, the Danish artist, Gerda Christoffersen. The two of them attended gatherings in Helen's home while they lived in the city in the 1950s.

Helen Marshall_1958. Photo source: Laura Davis collection, Canadian Bahá'í Archives.

Helen's continued role in the forefront of Bahá'í activities in the region is also evident in a 1968 list of six delegates elected from Southern Alberta to the National Convention. Also on that list, were her friends Samson Knowlton and Sylvia Demers. She attended the World Congress at the Royal Albert Hall in London in 1963 and shared her memories of the occasion with me. She expressed a special thrill at seeing fellow believers of every race and nationality, dressed in their national costumes, arriving in the great hall. She commented not only on how beautiful and diverse they were, but on how joyfully they mingled; "Like a world embracing family," she said. The London papers were full of news of the event, and city buses contained signs and billboards regarding it. She said it became a huge presence in the city.

An especially fond memory for her at that Congress, was seeing the elderly Aboriginal Australian Bahá'í, Fred Murray, address the gathering and recount his life in the face of intense hardships which he had endured. He is reported to have said, "When I was a baby my people died… I thought I have no people! But now I am a Bahá'í—you are all my people." According to Margaret Bluett, quoted in a *Bahá'íblog.net* article, he said, "I have come like a giant kangaroo across the world to stand on this stage and tell the world how happy I am to be a Bahá'í." Recently, I came across a *YouTube* video of Fred's comments to the Congress. He added that he had never been on an airplane before, "…hopping across Australia… happy to see the faces here… all colours of flowers…" He referred to Rúhíyyih Khánum as a mother to him. "Great love come from Haifa… Rúhíyyih Khánum sent for me… that's her there," he said, pointing. *The Bahá'í Blog*[107] article includes a photograph of 'Uncle Fred' sitting beside Rúhíyyih Khánum at the Congress, beaming as he rests his head on her shoulder. She appears mutually delighted, remembering him from her travels in Australia when he taught her to throw a boomerang. How I would have loved to have watched that lesson as it happened.

Helen also had a particular regard for Rúhíyyih Khánum. While still living in her treasured Calgary home on 18th Avenue, Helen hosted this woman during her 1960 visit to Alberta, the same trip during which Rúhíyyih Khánum visited Peigan Reserve, a two-hour drive south of Calgary. Helen told me that at the time, her own mother was still alive, and living with her. Helen's preparations for the occasion were so extensive that her mother remarked, "Helen, it's as if the Queen is coming." Helen said she had to concur. Her guest's rank, accomplishments, and position as widow of the departed Head of the Faith, Shoghi Effendi, were indeed awesome to her. In addition to this, Rúhíyyih Khánum was a Canadian. "She was ours. We felt a special claim to her," said Helen.

In her seventies, Helen sold her Calgary home and moved to the Windward Islands in the Caribbean to assist the Bahá'í community there. It was a monumental decision to sell the home that had anchored her life for so many years and had provided her with income. She did so in response to the House of Justice call for 'pioneers' in 1975.

---

107 *Bahá'íblog.net: https://www.Bahá'íblog.net/2020/04/a-tribute-to-fred-murray-retracing-the-story-of-uncle-fred/*

                                              Helen Marshall

When she returned from the Caribbean a few years later, she moved to Carstairs just north of Calgary, again for the purpose of strengthening a fledgling Bahá'í community. Her presence was key to the 1979 formation of a Local Spiritual Assembly in the town. She returned to Calgary a few years later, to an apartment near her daughter's home and eventually to a seniors' residence with varying levels of care.

Helen Marshall reading a prayer.
Photo source: Marie Lucas.

The other distinguished guest that Helen hosted while still living on 18th Avenue, was Hand of the Cause of God, Tarazu'lláh Samandari. Though he made this visit in 1967 before I even knew of the Bahá'í Faith, the effect of his visit lingered even for me, personally. When I moved into the suite he had stayed in seven years earlier, Helen made sure I understood the significance of his presence. This very elderly Persian gentleman had attained the presence of Bahá'u'lláh on three separate occasions and was the last living man to have done so.[108] It was at the advanced age of 92 that he made the speaking tour across Canada in the company of his son, and when in Calgary, stayed in Helen's home.

The precious, though admittedly remote connection for me to Tarazu'lláh Samandari, is in a sense, absorbed into Helen's furnishings that the man touched while in her home. When my husband, Dave, and I rented Helen's main floor suite in 1974; as we moved in, she reminded us that Tarazu'lláh Samandari had

---

108 An account of one memorable day spent in Bahá'u'lláh's presence when Mr. Samandari was a youthful pilgrim to the Holy Land in the 1890s, is included in Appendix G.

Helen Marshall (front left) in a play at Sylvan Lake Summer School. Photo source: Joanie Anderson's Sylvan Lake collection.

slept in the bedroom which would now be ours, and had bathed in the tub we would now be using. She later gave me several smaller pieces of furniture which I still treasure in my home. I see them daily; a semicircular side table holding a reading lamp, and a wooden chest in my dining room which contains my table linens. A samovar sits atop of that. I have told my children the story of the pieces, hoping their significance lingers for another generation.

12   Allison and Earl Healy

llison Healy has a smile that lifts a heavy heart. Her face lights up when she sees you, and there is music in her voice as she greets you. This dear woman lived at Kainai throughout her adult life, but came from Siksika where she was born in 1942. Like others of her generation, she was forced to live at residential school from the age of five. How is it that her face beams, and she chuckles so readily? There may be clues in her story.

Her family name was Melting Tallow. Her father, Matthew Melting Tallow, was from Kainai and her mother, Mary Alice Running Bird, from Siksika First Nation. They met when he came to Siksika as a young man to work in the nearby coal mines[109]. Allison was the first in her family to become a Bahá'í. Her siblings, Dorothy and Erwin, followed her as time went on, as did their mother, Mary Alice.

Her husband, Earl Healy, was a much-loved traditional dancer, born at Kainai in 1937. Commenting on his entry into traditional

Nonie Bride and Allison Healy in Airdrie. Photo source: Joan Young.

---

109 There is a video profile of Allison's mother, Mary Alice Running Bird, at Blackfoot Crossing Historical Park indicating this.

dancing as a significant part of his life[110], Earl said, "I wanted
something to keep my mind moving, not to ever think
backwards… something to be proud of myself." He was also
required to attend residential school as a child, and for him,
part of that legacy was drinking in his younger adult years. He
was able to win the battle with alcohol addiction in 1975 and
enrolled as a Bahá'í thereafter. One of the stories that remains of
his family background[111] is that his great-grandfather, Joe Healy,
had been a prominent interpreter on the Reserve. As an infant,
Joe's family's encampment had been raided by another tribe
and he was the only survivor. Whisky traders passing through,
found him and took him home to Fort Benton, Montana, and
raised him. Healy was the name of this adopting family. Joe's
great-grandson, Earl, would go on to become an ambassador
for both his culture and his Faith, in numerous countries
throughout the world. He left this world, leaving many bereft,
in November of 2006.

Some of the details of Allison's life were recorded by Elaine
Zavitz in an interview in the summer of 2015. Others came
from comments she made to filmmakers for *The Path Home*,
a documentary contribution of the Bahá'ís of Canada to the
dialogue around the Commission in 2016. Still more came from
Chelsea Horton's 2013 doctoral thesis. Elaine and Allison had
become good friends serving on the Alberta Bahá'í Council[112]
together for many years—along with Pat Verge. The three of
them frequently travelled together. Allison's service on the
Council began in 1996 and went on for twenty years. It required
her to move about in urban, non-Indigenous circles, which I
observed her to do with grace and courage. In speaking of her
residential school experience with Chelsea Horton, for

------

110 Pat Verge quotes Earl on nativeBahá'ís.com website
111 Also referred to on the nativeBahá'í.com
112 The agency created to coordinate and promote Bahá'í activities
     throughout the province.

                                    Allison and Earl Healy

Chelsea's UBC thesis titled *All is One: Becoming Indigenous and Bahá'í in Global North America*, Allison said the following:

"...being in a residential school I felt cut away from who I am... assimilated into another culture... I lost my true identity as an Indian person. And then especially hearing that everything about our culture was paganism... I never did hear anything good about being an Indian..."

In *The Path Home*, Allison smiles as she shares that she was a 'good reader' as a young child, which a nun who was an early teacher liked and rewarded with candy. Speaking so kindly of one of her early teachers, may have been her way to resist sounding too harsh or negative in her recollections, but tears soon came to her eyes as she shared that she was "...very mixed up coming out of the boarding school... We couldn't even smirk... we had to be so still, like statues..." Indeed, as she spoke about going home and sitting behind her house during the brief periods she was allowed home, she could scarcely continue speaking for the emotion it aroused within her.

Earl and Allison's home over the years, was in the valley of the Belly River. Cottonwood trees grew along the river here near their house, and according to the kids, rattlesnakes lived in the gullies they pointed out, as we took a walk one hot summer day when they were young. The dry earth on the sun-bleached hillsides supported tufts of grass and prickly pear cactus. There were six children born over the years: Barry (Farron), Jerilyn, Lisa, Earlene, Nancy, and Joey.

The children experienced ways in which the legacy of residential schools affected their parents and continued to present challenges to them. An indication of the impact came from a comment one of their daughters made about her mother's reluctance to speak the Blackfoot language— something she made great effort to learn for herself, as she got older. The harsh dictates of residential school prohibition against speaking your own language cast a long shadow. And it was not the only one. Despite the shadows, both Earl and Allison made efforts to thrive, and in their adult lives travelled the world giving people joy and spreading light. More about that in a bit…

Allison's early educational experience after residential school at Siksika, was finishing grade eleven at a mixed Catholic day school in Red Deer, then taking certified nurse's-aide training. Her first job was at the Charles Camsell Hospital in Edmonton, one of the 'Indian Hospitals' Canada created for the segregated treatment of Indigenous people. Allison met a friendly nurse there who, to her surprise, she encountered again in the years to come at Bahá'í meetings. That friendly nurse was Pam Sherwin.

During her time in Edmonton, Allison visited an aunt on the Blood Reserve (Kainai), who suggested she take a job there. Her aunt lived close to the Indian Hospital on the Reserve—which was not hiring at the time—but just across the road, and off the reserve was the municipal hospital. Allison applied and was immediately hired.

One of her cousins worked in a nearby restaurant so Allison frequently dropped in. One day, she passed by a young man in the doorway as she was leaving. There must have been a discernible spark between them, or perhaps Earl asked about Allison, because the cousin later asked, "Do you know that guy? I never see him here, but all of a sudden he keeps visiting the restaurant."

The young man was Earl of course, and the two were introduced by Allison's cousin—who also happened to be Earl's cousin on the other side of the family. She invited the two of them to her place for supper together. A relationship blossomed and they married in 1966. It took time for their wedding to be arranged because Earl was Anglican and Allison was Catholic. Both were reluctant to change Faiths at first, but Allison agreed to attend a weekly class taught by the Anglican minister and in time decided she would convert. The aspect of Anglican

     Allison and Earl Healy

practice she liked was not having to confess to a priest—
something she had never felt entirely comfortable doing.

Allison said the experience of comparing religious beliefs
started her interest in learning about other Faiths. It was her
cousin, Diana Melting Tallow, who introduced her to the Bahá'í
Faith in 1970. At some point along the way, she was travelling
in a car with Siksika Bahá'ís, Ed and Jean Many Bears. She asked
Jean why she 'liked' the Bahá'í Faith so much[113]. That was when
Jean had replied, "It's because when I hear the Bahá'í prayers, I
can smell God."[114]

Joyce McGuffie and Eva Statz were among several Bahá'ís
who lived in Cardston at that time and frequently visited
Healys. Allison admitted she had not been accustomed to
having white people in her home and was nervous about it:[115]

*"At first I would forever be apologetic about my home
situation… But the Bahá'ís who came were so cordial and so
friendly. They were just part of the family… my husband is
so open… and if they happened to come while we're eating
he'll tell them, "Sit down, eat with us." …they'll sit down
and eat whatever we have and then after they'd help with
the dishes and play with the kids and they were just right in
with the family and I soon forgot that they were White."*

Sometimes, Joyce and Eva came with visual aid materials
such as Bahá'í films from the Holy Land, but they talked about
Christianity as well. Allison said she not only learned more
about Jesus, she also found her interest in Bahá'u'lláh aroused.
Joyce and Eva came frequently between 1970 and 1972 and by
then Allison said she felt sure of the truth of the Bahá'í Faith

---

113 See story of Ed and Jean Many Bears, Chapter 6

114 The full story of this conversation with Jean Many Bears is included in
Chapter 6.

115 Chelsea Horton interviews. Horton, C. D. (2013). *All is one: becoming
Indigenous and Baha'i in global North America (T)*. University of British
Columbia. Retrieved from *https://open.library.ubc.ca/collections/
ubctheses/24/items/1.0074080*.

so signed an enrollment card. As she was signing it, Earl came running excitedly into the room. "Are you sure of what you are doing?"

She replied, "Yes, I'm sure." She told Elaine Zavitz this was the first choice she had ever truly made for herself, and she realized it was something 'no one could take away' from her. She said that ever since, despite challenges and difficulties, this deep, early learning is what kept her with 'the Faith'. She said she had remained firm because she was 'well-grounded' and understood what she had enrolled in.

Both Earl and Allison described becoming more involved in their culture and traditions, after becoming Bahá'ís. Their residential school religious training had said Indigenous culture and beliefs were wrong and should be set aside. The Bahá'í teachings encouraged cultural expression and believed all the world's religions were sources of guidance sent from the same Creator.

As mentioned earlier, Earl became a champion traditional dancer and won many dance competitions. He was proud of his culture and when he was asked to lead the Grand Entry at powwows, he felt honored to be the one to carry the Eagle Staff. He shared his dancing not only with people around the region, but also with Indigenous people in other countries. Allison often danced in her traditional regalia as well and said that when they visited Indigenous people in places like New Zealand and Siberia; where people were also in danger of losing their culture, "They'd get so excited to see us when we were dancing."

At home, Earl's friend, Reggie Newkirk, said it was initially Earl who encouraged him later in life, to learn traditional First Nations dancing regardless of his non-Indigenous heritage as an African American who had grown up in Brooklyn.

The Healy family were—and their children still are—tipi holders at Elbow River Camp at Calgary Stampede in the summer. Their tipi is one of twenty-six which are set up every year, enriching the Stampede experience immensely for those

     Allison and Earl Healy

Shirley Lindstrom, Martha Many Grey Horses, Dora Wedge and Allison and Earl Healy dancing at Vision Quest, Rawdon, Quebec, 1981. Photo source: Bahá'í Canada Photograph Collection, Canadian Bahá'í Archives.

Reggie Newkirk and Earl Healy 1982. Photo source: Bahá'í Canada Photograph Collection, Canadian Bahá'í Archives.

Two of Healy's daughters—Earlene and Nancy Healy. Photo source: Joan Young.

who visit. Their tipi has a water serpent design, with elk, deer, and the Big Dipper painted on it, a design having been passed down in a proper transfer ceremony by a relative of Earl's.

Elbow River Camp has been part of the Calgary Stampede ever since its inception in 1912, though it was known as 'Indian Village' until recently. According to an article[116] in *avenuecalgary. com* by Stephanie Joe, the creator of the Stampede, Guy Weadick, was determined to include both 'cowboys and Indians'. He had to navigate the rigidities of the Indian Act in order to include First Nations people and culture in those years. With effort, he got permission for temporary exemptions to the Indian Act each summer, that would allow the people to travel off their reserves wearing their traditional clothing and sharing aspects of their normally prohibited culture.

Pat Verge, in an article for *IndigenousBahá'ís.com*, describes Earl and Allison as wonderful hosts to the many visitors who came to their tipi at Elbow River Camp over the years:

"…the Healys display traditional outfits made of hide, pieces of clothing heavy with beautiful beadwork, and bustles made with the sacred eagle feather. They include items showing the traditional way of life such as bone utensils, rawhide bags to store dried meat, mint tea, and pemmican (a mixture of crushed dried meat, berries, sugar, and fat). The tipi smells fragrant with fresh sage…"

116 https://www.avenuecalgary.com/calgary-stampede/the-story-behind-elbow-river-camp/

                    Allison and Earl Healy

Donna Coey and Nancy Healy at Elbow River Camp, Calgary Stampede 2023. Photo source: Joan Young.

After Earl passed away and as Allison aged, her family, including her grandchildren and great-grandchildren, eagerly carried on the tradition, bringing Allison with them. Earlene said, "We take great pride in our culture, and it really brings our extended family together. Some of us only get to see each other at the Stampede in the summer."

One of Allison's memories from her early years as a Baháʼí (perhaps it was just prior to enrolling) was missing the visit of well-known and much loved African Baháʼí, Hand of the Cause of God, Enoch Olinga[117], who came to visit Kainai in the summer of 1970. She found out about it afterwards and, unable to know the future and the lovely encounter she would one day have with him, was very disappointed.

Reggie Newkirk recalled that Mr. Olinga also visited Lethbridge during that trip and gave a fireside talk at Enid Wrate's home. He

---

117 Hand of the Cause of God was a title given to a number of early Baháʼís whose services and leadership had been exemplary, and Enoch Olinga was one of them.

describes the talk as, "…a brilliant presentation on the veracity of the spiritual/traditional experience of First Nations, linking it to Indigenous traditions in the part of Uganda, from which he came. Then he brought up… the contribution they (Indigenous peoples) could make to humankind. It was a presentation 'straight from his heart' and it resonated with many of the attendees…"

Allison recalls that Barbara Healy, Earl's sister, told her that her cousin, Diana Melting Tallow, took Mr. Olinga to the airport when he was leaving, and that Barbara had been sitting in the backseat, nervous to be travelling in a car with an African man she'd never seen before. In Blackfoot, Diana told her not to be scared of him, and that he was a very holy man. At that moment, Enoch turned to Barbara, and introduced himself. The following weekend, when Barbara came home, she repeatedly told the story about the black man she had met, with great excitement. She said that when he spoke to her, she felt her fears disappear and that she couldn't emphasize enough what a nice man he was and how much she liked him.

Allison got her opportunity to meet Enoch Olinga herself, before he passed away. The opportunity came at the 8th International Conference in Merida, Mexico, in 1977. She described it as her 'first big trip', which she attended with her cousin, Diana, a more experienced traveler, who had made a point to take Spanish courses before she went and generally acted as Allison's guide and mentor on the trip.

In Merida, Allison saw Mr. Olinga walking by with some other Hands of the Cause and ran after them in great excitement. She touched him from behind, surprising him. He turned around and said her name. She felt recognized at a level of the spirit, saying later that it happened too quickly for him to have read her name tag. Whatever the case, Allison treasured the moment for the rest of her life. When he was assassinated in the unrest in Uganda in 1979, Allison was pleased to have been personally informed by well-known Canadian Bahá'í, Angus Cowan, in a telephone call.

                                    Allison and Earl Healy

The Healys travelled to New Zealand in 1996. When they walked into the National Bahá'í Office in Auckland, hanging right in the front foyer, was a big picture of Enoch Olinga. She said it startled her and felt significant. He was known to the Bahá'ís as the 'Father of Victories' in spreading the Bahá'í Faith in Africa.

Allison was in New Zealand with Earl, as part of a 'teaching exchange', an opportunity to share both their culture and their Faith with the Maori people. Pat Verge recalls that Maori Bahá'ís had come to Alberta a few years earlier, in 1992, and that the Healys had taken them to Stoney Nakoda near Banff on Christmas Day, to a Round Dance. Their visit to Alberta was part of a North American tour they were making in 1992, following the Bahá'í World Congress in New York City. It was at the New York Congress where they first met and connected with the Healys. A picture of the Maori group visiting Morley is included in Pat Verge's book, *Equals and Partners*. Earl and Allison were delighted to see these people once again, during their 1996 trip to New Zealand.

The couple travelled to many Bahá'í gatherings on this continent as well. Among these events were a visit to the Temple near Chicago, to Indigenous Councils held in Yakima, Vancouver Island, and Ft. Qu'Appelle, a 1981 Indigenous Council called 'Vision Quest' in Rawdon, Quebec, and a big international conference in Montreal in 1982. Allison also frequently travelled to Canada's National Bahá'í Conventions— often held in Toronto—as an elected delegate from southern Alberta. In summer, the family also attended Bahá'í Summer Schools held at Sylvan Lake. In 2007, after Earl passed away, Allison went on pilgrimage to the Bahá'í World Center in Haifa, Israel, with her cousin and her sister—Diana and Dorothy—a memorable experience for the three of them.

Earl's first big trip off the North American continent was to Dominica and St. Lucia[118] with Arthur Irwin, where

118 The Canadian Bahá'í News, March/April 1982 report

Allison and Earl Healy with Counsellor Farzam Arbab. Photo source: Bahá'í Canada Photograph Collection, Canadian Bahá'í Archive.

they spent four weeks visiting the Indigenous Carib people, deepening them in their understanding of Bahá'í teachings and in encouraging the revival of their ancient Carib language and culture. Earl and Allison went to Russia twice in the 1990s, travelling to Yakutsk, the northern city in the Sakha Republic where many Russian youth were becoming interested in the Bahá'í Faith. Allison recalls the first trip to Russia saying, "It was a very hard winter that year, but it was so exciting to meet these youth… some of them had only been Bahá'ís for a few months, and some the same day…" Their second trip to Russia was in the same area, with a stopover in Moscow in the summer of 1999, with 'a lot of mosquitoes'. Kevin Locke, an American Bahá'í and well-known hoop dancer and cultural educator of Lakota background, was with them on that trip.

In 1983, years before they were invited to go to Russia, they gave their daughter, Earlene, the opportunity to attend the New Era International school in Panchgani, India. I asked Earlene how that had come about. She said that at the 1983 National Convention, her mother met another Bahá'í who had a son and daughter attending the school who told her about it.

Allison and Earl Healy

When Allison got home, she sat her three daughters down and asked if one of them would like to go. Earlene was the one who volunteered and within a few brief months, she was joining a small group of other Canadian youth for the flight there. She explained that after the initial excitement, most of them felt homesick and wanted to come home. She also considered coming home at Christmas break, but in a phone call with her parents, her father offered to come visit during her Christmas break. He did, and discovered that Earlene's choir (her chosen extra-curricular activity) was touring over their break. Earl travelled with it for three weeks and thoroughly enjoyed himself.

During the tour, he is reported to have joked, "Well, I learned we are not from India. And my next visit will have to be to Russia because they say our people came from over the Bering Strait[119]." It seems he may have had a premonition, because at that point there had been no indication that he and Allison would soon be invited to go to Russia.

Of the students from Canada, only Earlene and a fellow student named Nicholas, stayed at New Era for the second semester. When it was over, one of her teachers invited her to go on a 'travel teaching' trip to Sri Lanka with a group. She called home and asked if her ticket could be changed and her trip extended. It was changed and when the trip to Sri Lanka was over, yet another travel opportunity came up, so she asked for another extension.

The girl who had once considered coming home early got permission for a second extension to her stay in India. At that point Earl told Allison, "If Earlene asks again, say no." He admitted he had become concerned their daughter might get married there and stay for good.

Allison's travels and services to her Faith included going to Otavalo, Equador, in 2001 to attend training in the Ruhi

---

119 The theory that Indigenous North Americans arrived from Asia over the Bering Strait, has now been seriously questioned.

Institute[120] as a tutor for the program. For years, she frequently supported the Bahá'ís on Stoney Nakoda First Nation in this capacity, but she did so in other ways as well. "She is much loved at this reserve," said Pat Verge, also a longtime friend of the people there. Pat pointed out that Earl was related to the family of the late Nakoda Bahá'í Elder, Beatrice Poucette, so there were family ties to Stoney Nakoda as well.

After Earl passed away, Allison regularly attended the annual Harper Mountain Indigenous Gatherings near Kamloops, BC. Bev Knowlton and Nonie Rideout usually travelled with her. Nonie, who lived in Banff for many years, often drove. Bev recalls the long drive through the mountains from Alberta being lightened by Nonie's funny stories. She said she and Allison were kept laughing by often outrageous tales they could not always determine to be true or not. One of the tales that kept them chuckling for miles began with Nonie asking if they knew she had a famous ancestor. Both women said no, so Nonie continued saying, "Yes, he was the last man to be hanged in Canada." Their laughter went on throughout the weekend whenever the thought came to mind, as well as late into the night as the three of them lay in their beds in a shared hotel room.

Allison Healy and Joan Young at National Convention in Toronto. Photo source: Joan Young.

---

120 Bahá'ís around the world are engaged in a process of learning to build capacity to apply the teachings of Bahá'u'lláh toward the transformation of society. The Ruhi Institute carries out action and research in the field and has developed—and continues to refine—a series of course materials for various age groups.

     Allison and Earl Healy

My own memories of Allison feature a beaming smile whenever we encountered each other, and her melodious voice saying, "Hello…" lingering on the 'o' in the loveliest way. "It's so nice to see you!" This greeting warmed my heart from the time her children were young and I visited them on Kainai First Nation, till she aged and lived in a nursing home in Fort Macleod. Her recognition was like a light suddenly turning on.

Allison is still alive at the time of this writing. Her spirit, which has shone so brightly will, no doubt, gleam even more brightly in the world beyond. There will be legions of people left behind from many races and places, who love and remember her. More will be awaiting on her arrival.

13 Sylvia Demers

I last visited Sylvia in her basement apartment in Calgary, in April of 2016. She was in her late eighties, frail, and suffering from 'sciatica' which gave her almost constant pain. Yet she insisted it was not too much trouble to climb a flight of stairs to let me in, and later, to let me out. As I entered her apartment, I saw stacks of books and papers on most of the available surfaces. She offered me tea in the living room, and we sat beside each other on the couch, but not before she removed a pile of papers. I had always known her to be a reader, a letter writer, and a board member of various organizations, but I could not shake the feeling that mounds of information may finally be starting to challenge her formerly efficient grasp.

By this time, she had sold the home she lived in for many years, with her mother in the Bankview district of the city. It was a lovely, white two-story home set on one of the many hills in the area, with a long flight of steps rising from the sidewalk to the front door.

Stories demonstrating her unflinching determination, her ability to keep her chin up, to do the right thing, and be of continual service to others, abounded among people who knew her. At her funeral, Fariborz Birjandian, who arrived in Calgary in the 1980s with his family as an Iranian refugee, said Sylvia walked a long distance to his family's bare, new apartment during a snowstorm, to deliver home baking she had made for them. Then, seeing how they lacked furniture, she showed up a few days later with a table and chairs crammed into her car. To me, this story exemplified quintessential Sylvia. She saw a need and addressed it, in completely practical terms.

I asked some new Chinese Canadians I met at her funeral what she had done for them when they arrived in the 1990s. "Everything. She taught us English, tutored the kids after school, showed us how to find a doctor, brought food, and found us the things we needed."

During that last visit in 2016, she said, "There are still newcomers from a variety of countries who hear that I tutor English for free and show up at my door looking for services." It was not long after, as the result of a health crisis and with the help of her friend, Diana Shaw, she moved into a senior's facility in Okotoks. She passed away on March 11th, 2018.

Where did this remarkable woman come from? In the literal sense, she came from a farm in northern Saskatchewan, the daughter of Jewish immigrants from Poland. Her maiden name was Plotkin. While still a child, she moved with her mother and two brothers to Calgary. As a young woman, she joined the military. The crisp efficiency and brisk execution of tasks that I saw her accomplish in the Bahá'í community over the years, may have been in part, a remnant of this early training. But her sterling individual qualities were uniquely hers. They were qualities that she was not only born with, but that she had refined with great determination. She held herself to a singularly high standard.

She joined the Bahá'í Faith in 1955. I was curious as to how she first heard of it. Catharina Ankersmit of Canmore, told me that when she first arrived in Calgary from the Netherlands in 1955 and sought out the Bahá'ís, Sylvia was already attending 'firesides' conducted by Helen Marshall and Gordon and Barbara Scott. She joined the Faith shortly thereafter. At a 2016 Naw Rúz[121] party at the home of Judie and Michael Bopp in the Wildcat Hills west of Cochrane, Khosrow, a Persian Bahá'í who

---

121 Naw Rúz is the the Bahá'í new year, celebrated at the spring equinox, March 20 or 21.

                                        Sylvia Demers

I had asked at Sylvia's funeral whether he knew how Sylvia first learned of the Faith, approached me and said, "I've asked my brother. He knows."

He related that his brother had been driving somewhere with Sylvia in the 1990s and mentioned an upcoming trip he was planning to take to Chicago to see the Bahá'í Temple there, on the shores of Lake Michigan. She then told him that she had been to Chicago in 1953 to visit an uncle. They had taken a drive around the lakeshore and come upon the beautiful temple in nearby Wilmette. Their curiosity aroused, they stopped, went in, and got some Bahá'í literature. She continued her investigation of the Faith on her return to Calgary.

Sylvia's service to her Faith once she joined it, was conscientious and sustained. While most obvious may have been her many years serving as secretary of the Local Spiritual Assembly of the Bahá'ís of Calgary, her work with Summer Schools, organizing the many activities of a growing community, and serving the needs of its individual members, was also remarkable. I found her name on a 1968 list of delegates elected from Southern Alberta to the National Bahá'í Convention, an indication of the esteem in which the community held her.

When I asked her about her experience in the Bahá'í community during the early years, she said that in the sixties, individual Bahá'ís would arrive in the city on a bus—or have hitch-hiked from somewhere else in Canada—and would call her at work. They needed a ride, a place to stay, or simply information which she would help them find, or provide for herself. This was just one of the demands made on her time. I recall Sylvia giving me a ride to attend a Feast with her at Siksika First Nation, an hour's drive east of Calgary in the early 1970s. That was the first opportunity in my life to spend time in a First Nations home. She supported the Bahá'ís there in their efforts, and helped deepen their knowledge of the Faith—which at that time was still very new to them.

Sylvia Demers as a young woman. Photo source: Joanie Anderson, Sylvan Lake collection.

For years she was employed as an administrative assistant for two American oilmen (brothers) who had come from Oklahoma City. They brought their aging mother up to Calgary as well, but according to Sylvia they found caregiving 'not to their liking'. They preferred that she, their employee, check in on their mother several times a week; which she dutifully did for years, on her way home to look after her own mother. Her employers had heard of the Bahá'í Faith back in Oklahoma and were sympathetic enough that when she needed to attend Bahá'í meetings or pick up one of the travelling Bahá'í young people mentioned earlier, they would allow her to do so, and make up the time later.

There were two periods of time when she moved away from Calgary, each for a few years duration and married someone. I never met either of her husbands, and as far as I know, true to form, her weddings (and divorces) were completely private. I experienced her as far too private a person to ever ask about her marriages. All I know, is that her last name changed from Plotkin, to Scott, to Demers. And I recall her close friend, Helen Marshall, in whose home I lived as a student, telling me that the Scott husband had been a psychiatrist in Connecticut.

Sylvia's closest long-time friend, a woman named Margo, is reported to have also commented on her extraordinary demand for privacy in personal matters. She observed that when Sylvia was changing the subject away from herself, she would characteristically say, "And how is your family?"

Sylvia Demers, Hand of the Cause of God, Enoch Olinga, Peter Rempel, 1970. Photo source: Canadian Bahá'í Archives.

In the late 1980s, Donna Coey recalls riding in the back of a car with Sylvia to a Bahá'í meeting in Edmonton. Sylvia was sitting in the middle with Donna on one side, and a Persian newcomer on the other side. It was an old car owned by one of the young Persian men who was still a struggling student, and it was in dubious condition. Somewhere along the highway, Sylvia said, "This seat's getting hot." They kept driving. She said it again. They drove on. Finally, Sylvia shouted, "My ass is on fire!"

That got them pulling over. Smoke rose as they scrambled out of the car and ripped out the back seat which was, indeed, on fire. They threw it in the ditch, heaped snow on it, stomped on it, then put it back in position and proceeded to Edmonton. My response to hearing this story is pure delight and surprise. I see Sylvia as the most proper of women, possessing impeccable English and the finest sense of decorum. To hear the choice of words she resorted to that day, shows another side of her; a side that was completely down to earth when necessary.

Pat Verge remembers Sylvia getting stopped for speeding on the way to Edmonton for another meeting. This one was with Don Rogers[122] who had just been appointed to the Continental Board of Counsellors. The policeman looked at the prim, elderly driver smiling at him sweetly, then glanced at the other passengers (young people of several races), shook his head and let her go with a warning.

I felt she had an almost uncanny ability to understand what people needed, and to facilitate connections between them. As time went on, she would often call on others in the Baháí community to fulfill a need that arose, instead of trying to fulfill most of the needs herself as she had done in earlier years. She sensed who had the ability, or could develop the ability, to fulfill a need and would benefit from doing so. Not long after I began collecting stories about early Alberta Baháís, I received a call from a lady who lived in Calgary—Eleanora McDermott— asking if she could interview me about the Sylvan Lake Bahá'í Summer School. She said she had recently been widowed and felt the need to be of service to the Baháí community. She had called Sylvia to see what she could do, and Sylvia had suggested she start by talking to Bahá'ís in order to write an article for the local Bahá'í Newsletter. She suggested Eleanora begin her research by talking to me. I lived in Carstairs, an hour's drive north of Calgary, but it turned out to be a wonderful opportunity for both Eleanor and me. Not only did we become friends, we began travelling together to visit other Bahá'ís in rural areas, most often at Piikani First Nation where she had grown up, the eldest child of Samson and Rosie Knowlton. Our

---

122 Otto Don Rogers, was an accomplished Canadian painter. He grew up on a wheat farm near Saskatoon and following art training in Milwaukee, taught in the art department at the University of Saskatoon throughout the 1970s. He was not only loved by his students, a significant number of them followed his spiritual path to become Bahá'ís. During this time, he was appointed to the Continental Board of Councillors, a Bahá'í agency, then appointed to the International Teaching Centre at the Bahá'í World Centre in Haifa, Israel. He continued painting there. His insightful work and vision is featured in the documentary *Approach to a Sacred Place*, available for download from 9 Star Media.

                                          Sylvia Demers

friendship, which had been facilitated by Sylvia, became the source of on-going Bahá'í activities which continued long after Sylvia's passing.

Sylvia never had children, and at the time of her passing, had three cousins surviving her, one in Vancouver, another in the US, and a third in Israel. The Vancouver cousin sent a lovely message to her funeral, expressing her appreciation to the Bahá'ís for their loving care of Sylvia in her last years. It was her friend, Diana Shaw, who Sylvia turned to, to help look after her affairs at the end of her life. It was Diana

Sylvia Demers funeral card. Photo source: Joan Young.

who would ask for Sylvia's tolerance and patience, when she wanted her to accept help. Until the end, Sylvia was fiercely independent, but would reluctantly say—on occasion, "I wish you wouldn't… but if it makes you happy, do it."

On other occasions Sylvia flatly refused gestures of kindness, assistance, and gifts of love. It was one of the mysteries of her fiercely private and complex personality which even her closest friends did not understand. "I'm so sorry to be a burden," she would often say in her last years.

A note found among her belongings after she passed away expressed one more trait this dear woman possessed. "Avocados $2.69 each today. Too expensive—don't buy." Sylvia loved avocados. Self-abnegation and Sylvia; they went together.

14 Del (Delores) Craig

"Stay for lunch," Del said, every time I visited. Despite being confined to a wheelchair and living in a senior's lodge, she offered enthusiastic hospitality with a spirit as bright as ever. During the summer of 2015, she was living at the Strathmore Senior's Lodge, an hour's drive from her hometown of High River. Del and her entire town had been evacuated during the historic flooding two years earlier when heavy rains stalled over the eastern Rockies, adding to a sudden thaw of the snowpack. It overwhelmed the region's rivers, and large areas of the plains of Treaty Seven Territory sat under feet of water. Not only had Del's hometown of High River suffered devastating loss and total evacuation, five years later, Siksika First Nation just east and south of Strathmore, still had almost a thousand people waiting for permanent housing.

Looking around her temporary, single room accommodation in Strathmore, I observed a cheerful and productive spirit still at work. There was a quilting project at her sewing machine, a set of oil paints, and a stack of hand-made greeting cards on her desk. Multi-colored necklaces, artfully arranged, decorated an entire wall in her bathroom.

I first encountered Del as an education student in Calgary in 1970. At her invitation, I took a bus out to her home in the Ogden area of the city on Sunday afternoons, to teach Bahá'í children's classes which included her youngest daughter. She was a single mother at that time, with one child, Brenda, still living at home. We would be joined by the Nicholls children[123], Dawn and David, among others. She earned her living being a cook, taking boarders into her home, and cake decorating to supplement her income.

In one of our early visits in her Strathmore senior's apartment, I asked how she had become a Bahá'í. Though born in Edmonton, she had grown up in Manitoba in a French speaking family and community, and had married there. A shadow passed over her usually beaming face as she explained that she had married a man who was prone to violence. Her sister, Doris, had moved to Calgary and become a Bahá'í. Their mother, Yvonne Morin, had moved in with Doris and had also joined the Bahá'í Faith. Upon hearing of her mother's conversion, Del said she had felt indignant; as if her sister must surely have 'hood-winked' their mother. Del's marriage in Manitoba became intolerable so she told her husband she was leaving with the children. He threatened her with a kitchen knife, demanding she stay at knifepoint. She said she stood stock still, looked him in the eye and said, "If you have to do this, go ahead. Get it over with. Now!"

He didn't 'do it', and at Doris's invitation, she was soon on a bus to Calgary with the children. Staying with Doris, she found herself increasingly attracted to Bahá'í teachings. When the famous and beautiful Florence Mayberry, author and Bahá'í speaker, was scheduled to speak to the Calgary Bahá'ís, Del wanted to hear her too. She made one of her beautiful cakes for the event and eagerly watched Florence interviewed on television.

"But you can't come," Doris said, "This meeting is only for Bahá'ís."

"What?" Del protested. "That's ridiculous."

"That's the way it is," said Doris, heading off to bed.

By 2 am Del could not stand it. The thought of being left home to babysit while exciting things were going on, was

---

123 See chapter 17 re Miriam Nicholls

                    Del (Delores) Craig

too much to bear. She got up and knocked on Doris's door. It opened a crack, and an enrollment card was thrust into her hand. She signed it then and there.

Del's childhood was the subject of lunch conversation on another visit. Over tomato soup and sandwiches, she told me that her mother became very ill when she and her siblings were young. The children ended up with no one to care for them except the Catholic Mothers of the Good Shepherd Orphanage. Del, one of the older siblings, said she was beaten mercilessly for 'sins' such as helping her little sister get up at night to go to the bathroom so she would not wet her bed. She remembers being beaten so badly that blood was splattering all over the nun's face and clothes.

"I left my body and was watching the scene from above. All I could think about, was to wonder how she'd ever get all that blood off her clothing."

Young Del also ended up in a solitary confinement cell in the basement at times, a small cell designed for a child. I could not quite believe what I had heard her say, so I questioned her. "Just like a prison cell," she confirmed. "Just a concrete floor, a blanket to lie on, and a pot to sit on. That's all… and these were the Sisters of the Good Shepherd…" She shuddered and looked away.

Fortunately, Del's mother, Yvonne, recovered and was able to reunite with her children. But trauma must have lingered. How could it not? Del's account sounds very much like the experience of residential school for Indigenous children. The perpetrators were people from the same set of institutions. Perhaps it was this common childhood experience that explains, in part, Del's unusually close friendship with Rosie Knowlton in the years she lived near Piikani. In fact, she and Jack, the man she called 'the love of my life' were married at Knowlton's home prior to their move to Africa. Rosie's daughters recall how intensely their mother missed Del when she left. Utterly bereft, she said, "All the Bahá'ís leave me."

Bahá'ís were indeed a highly mobile population in those years, often moving to fulfill a goal of expanding their community somewhere else around the world. But it certainly took its toll on people like Rosie, and my heart goes out to her.

Del experienced further tragedy in her life as a mother when both her sons died young. Ronald was killed in a car accident when an axle broke on the car that he was driving—a car that his brother Bob had purchased for him. Unable to shake off feelings of guilt and responsibility for his brother's death, Bob committed suicide four years later. "Those boys were so good to me…" she said, looking wistfully out the window. She then spoke fondly of her two surviving daughters, Claudette who now lives in Guelph, and Brenda who lives in High River.

I asked Del about a black and white group photo hanging above her bed. She explained it was the attendees of the first Bahá'í Summer School at Sylvan Lake, in 1967. Numerous faces were still recognizable to the two of us as we examined it more closely. Samson and Rosie Knowlton, Ed and Kay Muttart, Del and her daughter Brenda, her mother Yvonne Morin, Ron Parsons, Enid Wrate, Enid's daughter Cindy, her son Bevan, Angus Cowan, Helen Marshall, Joyce McGuffie and Dale Lillico were among them.

Del talked about the challenge of cooking for a crowd over the first ten years of the camp's operation. She had made cooking for people her special form of service. Though not a trained chef, she was a professional cook. She had cooked in restaurants and work camps and said that her skill was making tasty but inexpensive food from scratch, that people would enjoy. "The bean-sprout and tofu style of feeding people were not my way," she said, smiling. She said she always looked to Ed Muttart's[124] face to see his reaction to her cooking. He clearly held a special place in her heart, and her fondness for him seemed undiminished by time.

---

124 Ed was the owner of the property at the facility's beginning, though he later donated it to the National Spiritual Assembly.

Early Sylvan Lake Summer School Committee: Reggie Newkirk, Del Craig, Forbes Campbell, Morine Fraser, Marian West, Hasan Rushdy. Photo source: Joanie Anderson, Sylvan Lake Archives Collection.

In those first years, physical conditions at the camp were rustic, to say the least. In the kitchen, Del set up a gas stove and long tables with tubs for prep work and washing dishes. There was no electric power—so no refrigerator either. Despite health regulations being more relaxed at that time, when the health inspector saw the facilities, he threatened to close them down. Del said she was able to talk him into letting them stay open by explaining plans for improvements to be made before the next year. To keep food cool, she set containers in the stream that trickled down to the lake near the dining hall. For even more cooling space, she got helpers to dig a hole in the ground and place blocks of ice and sawdust in it, the way early settlers

once did. She covered the hole with a sheet of plywood, "…
so nobody would step on my food," she explained, gesturing
with her hands and smiling. It occurred to me that her focus
seemed exclusively on feeding people, not the safety of their
limbs in the event they stumbled into her storage pit. I had to
wonder later, if towards the end of her life, some of her concern
about getting to lunch on time and dwelling on what would be
served that day, might be more than a reflection of her work
experience as a cook. I considered it was possible that her time
as a child in the orphanage might have left her fearful of not
getting enough to eat. I wanted to hold that long ago child in
my arms and reassure her.

While speaking about the years she spent cooking at Sylvan
Lake, she recalled that one evening, she ran out of gas before
supper. Ed Muttart rushed into town in his jeep to get more. To
keep people from getting too restless, John Robarts was asked
to give his talk during the supper hour, a talk which had been
meant for later. She chuckled at the alarm the situation could
have caused, but appeared unsurprised at how well it worked
out in the end.

She met the 'love of her life' in the mid 1970s. She had gone
to Bauser Bahá'í Summer School in BC to cook one summer,
and left her mother looking after the house and its boarders in
Calgary. While away, a new boarder arrived named Jack Craig.
Her mother was so impressed with Jack's character that when
Del returned to Calgary, Yvonne orchestrated having the two
of them get to know each other by pulling out board games at
night and insisting they both play. Del had not been looking for
a husband and had no real interest in getting to know this man
either. To her surprise, it was the beginning of what became a
long, happy marriage.

Their 1977 wedding was hosted at the Knowlton's home on
Piikani First Nation: the first pieces of wedding cake, a product
of Del's highly accomplished cake decorating skills, were
served to her mother, Yvonne Morin, and to Samson and Rosie

                                    Del (Delores) Craig

Del and Jack Craig Photo source:

Knowlton, guests of honour and dear friends. The Craigs were living just west of Piikani at Lundbreck after their wedding, when one day Jack simply stated, "I want to be a Bahá'í too." Del believed that she and her mother were only part of the influence on Jack's decision. She believed the Knowltons may have been a greater influence on him because he saw the beneficial effects of the Teachings so clearly in their lives.

I asked Del how Jack felt about the idea of pioneering[125] to Africa when she first proposed it. She replied, "Jack would have done anything I asked him to…" She said it in such a way, that I believed he truly would have. She said her desire to 'pioneer' was a direct result of the inspiration and urgency of a talk given by Hand of the Cause William Sears, which urged a heroic

---

125 Pioneering—a term used by Bahá'ís to refer to living in a place for the purpose of assisting the growth and development of a Bahá'í community there, while being self-supporting.

response to the needs of the time. The Craigs arrived in Africa in 1981, in Bangui, the capital of the Central African Republic. A significant twenty years of their lives were spent there, far from Treaty Seven Territory. However, the land where their life together began, was where they returned when health and age demanded.

Del and I frequently spent time sitting next to one another, looking through her photo albums of Africa. Each page would invariably evoke memories. She had little hand drawings between photographs, and had included plane tickets and telegrams. Some pages included miniature cut-outs of African animals on the borders, prompting me to ask if she had encountered any lions or elephants while there:

"Oh no, we didn't see them. But we always heard the elephants at night. It was a lovely sound… But a snake once came in our house, a black mamba. We managed to chase it out. The locals tried to find it to kill it, but it vanished into the night. They eat snake, you know. It made this loud screeching sound that I'll never forget as it leapt off the veranda, straight like an arrow."

Del shuddered as she demonstrated the snake's movement with her right arm.

Jack was a skilled heavy-duty mechanic and got a job at a lumber mill within ten days of arriving. He soon discovered that his employers were stealing from the government, having seen large pieces of equipment loaded onto trucks and being driven away. Afraid he would report them, his employers fired him. Jack decided not to pursue the matter, having been advised that doing so would shut him out from other jobs in the country. Knowing that the Central African Republic had been colonized by France, I asked if Jack spoke French. "Oh no," replied Del, "But all the manuals were in English so he was okay. Mind you, he could fix anything without a manual. He was just so good at it…" Del was herself fluent in French, having

     Del (Delores) Craig

grown up in a French-speaking family, and said that her French was quite adequate in Africa but that on their stopovers in Paris, she had trouble making herself understood.

The Craigs bought a farm with the settlement money Jack received from the sawmill. The farm was a coffee plantation and Pygmies were their main labor force. In fact, a whole village of Pygmies became Bahá'ís while Jack and Del were in Africa. "But the Bahá'í teachers had to be invited to their villages in the forest or they'd never find them—they could be invisible," she explained. There was not a house on the plantation when they first purchased it so they contracted a local crew to build one. Work proceeded so slowly that Del and her Italian lady friend, Marinella, decided to stay on site to help with the construction themselves. "Yep, we laid mattresses out on the ground and got to work," Del said.

Despite Marinella's strong fear of spiders, they were soon pitching wet clay into a form made of tree branches that had been woven together. Their presence and determination kept the men working and within weeks, the Craigs had a house. Del explained that mud houses were very cool in the heat of the African sun. "Butter wouldn't even melt in them during the day." Thinking about building that house and making so many things 'from scratch' in Africa, Del smiled wryly. "I could build you a house now," she asserted.

Besides coffee, the Craigs had an acre of bananas, and they grew dry rice and peanuts. They even had some orange trees from seeds they brought with them from a pilgrimage to Haifa.[126] They also had some local fruit; a small pear-shaped fruit which Del had forgotten the name of, as well as pineapple and papaya. Food was plentiful and organic. It was inexpensive if you grew your own. The grocery stores varied in what they sold but usually carried spices and a range of basics. There was a French supermarket where they could buy almost

------

126 Haifa, Israel, is the location of the Bahá'í World Centre. Its famous gardens include many orange trees.

anything for a price, and another supermarket where the Craigs occasionally bought butter and a $2.00 toffee apple, a favorite treat reminding them of Canada.

Another favorite dessert made at home was to slice a papaya in half, load it up with yogurt, sliced banana, and other fruits. "You could make your own yogurt any time, just by setting out a jar of milk. The air was always the right temperature." Del said she never acquired a taste for the African staple, manioc. The locals ground it and left it on the earth to dry, then swept it up and cooked it later. Del bit into a pebble in the first batch she tried. Perhaps it was that pebble that put her off, but she said it also tasted like 'old socks'. When she prepared it to feed to other people, she spread it out on a table instead of the ground. "That kept the pebbles, and the chickens, out of it," she said. She kept chickens for eggs, and also hatched new chickens to become meat later on. The eggs for hatching chicks had to be brought into the house because snakes would eat them if left outdoors.

She then surprised me then by saying, "We ate termites too—they were good! We just fried them up and they tasted like bacon bits." Plantains, another staple, were fried or boiled but also 'not very tasty' according to Del. She enjoyed the mushrooms they picked, which had to be gotten at just the right stage of growth 'before they got wormy'. "They seemed to appear from nothing overnight", she said. The locals liked mushrooms too, but not beans which Del had given them seeds for. She said the beans that they grew from those seeds were all returned to her when they matured. The people did not have a taste for them and considered them to rightfully be hers anyway.

Her cooking facilities in the Central African Republic were primitive, but Del didn't mind. In fact, she found it a challenge. Her first oven was a hole in the ground, where, when the wood burnt down, she put bread in and covered it. "Oh, that bread tasted so good…" she said, beaming. Soon Jack built her an above-ground stove and oven. The stove top came from the bottom of an old truck and the oven was framed with half a

   Del (Delores) Craig

culvert. The culvert was covered with hand-made bricks and mortar, so it would retain heat. Clay for the bricks came from termite hills where it had been perfectly loosened and crumbled by the little creatures.

They also built a bath house and toilet on the plantation. A deep hole was dug, walls built around it, and a thatched roof made to cover it. Two holes cut into a plank served as toilet seats. A bucket of lime was thrown down the holes from time to time to limit odor. There was another bench to sit on while bathing, and slats in that part of the floor drained the water. To bathe, they brought buckets of warm water in and set them on the bench. She kept a big tub of hot water on the banked coals of her wood fire for this purpose, saying that the hardwood from the African forests burned especially hot, excellent for cooking and heating water.

Family pets included a rescued boxer puppy that roamed their house and yard. A small monkey clung to Del and Jack like a baby, and when it died, they missed it so intensely they never got another. Del's mom, Yvonne, joined them for three of their years in Africa. She had followed Del to so many places previously that the pattern was a bit of a family joke. However, no one anticipated she would follow Del to Africa. When I asked if her mom had enjoyed her time there, Del replied, "Oh yes. And she loved gardening. You couldn't get her out of the garden… and everything grew so abundantly there. Even the stakes in her tomato patch would sprout and grow." Del and Jack's teenage daughters, one from each of their previous marriages, were with them in Africa for a while as well.

Del said the people she met in the country were so uncynical, so spiritual, and so connected to nature that they would even say a prayer before cutting down a tree. Many missionaries had been teaching there before the Bahá'ís arrived but Del said the locals knew there was a difference between them and the Christians they had encountered—the Bahá'ís would actually associate with them as friends and equals.

At first, the Bahá'ís would meet in homes, but soon built their first Center, a small, thatched roof structure. Then came a larger one like it, then a much larger one which they also outgrew. Finally, the community divided up into twelve sectors for meetings. The Craigs supplied meals and a place to stay for visiting Bahá'í 'teaching teams' throughout much of their time in Africa. Another family of Canadian pioneers arrived just after the Craigs did; Jane and Neil Macmillan from British Columbia.

Del recalled observing the Bahá'í Fast[127] in Africa during March being easier than at home. Italian Bahá'í pioneers would come to visit from the city and they would all sit together in the river to cool off while waiting for sundown when they would break the Fast together. "It felt so good, you forgot you were waiting for the Fast to end so you could finally have some supper."

While recalling sitting in the river with friends, Del also remembered that, early in her time there, she heard what sounded like music coming from the river. When she investigated, it was a circle of people standing in the water, slapping the surface in such a way as to make not only rhythm but pitched melody. She had never heard anything like it and the skin on her arms tingled with its loveliness. One of the things she missed intensely upon returning to Canada was the music and dancing. The Africans sang, clapped, and danced at all the Feasts[128], often with babies hanging on their backs. They played hand-made instruments such as xylophones made of hardwood. Our Canadian Feasts paled in comparison in her estimation. As she spoke, I found myself longing to be present at an African Feast.

Del was so delighted by African music and she arranged for a film to be made of some African Bahá'ís' playing and singing

---

127 The Bahá'í Fast is observed in March, from sunrise to sunset for nineteen days, with exemptions for children, the elderly, and those with health conditions and nursing or pregnant mothers.

128 She was referring to the Bahá'í Feasts held once every nineteen days, the regular community event of worship, fellowship and sharing of food.

                    Del (Delores) Craig

songs, the words to which were mostly in Sango. She felt the singers were so good they ought to be appreciated and wanted to send the film back to Canada. She used her own movie camera and got a woman she knew to operate it, filming in her yard. She had the singers make their own matching dresses for the film. When filming was complete, the group had a celebration of dancing because they were so pleased with their work. To Del's great disappointment, the sole copy of the film disappeared when she sent it to the embassy to have a copy made. She still regretted that loss as she spoke of it in 2016. On another occasion, she also once filmed some of the local people dancing. When they saw the results projected on her wall, they howled with laughter, never having seen themselves on film before.

Del taught sewing classes while there and showed me a picture of a float they put in a parade in Bangui, which consisted of sewing machines bolted onto a flat-bed truck which Jack borrowed from the American embassy where he worked. The women from Del's sewing classes sat with the machines, wearing matching dresses they had made. The President had been seated, watching the parade impassively till that point but when he saw this float, he suddenly stood and applauded. Del smiled with satisfaction as she recalled the moment. "Of course when he stood, everyone else did too." The President's wife then bought much of the women's sewing work from the market for family members. Proceeds from the sales went to purchase more material for classes.

The Craigs sold their farm after a time and rented a house in town which they turned into a Peace Corps transit house for American youth coming into the country. The volunteers were in Africa for two-year time periods and they came back to the transit house when they got sick, or to collect their pay. Another of Del's ideas to supplement income from the Peace Corps, was to purchase a dry-cleaning business. Jack was dubious about it at first but maintained the machines for her. The business turned out to be a fine supplement to their income and employed numerous local people who Del said were loyal and hard-working. "Only one had to be fired", she added. She called their dry-cleaning business 'Best Press'. "Why not? We were good," she said, smiling with satisfaction.

The Craigs would invite their employees in for a meal sometimes, unusual since white employers did not usually socialize with Africans under any circumstance. One day Del invited them to have a swim in her pool. They were hesitant at first, but finally accepted her offer. Once in—and certain they were welcome—they were reluctant to get out. After that, when lunch time came, they could hardly wait to get into the lovely pool. On occasions when the cleaning machines broke down, employees would insist on scrubbing by hand in the yard in tubs despite the smell and sting of the chemicals, such was their loyalty and dedication.

Jack developed a brain tumor while in Africa and returned to Canada for surgery. Back in Calgary, miraculously, other patients on the waiting list cancelled diagnostic scans as well as surgeries, so Jack was able to get to the top of the list. After surgery, they returned to Africa where he began to have seizures. Del was grateful they had been able to return to Africa because in Canada, Jack would not have been allowed to work in the kinds of jobs he was qualified for. In Africa, when he had a seizure, his trainees simply laid out cardboard for him to lie on and kept him safe. The men were proud to have been taught by him, an unusually gifted mechanic who could go to bed at night contemplating a mechanical problem and wake up next morning with the solution in mind.

I asked her about civil unrest while she was there. She said, "Yes, there were three civil wars while we were there, tribal wars for power and the presidency." She said this with nonchalance but looking at my furrowed brow, clarified they never really felt in danger, even though there had been shooting at night at times—sometimes with soldiers shooting from the fence on their own property.

                                                      Del (Delores) Craig

I continued to stare at her in disbelief and then it occurred
to me that the woman I was speaking to, had faced a much
more imminent threat of death at the point of a knife back in
Winnipeg, so perhaps she was more prepared to face it than
many. She went on to describe one of the assassination attempts
on the President which involved three men scaling his fence
intending to shoot him, but as they did so, one shot himself in
the foot, ending that particular attempt. To her it seemed a bit
of a joke. On another occasion she said Jack's truck was stolen
by one faction, and reclaimed for them by another; such was
the regard between the Craigs and so many of the local Africans
who knew them. On another occasion, a twelve-year old kid
threatened her with a gun thrust into her open kitchen window.
She swatted him away, shouting, "You should be in school!" at
which he promptly fled.

I asked Del about the state of the country now. She sighed,
"There seems to be genocide…" The Craigs returned to Canada
in 2001 and within the year Jack was in hospital in High River.
He stayed there for nine years, dying of Parkinsons in 2010.
It was during these years that a band of musicians she had
known in the Central African Republic toured in Canada. She
was able to go to Montreal to see them for a joyful and tear-
filled reunion which she showed me photos of. Among the
band members were some of the young men she had filmed
dancing in her house in Africa years earlier, the fellows who
had laughed uproariously to see themselves as dancing figures
on a wall.

Del was transferred back to a newly built seniors' residence
in High River in late 2015, pleased to be near friends and her
daughter, Brenda, again. She continued to participate in Bahá'í
activities when able, and cling to prayer as a fundamental part
of life. Her Bahá'í prayer book, always at her side, was sheathed
in a hand-tooled leather case.

She said she still frequently dreamed of Africa—and Jack.
Del passed away in the summer of 2018. Her High River funeral,

Del Craig later in life. Photo source: unknown.

attended by family and friends, consisted of Bahá'í prayers and writings said at her graveside under a hot August sun. I had the feeling that she may be watching us gather there at her grave, but now, very likely with her beloved Jack at her side.

Del (Delores) Craig

15   Catharina Ankersmit

◇◇◇◇◇◇◇◇◇◇◇◇◇◇◇◇◇◇◇◇◇◇◇◇◇◇◇◇◇◇◇◇◇◇

"Bring her in!" Catharina insisted. It was a mild winter day in 2017 and I had taken a drive with my dog out to Canmore where Catharina lived. Canmore, a beautiful mountain town near Banff, is a destination spot for skiing enthusiasts in winter, hiking adventurers in summer, and day-trippers like me who are exhilarated by the beauty of the mountains. As she invited me in, I explained I may not be able to stay long, because my dog was out in the car and had gotten wet. I had let my big Labrador retriever, Molly, out for a quick walk and bathroom break before going in to visit, and she had bolted into nearby Cougar Creek at the sight of ducks swimming by. I was concerned that if she came in still wet, she would be all too pungent for Catharina's fourth-floor luxury condo. Catharina would not hear of leaving her shivering in the car, so I went back out and got Molly.

With a few old towels, we dried the dog off together and then let her run free. To Catharina's delight, the

Catharina Ankersmit wearing a traditional Norwegian dress. Photo source: Catharina Ankersmit.

dog went straight into her bedroom closet and sniffed out a toy left by a little dog who had lived with her several years earlier. Molly brought it into the living room where we drank tea, and she proceeded to chew the toy. I love this memory of Catharina. The afternoon sun flooded in through the windows, briefly warming our faces before it began its mid-afternoon descent behind the high mountain range just south of her neighborhood. She lived two more years after that day…

In 2018, for her 90th birthday, Catharina published a memoir titled *The Nut from Nijmegen* with the help of her daughter, Laila. Another daughter, Ingrid, instigated some earlier recording of memory which contributed to the book. I attended the milestone birthday celebration held in the Canmore Opera House, a replica log building of the original, which stood next to the condo complex where Catharina had lived since 2003. Given her advanced age and declining eyesight, her son, John, had been living with her for several years as her caretaker. She took evident pleasure visiting old friends that day, and in introducing them to each other. She introduced me to the woman who had shared a hospital room with her when her first child, Mary, was born. The woman was still a dear friend.

Catharina grew up in the Netherlands, a young teenager during World War II with hunger, deprivation and danger her constant companions. Born in 1928, she was the second of four daughters of Albertus Ankersmit and Dina Hendrika van Tuinen, living in the city of Nijmegen near the German border. In her memoir, she shared remarkably precise images of a distant childhood:

"My earliest memories are of the flowers on the wallpaper in the room where my crib was at Charlottenburg, my grandmother's house… It was after I started school that we moved to the house on the Berg en Dalse Weg where my parents spent the next 36 years… I do remember the snow

                                            Catharina Ankersmit

drops blooming in the unkempt grass, and the crocuses in the garden behind the house. That garden gave me a good feeling…"

In a document she sent me in 2017 titled, *Catharina – My Bahá'í Life*, she spoke of her parents and the comfortable relationship which existed between them, calling them 'each other's best friend'. She said they did not belong to a church, and religion was not discussed in the home. She described her father as an open-minded man from a Mennonite background who advised her "…never join a religious or political group, as these are things you might have to give up your life for…" She referred to her mother as a 'free thinker' who had an interest in eastern religions and who read Tagore and Krishnamurti. She said her mother "… instilled in us so much love, meaning, and feeling that after her death for years I thought of her every day, and I often still do when I hear the songs she used to sing, or see wildflowers, especially daisies…"

World War II brought an abrupt change to the almost idyllic life she had known. "On the tenth of May in 1940, the Germans got up early and walked into our country." [129] The German occupation of the Netherlands could not have been more simply put. She goes on to describe conditions as they worsened:

"In winter we wore wooden shoes, or shoes with old car tire soles… only enough coal to heat one room, and gas and power were only available at certain times. There was no more meat, no more sugar, no more tea or coffee, very little bread and it was not made with wheat, no butter, no oil, no fat. By 1944 there was not much except potatoes, and sometimes there were frozen ones among the good ones." [130]

In *Catharina – My Bahá'í Life* she speaks of the effect of the war on her thinking as a young woman:

---

129 From *The Nut from Nijmegen.*
130 ibid

"When the war was over, I spent a lot of time thinking about a way in which we could secure peace in the world… how could a 'Christian' nation like Germany be so inhuman to the Jews. How could the world stand by and let that happen? I decided that Christianity had totally missed Jesus' message of 'love thy neighbor' and of peace and goodwill amongst men. I rejected religion, but not the teachings of Jesus. I also felt that the other great world religions had the same status and validity as the Christian church."

At the age of twenty-one Catharina went to work in England for six months, caring for an elderly man in Brighton. She joined the International Friendship Club whose goal was international peace. It provided her with the opportunity to meet young people from other countries. She said she joined them because their 'cause' mattered to her. Her independent thinking had already decided that what the world needed was an international governing body, motivated by a true concern for the welfare of all humankind.

When the job in England ended, she found employment as an au pair in Norway. While there, she attended a camp with the International Friendship Club where she met Elinor Gregory, an American Bahá'í with whom she 'hit it off fabulously'. They soon found themselves taking a trip together during which Catharina challenged Elinor to explain how religion could help the world's ills, given its dreadful record. Catharina tells the story as follows:

"On the train we talked about prejudice. Elinor told me she loved Holland, but I said I thought Holland was actually a narrow-minded country. She had to explain what the word 'prejudiced' meant, because I was not sure. [Catharina's English was still improving.] That is how we got to talking about religion and how we could ever have peace with so many religions, politics, armies and so on. Elinor started to bring up the oneness of God… She even mentioned the

    Catharina Ankersmit

word 'Bahá'í' a few times, so finally I asked her what it meant. She told me about Bahá'u'lláh, and I was at first shocked that it wasn't actually Jesus who came back, but another Messenger fulfilling prophecies. Towards the end of the weekend, I asked her if she could give me a book 'that man' had written." [131]

Elinor invited Catharina to a 'fireside meeting' in her home at which time she lent her the *Kitab-i-Iqan* (*The Book of Certitude*) by Bahá'u'lláh. Catharina was struck by a statement on its second page about the standard for true understanding and recognition of God and His Prophets. It said, "…inasmuch as man can never hope to attain unto the knowledge of the All-Glorious, can never quaff from the stream of divine knowledge and wisdom, can never enter the abode of immortality, nor partake of the cup of divine nearness and favour, unless and until he ceases to regard the words and deeds of mortal men as a standard for the true understanding and recognition of God and His Prophets."

"This really struck me," she said. "All those different Christian churches were founded on the interpretation of the Word of God by mortal man, and they are so sure of being the only ones who are right that they denounce all the other churches… I had to let that sink in for a bit." [132]

Still, Catharina said she felt the urge to prove some aspect of the *Kitab-i-Iqan* unacceptable, but upon further thought said she could not find any point she actually objected to. Indeed, upon reading a second book, *The Renewal of Civilization* by David Hofman, she described herself as "…on fire by this time and knew I had found the answer to the way to Peace."

Speaking further of her attraction to the new Faith, she said that in the following weeks she found herself thinking, "I will be a Bahá'í someday… which stopped me in my tracks because

---

131 From *Catharina – My Bahá'í Life*
132 ibid

I knew that if I joined a religion, it might cost me my life…"
She recalled her father's warning. But she must have made her
decision shortly thereafter because she is recorded as having
attended her first Feast on October 15, 1950. Feasts are one of
the few Bahá'í events open to enrolled members only. "I had
written a long letter to my mother telling her all about this new
religion. Before she could even answer me, I realized it did not
matter whether my mother approved of the religion or not,
because I knew for myself that it was true."

From Norway, Catharina travelled to Switzerland, staying
and working in the city of Lausanne on the shores of Lac
Leman, where the Bahá'í European Teaching Committee
had its headquarters. Being there put her in touch with well-
known Bahá'ís including Zikhrullah Khadem, Ugo Giachery,
Dr. Hermann Grossman, Dr. Muhlschlegel, Ian Semple, David
Hofman, Edna True and others. Thereafter, she returned to the
Netherlands and applied for immigration to Canada, arriving in
Ontario in 1953 and living with relatives in Georgetown, near
Toronto. For two years she recalled taking the bus forty miles
to Toronto to attend Bahá'í Feasts on Bloor Street, where she
met well-known Canadian Bahá'ís: Peggy Ross, Laura Davis,
Michael and Elizabeth Rochester, Betty and Douglas Martin,
Edith Blakeney, and Allan and Evelyn Raynor.

In 1955 she moved west to Alberta, getting a job in Calgary.
She associated with the Bahá'ís there and soon found herself
a member of its administrative body, the Local Spiritual
Assembly. Her outstanding memory of its meetings was the day
in 1957 when the members heard that the Head of their Faith,
Shoghi Effendi, had passed away. "We felt so lost and adrift," she
said.

Other Bahá'ís who she remembered living in Calgary at the
time were Barbara and Gordon Scott, Helen Marshall, Mary
Campbell, Sylvia Plotkin (Demers), Dale Olivier (Lillico), and
Nora Harrison. Rudy Amartey, a dashing young man from
Ghana, was also a member living there—though he only stayed

                                          Catharina Ankersmit

Richard Stanton, Kathy Ankersmit, Charles Lightfoot, in Edmonton at the site of HBC Fort Edmonton, between the North Saskatchewan River and present Legislature buildings, ca August 1955. Photo source: Canadian Bahá'í Archive.

a short time—and he and Catharina became close. Their brief relationship resulted in a pregnancy, much to Catharina's alarm. There were communications and misunderstandings between them after he left, and in the end, she chose to have the child and give it up for adoption. It appears to have been an agonizing decision for her, and she describes her dear friend Mary Campbell as being her companion and mainstay during that difficult period. Her concern for the baby, Mary, (named after Mary Campbell) never left her, and she wanted very badly to know what had become of the child. She described her reason for not reaching out to contact her daughter as the years went on, as a 'lack of courage'. However, she describes the reunion that took place at Mary's initiative, years later at Olds College where Catharina worked, as "The happiest day of my life."

In her words, "I went back to the office and there was a dark-skinned young woman giving me a strange look. Then she said, 'Are you Catharina Ankersmit?'[133] I blurted out 'You are my daughter!' I sat down and this enormous feeling of happiness

---

133 From *The Nut From Nijmegen*.

and gratitude came over me. I was so happy, there are no words to explain, and I got up and threw my arms around my child.

After Mary was born and adopted by a Calgary family, Catharina married Erik Poulsen, a Danish immigrant with whom she had six more children and lived on farms in the Rimbey and Bowden areas near Red Deer. Recalling the years of raising her children on the various farms Catharina says,

"The first year our crop looked very good but it froze on the eighth of August and that was the end of the crop… If it was not too cold the cookstove kept us warm, but when it got to minus twenty, Eric would light the furnace in the basement and the heat would come through one grate in the floor… The next spring Erik seeded the whole farm to grass and we borrowed money to buy four milk cows… We got a cream can and once a week we took the cream to the creamery in Rimbey and received about $10. That was our income, and it bought the groceries. We grew our own vegetables and we kept one pig to eat and sold the rest…"[134]

She goes on to tell about having to look after both the cows and the children when her husband began a job away from home. She would load up a sleigh with bales of hay to drag along to feed the cows, and would carry five-gallon pails of water to fill the water-trough. One day she slipped while carrying buckets of water, and in the extreme cold, got soaked. Her clothes froze before she got to the house. She had to change before she could attempt the task again, this time with even more ice to negotiate. She said, "I think I really felt sorry for myself then." What strikes me now, is how rarely she did appear to feel sorry for herself, and how vigorously she tackled her difficulties and challenges.

The Bahá'í camp, the Sylvan Lake Summer School, was just a half hour's drive away from her farm and I remember seeing her arrive there in the 1970s with a string of blonde children, their

---

134From *"The Nut From Nijmegen"*

                                          Catharina Ankersmit

hair gleaming in the sunshine. Catharina recalls camping there in two tents, bringing 'two hibachis and lots of bedding' and settling in for two weeks of classes, helping around the camp, and socializing. Many years later, at Catharina's funeral, I heard two of her children, Kirsten and John, reminisce with the camp chef, David Sherwin, about helping him in the kitchen, when they were young. John became Ed Muttart's summer assistant as a twelve-year old boy, helping Ed maintain the lakefront property and planting trees. During a 2017 Reunion on the property, Ed pointed out the many trees that John had helped him plant.

At age fifty-seven, Catharina moved to Edmonton to attend university. Having already taken numerous adult education courses while working at Olds College, she began classes on campus noting that her daughter, Laila, was also studying there at the same time. She expressed surprise at her own success with the courses. "I finally got a degree," she said, smiling.

Speaking of her early education she explained, "I did not do well in school; I was restless, critical of the teachers and I thought there were more important things than the stuff we had to learn in school."[135] I found the notion that she had not done well in school surprising, given how informed she was and how widely she read. In fact, sitting in her Canmore living room with its balcony view of the mountains, I was keenly aware of the entire wall of books across one side of the room, a remarkable collection for a person who 'did not do well in school'.

Sandy Taylor, a Bahá'í friend of hers in her later years, also noticed Catharina's intelligence. "As well as being impressed by her twinkling sense of humor and her unassuming manner, I am so very taken by her bright mind and the way she can speak fluently about almost any broad and varied topic that is raised in general conversation, and can frequently follow up this conversation by retrieving a relevant book from her large and extensive library…"

135 From *The Nut From Nijmegen*.

Friends meeting in Catharina's Canmore meeting room. Photo source: Joan Young.

Her dislike of school started early. According to her memoir, "I did not enjoy the first day of school, and no days after either. When the teacher noticed that I was left-handed, she did everything she could to make me use my right hand. This felt like it went against my grain and I developed a deep-seated dislike of school…"

I am also struck by her independence of thought, an independence which appears to have been seen as simple stubbornness by her first teacher. This independent thinking expressed itself in ways such as her strong support of Judge Reilly, the Canmore area judge who advocated restorative justice for Indigenous people, saying, "All our system wants to do is punish people. It doesn't want to fix things." She befriended people at Morley, attending picnics and other events with nearby Stoney Nakoda Bahá'ís when she could, and she had an early understanding of colonialism as it played out in Canada—an understanding which few Canadians possessed at the time.

Catharina Ankersmit

I observed her to speak directly and plainly. She meant what she said. She had no interest in pretense. She offered candid, individual thoughts on subjects and not the conventions which get easily spouted by many. I enjoyed her serious views on things, and at the same time, how quick she was to laugh and beam her infectious smile.

Following her retirement from work at age 65, she decided to spend a year in China teaching English. She described her decision as connected to the hope that she could share the teachings of her Faith with people there. She was characteristically modest about her ability to teach English and described a fellow teacher as 'a much better teacher than I was'. But she immersed herself whole-heartedly in the experience and said, "I could have stayed in China forever, but I wanted to see my grandchildren again, so I went back to Canada."

She bought herself a Chinese army coat before she left, which she planned to wear when she got off the plane to 'impress her

Catharina Ankersmit, front row centre, attending study group at Canmore public library. Photo source: Sandy Taylor.

family'—as she put it—a fine example of her self-deprecating
humour. A misunderstanding occurred as to where to meet them
in the airport, and it took ten or fifteen minutes to find them.
"Anyway I just about melted in my Chinese army coat, and was
very happy to see my family… that coat came off pretty quick."

She returned to China in September 1995 to attend the
United Nations World Conference on Women in Beijing.
Looking back on the experience later she said,

> *"I do think if the UN and most of the world's governments
> were made of women, we would have peace and not war.
> We wouldn't use up our tax money for armaments. I am a
> feminist. I don't mind saying so. Some women don't want
> to admit to it. It's the same with environmentalism. I don't
> mind saying that I am an environmentalist. We want our
> world preserved, so we can live in it."*[136]

At age eighty-eight, she was still volunteering in the
community and helping new Canadians improve their English
conversation skills. She was also an active member of a
Canmore book club until near the end of her life. Though her
eyesight was failing, and she needed a large magnifying glass
to read, she read anyway, something I watched her do at the
Bahá'í meetings she hosted in the conference room of her condo
building.[137]

Her tastes in music included the finest of the European
classics, and she was a frequent attendee of the Banff Centre for
the Arts concert series. But she also had a fondness for the '80s
pop group, ABBA. When she passed away, a wonderful touch
at the end of her graveside service was the sudden joyful sound
of ABBA playing from a daughter-in-law's cell phone, putting a
spring in people's step as they headed to their cars.

---

136 From *"The Nut From Nijmegen"*

137 See Appendix H for memories of Catharina shared by Bahá'í friends,
    May Cummings and Sandy Taylor. May's memories were prepared for
    the Swedish Bahá'í community which Catharina had early associations
    with, and where May had grown up.

                                      Catharina Ankersmit

Vintage truck owned by Catharina's eldest son, carrying her casket to the graveside service in the Olds cemetery. Photo source: Joan Young.

As I write these final lines about Catharina, my eyes are filling with tears. Today is the anniversary of her passing. I am envisioning the people in the next world who lined up to greet her when she 'arrived'. I imagine them beaming with more than their usual joy.

16   Miriam Nicholls

The steady hum of my car engine was lulling me into a meditative state. It was a beautiful fall day in Treaty Seven Territory, and I was headed towards the mountains of the Crowsnest Pass. The sunlight was softer, and the sky clearer, than in high summer. I was on my way home from Pincher Creek having visited Dale Lillico, and was passing the hamlet of Lundbreck where Del Craig had lived years earlier. A sudden longing to see yet another aging friend struck me. Miriam Nicholls lived in Blairmore, another twenty minutes west into the Pass. I had intended to turn north onto Cowboy Trail, otherwise known as Highway 22, which parallels the foot of the mountains, winding northwards through the Porcupine Hills but I changed my mind and continued westward. Soon, golden larch trees appeared, brilliant splashes of color on the mountainsides, inviting the hiker within me to climb up for a closer look and a stirring view of the valley below. But now I had a mission.

The visit turned out to be my last opportunity to see Miriam in her lifetime. It was

Crowsnest Mountain. Photo source: Joan Young.

2015, a year before she passed away. Not having called ahead, it took her a moment before she recognized me. A smile broke over her face when she did. It was almost lunch time so she invited me to join her in the dining room of the Continuing Care Facility where she lived. She was now confined to a wheelchair, but her mind was clear. As we talked, her daughter, Dawn, appeared at the table and said, "Hello Joan," as if she had seen me yesterday. She was on staff in the very nursing unit where Miriam was a long-term resident. Dawn probably had not seen me since she was nine or ten years old when I taught Bahá'í children's classes in Calgary, classes that included her brother David.

As we spoke, I asked Miriam about growing up in Toronto. She said her parents, the O'Hearns, placed a high value on social standing and had expectations which as an only child, she found difficult to meet. It seems they were also rather protective and perhaps overly concerned for their daughter's health and well-being. In a later conversation with David, I learned that Miriam had indeed experienced significant health issues as a child. It was understandable that she would have been considered delicate, given she had contracted a staph infection as an infant, which in those years became so severe it essentially confined her to bed until school age. As a teenager, her family moved to Anaheim in California for a few years, where she broke her tailbone in a skating accident. She was again confined to her bed, completing Grade 12 lying in bed.

Miriam Nicholls as a child in Toronto. Photo source: David Nicholls.

In a 2013 audio recording made by Amy Singh during a series of long-distance telephone visits, Miriam said that because her parents 'had each other for company', she felt not only free to, but needed to make her own way in life. This allowed her to consider moving out west when she enrolled as a Bahá'í in December of 1960. She said she first heard mention of the Bahá'í Faith in a 1950s television interview she had seen with Peggy Ross[138], but afterward she could not remember the name of the Faith. She had been working at Mutual of Omaha and getting rides home with a fellow employee[139] who stopped enroute one day, to drop something off at a brick building with a brass plaque on the door. She asked what the building was, and in response to his answer that this was the Bahá'í National Centre, she recalled the name and exclaimed, "But I've been looking for that!"

She went on to tell Amy, "I'd been very impressed with the Faith and wanted to get in touch with it but hadn't known how…" To learn more, she began attending 'firesides' held at Alan and Evelyn Raynor's[140] home. She came west in the summer of 1961 to attend the Bahá'í Summer School in Banff, flying to Calgary. She said that as the plane descended over the fields approaching the city, she 'felt drawn to the land', as if she belonged there. Remarkably, within three days of the Summer School concluding in Banff, she found a job in Calgary as librarian at the morning newspaper, *The Albertan*—a job she loved.

In speaking with me at lunch in 2015, she said she had feared that if she went back home to Toronto, she would 'never escape her parents grasp'. So, she informed her mother and her Toronto

---

138 Peggy Ross was a well-known Canadian Bahá'í who travelled extensively in her role as Auxiliary Board member, meeting Bahá'ís across the country and encouraging them in their efforts.

139 Miriam recalls this man's name being Jan Vander Veen.

140 Raynors were well-known members of the Canadian Bahá'í Community and contributed much to deepening the knowledge of the Faith among their fellow believers.

employer on the telephone that she was not coming back. "That went over like a lead balloon," she mused.

After Miriam's passing, I asked her daughter, Dawn, about her maternal grandparents; given what Miriam had said about them. Dawn recalled only seeing them once as a child and felt that while they may not have been all that wealthy, they were clearly upper middle-class. It is quite possible they disapproved of many of their daughter's choices, though they appeared to have shown some positive feeling towards the Faith Miriam adopted—at least initially. David said that Miriam's father had been an accountant, a man who was at the top of his field in Toronto. In 1961, with a steady job in Alberta, Miriam moved into Bowness as a 'pioneer'with the help of local Bahá'ís. Bowness was then a separate town just outside Calgary's western city limits, and within a year and a half of moving there, Miriam met her husband, Murray, who also enrolled in the Faith after their marriage.

Soon, the couple moved to Enderby in the interior of BC. However, they stayed in Bowness long enough to meet a young man, a door-to-door salesman, selling among other things, Christmas cards. "I don't need any Christmas cards, I'm a Bahá'í," Miriam had replied. The young salesman promptly asked, "What's a Bahá'í?" That young salesman was Peter Rempel, who went on to become a lifelong Bahá'í and a close friend of the Nicholls. He passed away in Lethbridge in May of 2020.

Over the years, Dawn heard her mom tell the story of meeting Peter. Though she was no longer sure of all the details, she thought Peter might have been selling Watkins' products when he first appeared at the family's door. Peter, in a telephone visit with Elaine Zavitz later in life, said he had met Miriam while selling Fuller Brush products, and that he had been offering a Christmas special. He went on to say he saw Miriam outside, hanging laundry on the line, when he initially struck up a conversation with her.

 Miriam Nicholls

Miriam recalls the details slightly differently[141]. She recalls watching Peter approach the house while 'washing the porch windows', and that he was wearing a dark overcoat. The sight of him struck her as significant because the night before she had dreamed of such a man approaching from the direction of the neighbour's house and walking up to her front door. The slight differences in how Peter remembered the moment many years later, and how Miriam recalled it, are incidental. The essentials of what happened are that Miriam shared what she believed to be the most important thing possible, her faith in the new Messenger of God, Bahá'u'lláh, with a person who was interested, and that that person found it to resonate with him as well.

To Murray's surprise, upon coming home from work the day Peter first arrived at their doorstep, he saw a stranger sitting at his kitchen table, a stranger who had been invited to stay for supper. It would turn out to be the first of many visits between them, one of which happened to include me in the summer of 1970, when I caught a ride back to Calgary with Peter, from a Vancouver Youth Conference. Of course, Peter stopped on the way in Enderby, which is not far off the Trans-Canada Highway, to visit his dear friends, the Nicholls.

In an essay series *One Bahá'í at a Time*, Susan Black records Miriam telling her about life in Enderby in the early years of marriage:

"During that time, Murray travelled to work in Kamloops and would regularly pick up hitchhikers and bring them home to our farm. A young couple who lived with us for a while… had a great wedding in our home. Murray, my husband, played the drums and other musicians gathered to entertain. I remember with fondness the sweet young girl asking me to make cream puffs. We had a lot of food, but I recall the cream puffs."

---

141 In her recorded interview with Amy Singh.

Despite the general lack of interest shown by the people of Enderby in her Faith—which she so badly wanted to share—Miriam persisted in efforts to bring it to their attention with ads in the paper and initiatives such as essay contests at the school. She spoke of friendly relations with a nearby First Nation, and her memories of this period included celebrating Holy Days with the neighbor kids bobbing for apples, corn roasts, and hosting Bahá'í friends such as Del Craig and her daughter, Brenda. Brenda was the same age as the Nicholls children and she and Del lived in Vernon at the time. In fact, when Miriam and Murray took a trip to the Yukon after he had a heart attack and was supposed to be resting, they left their two young children with Del to be looked after.

Teaching others about her Faith was a driving and life-long passion for Miriam, and her husband was often an active partner in the effort. For their trip to the Yukon, Murray painted, "TRY BAHÁ'Í" on the side of their camper. "We had so many inquiries!" said Miriam. "Once a university student acting as a flagman inquired so we gave him the name of the Bahá'í National Office on Bloor Street in Toronto, and he was looking forward to going to it when he went back."

Regarding the many nights Murray picked up hitchhikers on his way home from work, Miriam said she would always feed them supper and that they would spend the night before moving on next morning. They were most often young hippies, the 'flower children' of the sixties, on the road, exploring the world. Before turning in at the farm the evening before, Murray asked them to stash their drugs in the bushes. One evening when she was not feeling particularly well, Miriam recalled that thirteen hitchhikers arrived. She managed, with the help of a neighbour girl, to fix macaroni and cheese, as well as rice pudding for the lot of them. She said that after supper on nights like that, guitars would appear and they would sing the folk songs of the era. Murray, also a musician, would join in. The children would stay up and enjoy the music, after which the group would tell stories

   Miriam Nicholls

and frequently, Murray would tell them about the Bahá'í Faith. She said that two of the young people who stayed with them did choose to enroll as Bahá'ís while at their farm.

Remarkably, of all the hippy youth hitch-hiking in those years who had received such selfless hospitality, Miriam only recalled one young person coming into the kitchen to help her. It was an Indigenous girl, the companion of a young man who was 'running from the law'. Miriam was grateful for her help indeed. Murray advised the young man to 'give himself up to authorities', and a few years later he wrote back telling them he had taken Murray's advice and straightened his life out. Another young man sent back a Christmas gift of five children's books, lovely books that Miriam kept and treasured for years.

Dawn also recalled her father bringing home hitch hikers and that Miriam would feed them. She spoke of her mother's acute physical challenges at the time, saying she had been in a serious motorcycle accident while still pregnant with Dawn, and that Dawn was born not long after. Miriam was left with pain and a spinal injury that impaired her mobility. Dawn shared with us an image she was unable to forget, despite the passage of time. It was that of seeing her mother on the farm in BC, walking across the yard to feed the chickens. She had to grab her pant legs in order to lift up her limbs—one laborious step at a time. It is a strikingly painful picture, a delicate young woman raised in an upper crust Toronto home, struggling to do farm chores and raise her children—often alone—on a tiny farm in the interior of BC, and doing so without complaint.

Remarkably, in her interviews with both Susan Black and Amy Singh, she mentions none of the suffering of which she could have complained. Her only admission of difficulty was a comment to Amy on one occasion when she said, "After five years we were worn to a frazzle." Yet moments before, she clearly stated, "It was a wonderful life on the farm!" Though both were likely true, Miriam insisted on maintaining the more positive view of her life.

David also remembered his mother's inclination to look for the positive rather than dwell on the negative. He said, "I learned as a child, 'Look at the good points.' If there are nine bad points and only one good one, I was taught to look at the good one and not the bad. I have to say that my mom served and taught the Faith through word and example."

Miriam described their move back to Calgary from the farm in BC as a great relief from the financial struggles they had, yet she missed her animals, large garden, and 'thirty hens'. On this point David commented, "…the years lived in Enderby were hard physically and financially for both my parents, but I believe in many ways they were some of their fondest. My mom named all the farm animals. Two that I recall… the milk cow 'Bessie Butter Cup', and a pair of sheep, 'Lambie-kins' and 'Ramy-kins.'"

Murray had previously held a job while still in Calgary as a nursing orderly, and had been offered the same position in what sounded like orthopedic rehabilitation. Miriam described his aptitude for setting up the required pulleys and weights needed for traction in the healing process.

David shed light on their decision to leave the farm saying, "…in the spring of 1971 when they weren't sure how they could carry on in BC, a man drove into the farmyard one day and offered to buy the farm. So their prayers were answered, and they returned to Calgary."

During my 2017 visit with Dawn, she invited my travel companion, Donna Coey, and me to meet her and her husband for lunch in the nearby town of Coleman. I found her husband, Walter, to be a big-hearted and amiable man who proudly identified himself as 'a Friend of the Faith', a term he had learned from Miriam. Dawn and Walter's love and respect for Miriam was palpable. Dawn recounted her mother's keen mind and intense interest in history and human affairs. She said that when one of the family would ask for background information on almost any subject, Miriam would launch into an in-depth discussion of it. Dawn laughingly said, "We usually only wanted the short version, but she invariably knew what she was talking about."

Recalling his mother's knowledge in the field of religion in particular, David said,

"I remember different religious groups traveling door to door, teaching their beliefs. Upon coming to our house my mom would invite them in and have in-depth discussions with them regarding their religious teachings, meaning, and interpretations,while sharing the Bahá'í Faith with them at the same time. I would sometimes chuckle at the reactions of people in the discussions when my mom would refer to chapter, paragraph, and sometimes line in their own scripture, to illustrate her points or perspective…"

David's memory aptly demonstrates how much Miriam read and how informed she was. I can just imagine people coming to her door, intent on gaining a convert, and being utterly astonished that this follower of another Faith, was clearly more familiar with their Scriptures than they were.

Group meeting with Auxiliary Board member Don Rogers, (l to r) Don Rogers, Reg Wilson, Joyce McGuffie, Sylvia Demers, Miriam Nicholls and Counsellor, Angus Cowan, 1975. Photo source: Canadian Bahá'í Archives.

The Nicholls moved to Medicine Hat in their retirement, and Miriam's friends, Ivy Moore and Parvin Hemmati-Camphor, spoke of her with great fondness. They said they never heard her complain about anything, including her husband. Ivy recalled Murray's huge 'whack of keys' tied to his belt, his big cowboy hat, and his characteristically cranky manner. But she also noted his willingness to help people and said, "He would give you a ride anywhere." Apparently, when the couple first moved to 'the Hat' [142] and attended a Bahá'í Feast there, a little boy thought Murray was 'Abdu'l-Bahá because of his big white beard. Other local kids called him Santa.

He played in a band during these years and belonged to several local clubs. When he passed away, two hundred and fifty people attended his funeral. His funeral procession was led by a horse-drawn carriage, a moving sight which Ivy and Parvin found utterly fitting.

Miriam Nicholls, 1989. Photo source: David Nicholls.

Prior to moving to Medicine Hat—and after being in BC—the couple lived in Calgary for twenty-five years. I recall attending Feasts in their Renfrew area home in the mid 1970s. Miriam was elected to serve on the Calgary Spiritual Assembly during those years and was also appointed, at times, to the Summer School Committee in charge of overseeing programs offered at the Sylvan Lake Bahá'í Centre. Her outstanding recollection of serving there was the year the water source became

---

142 Affectionate and commonly used name for Medicine Hat.

 Miriam Nicholls

contaminated, giving most of the three hundred campers intestinal cramps and diarrhea. Miriam, the only committee member there at the time, had to close the facility down and ask people to leave. As they left, a few others arrived, and in Miriam's memory, were not only disappointed but expressed distinct displeasure at not being allowed in. Telling me this decades later, Miriam seemed unfazed by the irritation she had faced and sounded confident that her decision was the right one. I was surprised. I thought someone as kindly as Miriam might be more inclined to second-guess herself when faced with indignation from others.

She also mentioned how heart-warming it now was to have the teleconference visits initiated by which Amy Singh on Monday mornings. These were begun in response to the House of Justice calling for the holding of 'Devotional Gatherings' to enrich the spiritual life of the community. The group calls included various Bahá'ís from isolated communities scattered across the country, during which they would share prayers and selections from the Writings, as well as listen to uplifting music. Stories of an inspiring nature about individuals, especially those about 'Abdu'l-Bahá, were often included.

It was Miriam's friend, Donna Stirling-Zoller of Pincher Creek, who suggested they include Miriam when the calls began, and Miriam expressed heart-felt appreciation for the invitation. Her friendship with Donna also included Dale Lillico. The two women would drive out to Blairmore on occasion and take Miriam out to lunch at her favorite Chinese restaurant, where according to Dale, "The employees showed such love and compassion to our dear friend."

Harold Wright of Ulukhaktok[143] in the high Arctic was also a frequent participant in the Monday morning calls. It was Harold who first noticed that at times near the end of Miriam's life, she would drift off to sleep during prayers. They could hear deep, regular breathing so he or Amy would check to see

---

143 Formerly Holman NWT.

if she was still awake and get no response. On one occasion, they heard her repeating the prayer known as 'The Remover of Difficulties' under her breath along with Harold who was saying it aloud. Harold alerted Amy to Bahá'u'lláh's reference in the Writings about using this prayer in times of extreme difficulty, "Tell them to repeat it five hundred times, nay, a thousand times, by day and by night, sleeping and waking, that haply the Countenance of Glory may be unveiled to their eyes, and tiers of light descend upon them." [144]

It occurred to Amy and Harold, that Miriam was indeed praying while sleeping and that her whole soul seemed to be turning to its Maker. Amy paid the following tribute to her friend:

"Miriam's love and gratitude for these calls were outstanding. So was her nobility of soul, courtesy, cheerfulness, concern for others, and her deep, deep love for the Faith and the Bahá'í Teachings. Her love for the other friends who took part in these devotional meetings was evident, and the spiritual bond between us was strong, although most of us have never met one another in person. On days she was unable to take part, she unfailingly asked me to give her love to these friends, and they responded in kind, and kept her always in their prayers."

A 'collage' of images from Miriam's life has come together in my mind, a collage of scintillating highlights tucked between shadows of a darker, more somber layer of hardship which she so often endured.

She passed away on December 26, 2016, with her family at her side. Pat Verge and I attempted to attend her Blairmore funeral but were prevented by a blizzard with such ferocious winds that visibility on the highways was impossible. Some months later, I received a call from her son, David, who had

---

144 This quotation of Bahá'u'lláh's is taken from Shoghi Effendi's seminal history of the early Bahá'í era, *God Passes By*, page 119.

 Miriam Nicholls

heard I had an audio recording of her voice and wondered if he could have a copy. I passed along Amy Singh's 2013 recorded interview with her, my heart full for the young man who had recently suffered his own tragic loss of family in a house fire. Joy and sorrow…

17   Maxine Fraser

◇◇◇◇◇◇◇◇◇◇◇◇◇◇◇◇◇◇◇◇◇◇◇◇◇◇◇◇◇◇◇

The doorbell rang so I set the baby down and answered it. It was 1981 and I also had a two-year old toddler who was following me to the door. The tall, imposing, figure of gray-haired Maxine Fraser stood there smiling. She was on her way to other places, but I asked her if she had time for tea and a chat. She had dropped in unexpectedly on other occasions as well—on her way to visit people living further south, or in Saskatchewan, or Manitoba. She was living in Daysland, near Edmonton, at the time. She was many years older than me, but seemed to sense my need for encouragement in raising children, and she provided it generously.

Forty years after these visits I spoke to Amy Singh, requesting her memories about Maxine's life. She knew her better than I did and was a wealth of information, possessing letters written between the two of them, diary entries, and memories of visits and conversations. Other people who knew Maxine in Edmonton during the 1970s added their impressions and memories to hers. A few of their recollections included Maxine's periods of difficulty with mental health, which though worrisome to those who knew and loved her, appear to have never have lasted long, and from which she always emerged to go on to greater service and activity.

During the 1950s, Maxine was a single mother struggling to make ends meet. She once told Amy in her plain-spoken way, "My husband ran off with his secretary." Women had extremely limited options for a livelihood in those years if they were not able—or willing—to re-marry. Maxine chose to look after herself and her young daughter, Morine, with vigor and determination. The challenges of daily life are characterized in a 1966 letter written by Amy to her mother in Cutknife, Saskatchewan. Amy was a student at the University of Alberta at the time, and frequently visited Maxine in her Edmonton home:

> *"Last night Maxine invited me over for supper and I really had a nice time. She used to have six boarders to cook, clean, and wash for, but now they are all light housekeepers, so she has a lot more spare time. She used to look tired quite often but now her eyes just twinkle and she's so full of fun and mischief and energy that it's just amazing. She is separated from her husband and that's her only income, so I'm glad it has worked out this way because she has quite a weak heart and should only work about half as hard…"*

Maxine not only used her home as a source of income by taking in boarders, which involved cooking their meals and doing their laundry, she also frequently cared for foster children, many of them Indigenous, and for a time sold *World Book* encyclopedias. I recall buying a set of their children's books from her for my own young children.

At some point, she converted her Edmonton garage into a large room in which she opened a kindergarten. By 1965 it was no longer a kindergarten but was being used for Bahá'í meetings. The Bahá'ís called it the 'Big Room'. Peter Sorrel, a long-time Edmonton Bahá'í, says of Maxine during that period, "Maxine was the 'most special' Bahá'í in my life… She was the 'mother hen' of all us young people… She always had a piece of pie for us, which had both spiritual and practical benefit."

Robert Ogram, who became a Bahá'í in Lloydminster in 1969, recalls being invited by his high school friend, Greg Wagner, to attend a weekend event at Maxine's Edmonton home. This was one of the many occasions when Maxine demonstrated her concern and support for youth. According to Robert,

"At Christmas time Greg invited me to a 'live-in' at Maxine Fraser's home. This was a reference to 'love-ins' which were gatherings of the new counterculture - 'hippy culture'. So we (the youth invited) were to spend a long weekend at Maxine's home, studying some Bahá'í writings and socializing with other young Bahá'ís… Maxine made the meals with the help of others, arranged the bunks and sleeping accommodations and was generally a mother to us…"

Amy said that as a rather lonely young student away from home, she was grateful for Maxine's motherly influence, "… filling my stomach with wonderful home-cooked food, my head with sound practical advice, my heart with love for the spiritual teachings of Bahá'u'lláh and my vision with an example of service to others."

Maxine had legendary cooking skills. Numerous people recall her bountiful and delicious meals. According to Amy:

"Maxine was canny, in the dictionary sense of the word… shrewd, cautious, thrifty, knowing, wise… skillful and clever. She had a bountiful garden, though it wasn't large. I remember her talking about getting her meat from a butcher who knew what she liked… She bought fruit at her neighborhood store, getting what was in season and often at a reduced price because it was a little bruised or withered, but which made wonderful, stewed fruit and pies. She had a good relationship with the grocers where she shopped, and I think they saved things for her and marked them down…"

The house Maxine purchased in Daysland after leaving Edmonton in 1970, was a beautiful old, three-story home with plenty of room for the foster children. It needed repairs so she went through the process of having it declared an Alberta Heritage House. Doing so meant she had to let people tour through, but that provided the funding for repair and upkeep.

Her relationships with First Nations people in the region were numerous. She loved them and they loved her.

"Her deep love for, and sensitivity to, the Native people often resulted in mystical communication. Sometimes they had no telephone and there was no physical means to contact them… but when she needed them, they would show up—on her doorstep or wherever she was. I knew it to happen many times and grew accustomed to this mystery. They loved her and trusted her. And teased her too! I recall standing beside her car at Hobbema, while Roy Coyote with a twinkle in his eyes, whistled meadowlark calls and chuckled as Maxine first searched the landscape for the birds, and then caught on to his prank and laughed with us…"[145]

Robert Ogram also spoke of Maxine's involvement with First Nations and recalls having met the same man, Roy Coyote, who loved to tease Maxine. Robert and some other Bahá'ís spent a night at Roy's home near Hobbema, while attending another weekend event held in the area. Maxine would have been brimming with energy in gatherings such as these and would have fueled much of the activity. Robert continued:

"…I had returned (to Saskatchewan) and was involved with First Nations Bahá'ís. The Alberta Bahá'í community was hosting a gathering in the spring of 1976. It was called 'Spring Thaw'… Merv Krivoshein and Arlene were living in Lloydminster, and I think I was teaching at the school at Ministikwan, a Saskatchewan First Nations community. Merv and I were the drivers and, in two cars, we brought friends from Onion Lake (Seekasakootch) First Nation to this gathering in Wetaskiwin, Alberta. [The town of Wetaskiwin is just north of the First Nations community of Hobbema, now known as Maskwacis.] Ed Muttart from the Canadian National Spiritual Assembly was there.

---

145 Amy Singh's memory.

                                          Miriam Nicholls

She also had a love for children and delighted in their company. Amy said that children loved her; perhaps because she loved them too. She listened to them, was not condescending, answered their questions honestly, and was 'just plain fun.' A lovely memory Amy has, is of her son, Ranjit, going to stay with Maxine for a few days in Daysland as a young boy. Years after it happened, during a phone visit, Maxine told Amy about a conversation that she had with him during that visit. She said that the local library had been planning to throw out some shelves, but had given them to her instead. "When I put them in the veranda, Ranjit said, 'What's your husband going to say at you bringing in such junk?' I said, 'I don't have a husband, so I don't have to worry about that!' Ranjit said, 'What about that old man upstairs?' I had a boarder up there. I didn't think he was so old, but I guess Ranjit did. I just had so much fun! I enjoyed every minute he was here..."

There was also Maxine's exceptional empathy and understanding for adults, "...especially the sick, lonely, or vulnerable. But she was often disappointed and hurt by thoughtless or selfish people and had little time for the insincere..." said Amy. She described Maxine's faith as:

"... no superficial thing but had its roots deep in her heart. It was evident in her constant service to those around her: family, foster children, friends, neighbors, newcomers, university students, the sick, strangers, people of all races and religious backgrounds, particularly children and native people. She went out of her way to visit isolated people and acquaintances along the highways of Alberta, Saskatchewan and Manitoba... She had a deep and abiding love for God and His Messengers... a love for service, but disliked a rigid approach, preferring instead... 'to do things as the spirit

Numerous people who knew her, marvelled at her apparent closeness to the spiritual realm. She seemed to possess a degree of perception beyond what most people had. Glenn Cameron[146] who was a student in Edmonton at the time said, "She just seemed to know things that were not discernible by others, and I learned to trust her intuitive pronouncements more and more..."

He recalled the time Maxine phoned, asking him to get a slide projector from a certain location and take it to where it was needed for an event. He did not own a car, lived out of town in St. Albert, and had to hitch-hike to accomplish the request. He was also desperately trying to study for an exam next day. But trusting Maxine's judgement, he set out. Arriving at the location she had referred him to, he found no one there who knew anything about either a slide projector, or an 'event'.

So, Glenn put his thumb out to return home for an even longer night of studying. Hitch-hiking was commonplace at the time, so when a young man stopped his car beside him, Glenn opened the door and got in. Hoping there might be some redemptive value to what appeared to have been a wasted evening, Glenn decided to 'teach the Faith' to the young driver who had never heard of it before. The driver said little, but had a beatific smile on his face.

Years later, Glenn said, "The young man later told me that he had been at an impasse in his life… He was stoned and hadn't noticed me standing beside his car when he stopped at a light; he hadn't even noticed me getting into his car and only became aware of me when I started talking. It was a long ride from

---

146 Glenn Cameron is a Bahá'í who has now lived in Gatineau for many years and is the author of *A Basic Bahá'í Chronology* (and subsequent website *https://Bahá'í-library.com/chronology*). It is my good fortune that he is also my brother-in-law.

South Edmonton to St Albert and by the time we arrived he had learned enough to know that he wanted to learn more....” Glenn goes on to say that his Bahá'í roommates took over the conversation with the young man, and he resumed his study. Their guest, a talented musician, did indeed go on to become a member of the Bahá'í community. His name: Earl McAuley. Glenn mused, “He can thank Maxine for the opportunity he was given to learn of the Faith.”

Despite Maxine's dislike of a 'rigid approach', she could be a stickler for form when some of the new young Bahá'ís were not doing things quite as she thought they should be done. And she told them so in her direct manner which she described as 'calling a spade, a spade'. But others did not always appreciate her bluntness. Paul Bujold recalls 'fuming' through a Feast[147] which he and two young Bahá'ís had tried to rearrange in some way to accommodate a slideshow they wanted to share. Maxine had told them, “No, no. That's not how you're supposed to do a Feast...”

I also experienced her 'plain-spoken' manner. She once looked at the teapot from which I was serving her a cup of tea, and said, “That's an ugly pot.” Indeed, it was a misshapen, amateur potter's effort, which dribbled badly when poured. “I'll bring you a new one next time I come.” She did.

A shy young man from a proper Catholic background who had become a Bahá'í, said that at times, Maxine left him completely flabbergasted with her outspoken revelations. “She used to speak to me about auras and spirits trailing around us...” Apparently, she even blithely told him which undergarments she was grateful to no longer have to wear as an older woman in summer. “I was always gobsmacked with the things she said... but I laughed politely, and I loved her...”

Another aspect of this remarkable woman was her creative output and love of beauty. She seemed to turn simple things

---

147 A 'Feast' is the regular coming together of members of the Bahá'í community (once in 19 days) involving devotions, consultation about community affairs, and the serving of refreshments—however simple.

into ceremonies of gratitude. In *Braiding Sweetgrass*, the Indigenous author, Robin Wall Kimmerer, speaks of ceremony saying, "That, I think, is the power of ceremony—it marries the mundane to the sacred. The water turns to wine, the coffee to a prayer. The material and spiritual mingle…" Amy remembered Maxine's simple ceremonies of love and gratitude to the Creator saying,

> *"She loved beauty and expressed it in her poetry, paintings and photographs. She cherished her fine china, good furniture and good books, and delighted in sharing a meal of tasty and nutritious things she had cooked and created, often including produce from her own garden… Maxine dearly loved the prairies and everything about them—the people, the skies, the flora and fauna. Among my 'souvenirs' of her are: The image of her taking a bouquet of fresh bright spring-green aspen poplar leaves to someone in the hospital… A photo she took of a meadow full of wildflowers and grasses… A tiny watercolor painting of prairie crocus[148] she did on a scrap of paper in a few swift strokes when she lived in Daysland. She was delighted to hear I'd had it framed…"*

At times, Maxine shared her difficulties and troubles with others in such a way as to illustrate some life lesson. Robert Ogram shared a story which Maxine told him, saying it has stayed with him.

> *"She was talking about her travels to visit people, to encourage them, and to teach others. She had been discouraged on one trip and was driving down a road. Suddenly she saw a bright flower in the ditch. She stopped and backed up her car, rolled down the window and said, 'HELLO LITTLE FLOWER!' Her trip was then transformed*

---

148 Maxine's painting of the crocus was in a 4 x 5 inch frame and later donated by Amy to the Alberta Bahá'í Archives at Sylvan Lake.

 Miriam Nicholls

The stories included Maxine pulling a pair of Jamie Bond's[149] shoes off a shelf which she had saved as significant. I have to admit I cannot comprehend saving any mortal person's shoes after they die, as if they are a relic, but then, I am not Maxine Fraser.

In recognition of her capacity to inspire, encourage, and teach her Faith to others, Angus Cowan, then an Auxiliary Board member[150], appointed her as one of his first assistants to the Auxiliary Board for the Propagation of the Faith. She

Don Rogers with his assistants circa 1980; Maxine Fraser at far left of middle row. Photo source: Amy Singh.

---

149 Jamie Bond was given the title 'Knight of Bahá'u'lláh' by the Guardian, as one of the 254 Bahá'ís to be the first to move to a new country or territory during the 'Ten Year Crusade'. (He and his wife Gale moved to Canada's high Arctic in 1953).

150 The Auxiliary Board members and their Assistants are appointed to inspire and encourage the community as it follows the Plans developed by the elected institutions of the Faith.

was honoured and took her responsibilities with the utmost seriousness. Her photo appears in the July/August issue of *Bahá'í Canada* in 1976, along with a handful of other individuals who were the first to be appointed in that capacity.

At the time of Maxine's passing, Amy wrote,

"There are a great many people who loved Maxine deeply, appreciated her generosity of spirit, her love of God and Bahá'u'lláh, and the way she shared her life, her home, her Faith and her love. Those people are spread far and wide across the continent and around the world. In the words of Ted Anderson, 'She is one of the unsung heroes of the Bahá'í community'…"

Some years before her passing, Ted Anderson told her directly that he considered her an unsung hero[151]. I believe bits of melody may have now been whistled, hummed, and sung for Maxine Fraser. She is no longer completely 'unsung'. 'Ebullient', was Ed Muttart's immediate response when I asked him how he remembered her; meaning exuberant, buoyant, and effervescent.

Maxine left this world in 2002 in Slave Lake, Alberta, where she had been cared for in the last years of life by her daughter, Morine. At the time of writing, I was saddened to hear that Morine also recently passed away in Nova Scotia. Her perspective on her unusual mother would have been of great value. If I have misrepresented Maxine, perhaps she will pour me another 'cup of tea' in the next life and set me straight. I would hope that her daughter, Morine, would join us.

---

151 From Amy Singh's unpublished memories.

   Miriam Nicholls

18   Jean Hedley

In the spring of 2016, I visited Jean in her High River apartment, specifically to ask about her life. I had visited her on numerous occasions before, but this trip was special. Though I had known her for years, I had never asked her about the events leading up to her decision to become a member of the Bahá'í community. Two years after this visit, as she became less steady on her feet, she moved into a seniors' residence across town which offered meals in a common dining room. On one of the occasions when Jean Hedley met me outdoors following an exercise class she had just completed using walking poles, she was delighted with her additional stability and the exercise they offered.

She told me about first meeting her husband, Harv. They were both members of the United Church in Manitoba as young, single individuals, and met while working at a church camp in the late 1950s. She was the camp nurse and he a camp counsellor. Jean chuckled as she explained that Harv had admitted to her later, that he had initially considered her 'too young and frisky' to be seriously interested in. My first thought was that Harv must have been an unusually serious and shy young man. I would love to have known each of them at that time.

Shedding more light on the couple's early days, their son, David, in his father's eulogy at the time of Harv's passing in 2014 said,

> *"...By this time they'd begun to notice each other, Mom was looking for a date for a children's hospital dance, and*

the other nurses encouraged her to take the initiative and give Harvey a call… Mom calls him up and asks, 'Are you married or engaged or anything?' He replies, 'No I'm not married, or engaged, or anything.' They went to the dance together and it wasn't long before they were engaged and married…"

In the 1970s, the Hedleys had some friends whose youthful son, John Macleod, had been travelling and recently returned home. Since they had last seen him, he had become a Bahá'í through hearing of it from Shar Mitchell[152], and he visited them speaking excitedly of his new Faith. They could see that it animated him immensely. After a bit of conversation on the topic—to Jean's astonishment—Harv said, "I have a book about the Bahá'í Faith downstairs."

Jean said she had seen it before but the name had not made any sense to her, so she 'just dusted around it'. Harv brought up the copy of *Bahá'u'lláh and the New Era* given to him as part of an inter-faith exchange. After further discussion, John exclaimed, "But you guys are Bahá'ís!" Jean was struck by this pronouncement. What could that mean? It sounded like an honour, but she was very uncertain as to what it entailed. However, her curiosity was definitely aroused.

That summer she worked at the United Church camp, as nurse again. Harv, who was now on the Board of Directors had invited their young friend, John, to serve as a counsellor. Shar Mitchell was also working there and by this time, was a fairly knowledgeable, devoted young Bahá'í. She and John were animated 'teachers' of the Bahá'í Faith, discussing it with anyone who was interested, and making real effort to live and behave as its Teachings would have them do. Jean recalls many people at the camp being affected by their love for their Faith. She recalls seeing the two of them going off at lunch time to say prayers together. Her naturally generous spirit could hardly begrudge

---

152 Well known Canadian Bahá'í and author of *The Bridegroom of Baghdad*.

          Miriam Nicholls

them the time they spent doing so, but she admitted, "Part of me wanted to begrudge them the prayer time. I thought surely there was something else they could be doing at that time of day."

She was, however, particularly impressed by Shar's early morning rise, on a daily basis, to say prayers at the lake shore long before her day's responsibilities began. Reflecting on the attraction she felt to Shar's faith and personal character, Jean said, "You'd have become a Bahá'í if you went anywhere near her…"

Soon after, she went to a 'fireside' at Gerald and Stuart Hanks[153] home. Gerald explained that there was no clergy in the Bahá'í Faith. However, she was so impressed with his account of the story of this new Faith, that she told him she thought he would make a great minister. One of her questions to him was, "If this Faith is so fantastic, how come I've never heard of it before? I have so many friends and relatives that are ministers in the United Church. Something's wrong here."

Looking back, she smiled ruefully as she shared this, aware of how self-important the question sounded. She recalled the reply to her question by one of the quieter Bahá'ís in attendance, "Because it's too important to shout from the rooftops. We wait till we know someone is listening." She said his answer struck her deeply.

Bahá'í Summer School at the Peace Gardens was coming up. Harv had been invited to speak to the Bahá'ís about Christianity. He had become somewhat alarmed by what he understood to be the Bahá'í attitude towards Christ, which he heard described as a 'Prophet'. He felt Christ was much more than a mere prophet.

Ruth Moffett, a well-known and widely travelled American Bahá'í speaker, was teaching at the school. This would have been in Ruth's later years, and Jean's first impression of her was that

---

153 Gerald Hanks was a much-loved surgeon and family physician in Winnipeg. He was born In England and met his Irish wife, Stuart, in Germany after WWII. They emigrated to Canada in 1961 and became Bahá'ís in 1967. They were devoted promoters of their Faith, and joyfully taught others about it.

she was a rather frail, little old lady. But she quickly won Jean's respect with her knowledge of science, the history of religion, and abilities as a speaker. Jean said she had been praying during the Summer School about the looming choice of accepting Bahá'u'lláh as the new Messenger of God. When her friend, John, asked her what she was waiting for, she made the decision—a sort of leap of faith—to become a Bahá'í, then and there.

Shortly thereafter, Harv and Jean's eldest son, David, fell off a roof and sustained such a serious concussion that he lost consciousness and was rushed to hospital. Jean was back at camp when it happened, and it was John Macleod who drove her to hospital to be with her son. John prayed during the drive, repeating the short prayer of the Báb's known as the 'Remover of Difficulties' [154]. Jean prayed over her unconscious son in his hospital room while Harv met John in the cafeteria. Harv made the decision to also accept the new Faith under the traumatic circumstances of the day with the need for divine assistance feeling so urgent. Jean said that given the turmoil of the experience, Harv later felt some qualms about the decision he had made to be a Bahá'í, but with much prayer and consideration, he was able to resolve his apprehensions over the years.

The following year, in 1973, the Hedleys moved to Alberta. They had heard that the Bahá'í community could use more members in High River, south of Calgary. It was during these years that the plans for expansion of the Bahá'í community emanating from its World Centre, strongly encouraged the movement of urban Bahá'ís out of the cities to smaller centers to form Local Spiritual Assemblies, the annually elected administrative bodies that guide and direct the affairs of Bahá'í communities. Harv was able to find a teaching job in the area near High River, and a new phase of their lives began.

------

154 The prayer says, "Is there any Remover of Difficulties save God? Say, praised be God. He is God. All are His servants and all abide by His bidding."

                                    Miriam Nicholls

The family was thrilled to soon have visits from friends they had known in Manitoba such as John Macleod. Gerald and Stuart Hanks also came to visit, a significant reassurance and comfort to Jean and Harv. Jean said she felt blessed to have known this family at the beginning of her life as a Bahá'í. The Hanks' daughter, Brenda, studied at U of C and also visited the Hedleys at times. All the Hanks' children; Bruce, Brenda, Stephen, and Duncan were significant in their support and love for the Hedleys.

Harv and Jean served on the Local Spiritual Assembly in High River for many years. Their participation in the Bahá'í community in southern Alberta provided opportunities to interact with Indigenous Bahá'ís in the region as well. Jean fondly remembers serving on the Regional Teaching Committee with Diana Melting Tallow and Allison and Earl Healy. The Hedleys also had extensive contact with people at Eden Valley First Nation, located in the foothills west of Longview. They made efforts to support activities

Harv and Jean Hedley. Photo source: Jean Hedley.

Jean Hedley and Frank Royal at Siksika Bahá'í Center. Photo source: Jean Hedley.

there, collaborating with John Lefthand Jr, a Band Councillor. Earl Healy, well-known Bahá'í from the Blood Reserve, was a relative of the Lefthands and he and Allison often visited, assisting in the efforts to share the Teachings with people there.

The Hedleys also attended the annual picnics held at Piikani First Nation hosted by Samson and Rosie Knowlton. These events were an especially fond memory for Jean. She recalled Clarence Knowlton's band providing the music, and his wife, Alfreda, helping with hospitality. She said,

"I heard Samson, on one of the earlier times that I met him, praying in this wonderfully deep, booming voice. That's what I remember—his strong voice saying, 'Oh God, my King, my Adored One…' I think that's how the prayer starts. And as he went on, I thought how could anybody not be a Bahá'í around Samson Knowlton? And if I weren't a Bahá'í before that, I would have become one that day. That's what I was thinking. And then Rosie was always there doing her lovely hostess thing and being so friendly and welcoming. Such a hostess…"

She recalled Del Craig also assisting with the cooking at these events and the Knowltons' long-time friend and neighbour, Dale Lillico, usually in the middle of the work as well. Then there were major events such as the 1982 visit of distinguished guest, Rúhíyyih Khánum, to Kainai for a Native

                                     Miriam Nicholls

Council, which Jean and Harv attended. She also recalled teaching trips to Siksika with Shar Mitchell, when Frank and Judy Royal were their hosts, with numerous local people expressing interest in learning more.

In 1988, the Hedleys moved to Ireland and served as caretakers at the National Bahá'í Centre in Dublin until 1992. With Jean's Irish roots, she said Ireland felt like home, though she had never actually been there before. She described the Irish National Center saying the apartment they lived in was part of the third floor of the Center. Its rooms were spacious and handsome. There were offices on that floor as well, and a guest bedroom. The second floor had a general meeting room, as well as the National Spiritual Assembly's meeting room. The main floor contained a kitchen, bookstore, and storage area for tools and painting supplies. Harv maintained the Center, kept the gardens groomed, and painted it from top to bottom. Jean's fondest memory is of serving the Irish National Spiritual Assembly tea and homemade biscuits during its meetings, and listening to their delightful laughter on many occasions.

She said that the Center has been upgraded since they returned to Canada with a financial legacy left to the Bahá'í Faith by O.Z. Whitehead, the author of several books on early Bahá'ís of the West. Though royalties from those books are not likely to have added much to his estate, Jean mused that his family had significant means, though he himself lived very modestly.[155]

Jean went back to Ireland in the summer of 2015 to attend another Bahá'í Summer School and her face brightened at the mere thought of being there. She has been back at least three times since returning to Canada and said that she felt that her talents and abilities as an individual were more intensely utilized in Ireland than they had been in Canada, which had

---

155 O.Z. Whitehead was the actor, Zebbie, in the film *'The Grapes of Wrath'*. He was also a personal friend of Ronald and Nancy Reagan's. In Ireland, he held 'firesides' every Sunday in the basement apartment of the lovely old home he lived in, just down the block from the Bahá'í Centre.

Eleanora McDermott,David Sherwin, and Jean Hedley on a 2017 road trip to visit Dale Lillico in Pincher Creek. Photo source:Joan Young.

made the experience so gratifying. She said that on her return visits to Ireland, the Irish Baháʼís would say, "It's so good to see you back home, Jean."

As I reflect on my own experiences with Jean—most of them after Harv passed away—including the numerous meals she invited me to in her apartment and the road trips we took together to visit mutual friends, I am convinced that one of her outstanding 'talents and abilities' was her way of making people feel not only welcome, but the centre of her interest and attention. She was intensely present, showing that she valued what you were saying in clear terms. It was evident that she was happy to be with you. It was not flattery, it was an active and articulated appreciation, a beaming smile and hearty chuckle. She truly loved people with a generous love that beamed from her face. She glowed with the joy of loving others.

Harv passed away in June of 2014 and his funeral was held in the High River United Church. Hedley's son, David, wrote the

                                          Miriam Nicholls

following about his father in his eulogy, which recognized both the joy and sorrow in Harv's life.

> *"It's because he was no stranger to struggle himself, overcoming depression and other things at times… He always had the amazing support of Mom… was the ear to the Bahá'í community, family members, and his many interfaith friends; and his deep and abiding prayer life to see him through. He will be remembered as a steady, godly, patient man, the embodiment of gentle strength and leading by example rather than force. He championed education and went out of his way to help those who needed a little more attention. He was an outstanding example for his four children as a loyal, supportive, appreciative father and husband."*

The Hedley's four, much-loved children, left to carry on their legacy are: David, Duncan, Darren, and Ailsa.

19 Mabel Pine

Mabel Harriet Pine is the first known Bahá'í to have lived in Alberta for much of her life, though only part of her time was spent in the southern part of the province. I choose to conclude with her story because it seemed that at the end of my undertaking to look at people's lives—people whose common bond was their love for their Faith—a look back at the first champion of that Faith in their province, could be instructive. Her life and her efforts at creating genuine connections of love and respect among people she met, could be seen as the cornerstone of the Bahá'í community in the entire province. The origins of a mission can be so humble and seemingly insignificant, that the results surprise us when we examine them from the vantage point of time. Mabel's life could be seen that way—as a surprising composite of humble dedication to her Faith, surprising risk-taking, and stoic endurance of intense hardship. Bahá'ís are grateful for her persistence in her efforts to establish the Faith in the region, despite long periods of isolation, poverty, and poor health.

She stands apart from others I have written about because she lived here so early on, that fewer interactions between her and other individuals I featured could be uncovered. Individuals such as Helen Marshall would certainly have known her during the years she lived in Calgary in the 1950s, and others would surely have met her at provincial conferences. I found myself wanting to know more than I could. My knowledge of her comes almost entirely from a lovingly assembled binder of photographs and typewritten accounts made by her daughter, Allison Stecyk, titled *Mabel Harriet Pine: Unsung Heroine of Canada*.

Born in Bristol, England in 1882, Mabel's parents, Sarah and George Bray, were of Irish descent, living in an upper middle-class neighborhood with a 'position in society', as Allison put it. Mabel suffered from a speech impediment as a child, wearing a special plate in her mouth to help correct the issue. She had speech therapy to improve her abilities, but she said it was her father who actually taught her to speak. A particularly painful incident marked her early life when she swung her little sister around in fun near the fireplace, striking her sister's head on the stone surface, causing the child severe head injury. Mabel 'carried the blame for life', according to Allison.

As a young woman, Mabel was an active suffragette and reformer who cared deeply about human rights. Her parents, especially her mother, seems to have disapproved of her interests and activities. Despite that lasting disapproval, Mabel dutifully wrote letters to her mother until the end of her life. Contrary to her mother's wish for her to become a seamstress or a milliner, she became a caregiver to an aristocratic lady. She then took a position as a nursery governess in far-off Algiers, for the children of the British Consul. When that position ended, she went on to become governess to the children of a wealthy family in Valparaiso, Chile. The voyage to Chile was marked by a terrifying

Mabel Pine as a young woman in England. Photo provided by her daughter, Allison Stecyk.

fire at sea, followed by a fortunate rescue in which the passengers were brought to Buenos Aries. After travelling from Buenos Aries, Argentina, to Valparaiso, Chile, Mabel experienced the dreadful 8.2 magnitude earthquake of 1906, with its epicenter near Valparaiso. Allison recounts that Mabel survived the quake having been 'taught what to do' but Allison does not elaborate. Perhaps it was as simple as Mabel knowing to get out of the building and out into the open. While in Valparaiso, she had an earnest admirer who wanted to see her and repeatedly requested English lessons from her, but he was discovered to be a German spy, so that ended.

She made a brief trip back to England to visit family before moving on to Canada where she was unable to get work as a governess again, so took a tailoring position in a Vancouver sweatshop. I would like to know more about this experience as well, but not only is Mabel no longer present to expand on the subject, her only child, Allison, has also passed away.

While in Vancouver, Mabel heard that the city of Edmonton was a place

Mabel Pine nursing graduation. Photo source: Allison Stecyk.

where 'it didn't rain all the time'. It seems she did not enjoy the gloominess of winter in Vancouver so moved to Edmonton where she took nurses training and graduated in 1914. She married John Pine in 1918 and they moved to a farm where 'prairie fires, hail, and other extremes' eventually forced John to give up on farming and take employment with a grain elevator company. Mabel provided nursing help to people in the numerous small towns in which they lived.

Her first child died shortly after birth in the Drumheller Hospital, and her second child which must have been Allison, was born by caesarean section in Edmonton; a surgery that nearly killed Mabel and left her an invalid for some time. Allison described her mother's caesarean surgery as 'botched'. She said her mother had a near death experience at the time, in which her Aunt Sarah spoke to her and said she had 'a mission in life'. At a doctor's advice, the couple moved to Armstrong in the interior of BC in 1925, to improve Mabel's health. This is where she first heard of the Bahá'í Faith from two women who moved next door. The sisters, Mrs. Joyce and Mrs. Collin[156] were two of Vancouver's earliest Bahá'ís, having been taught the Faith by Jinabi Fadl, the erudite Persian teacher 'Abdu'l-Bahá sent to North America to accurately reflect the Bahá'í teachings, and who spent a week in Vancouver doing so in 1921. Mabel's daughter, Allison, felt that Mabel's immediate acceptance of the Faith gave her life a sense of purpose again, and helped her recover more fully from the caesarean section.

While living in New Westminster later in life, Mabel wrote some of her memories for the National Pioneer Committee describing her early encounter with the Bahá'í Faith in Armstrong:

"… for God works in wondrous ways his purpose to perform. When my daughter was small, my husband moved from Alberta to Armstrong, BC in the valley, as he wanted to buy a small farm around there. He could not find what he wanted so we returned to Alberta, but my daughter and I were left in a small house in Armstrong. The house next-door was empty and was later taken by Mrs. Joyce and Mrs. Collin from Vancouver. Both were Bahá'ís. From them I heard about Bahá'u'lláh, and I was able to accept His teachings at once. We left after that year, and they left too…"

---

156 Will van den Hoonaard, in *The Origins of the Bahá'í Community in Canada, 1898-1948*, says that Mrs. Grace Joyce and Mrs. Frances Collin had another sister, Mrs. Rhoda Harvey, who became a Bahá'í as well on the last day of Jinabi Fadl's visit, as did Mrs. Collin's son, Austin Collin.

Mabel's first on-going contact with an active Bahá'í group
after enrolling occurred the following year in England when she
went back for another visit with her family. Allison recalls being
there with her mother as a young child, and how disapproving
her grandmother, aunt, and even her primly dressed young
cousins were, of her tumbling about outdoors and getting dirty.
Mabel and Allison went on to stay in the home of Claudia
Coles, a distinguished American Bahá'í living in England,
where Mabel learned much more about the new Faith she
had adopted. She also attended meetings in the home of the
Romers, another American Bahá'í couple who were also living
in England at the time.

Back in Canada, Mabel moved to more small Alberta towns
with her husband who was transferred to various grain elevator
jobs. She had no other Bahá'ís to associate with during those
years, so often taught Sunday School in United Church settings
while being known as a Bahá'í.

Much of her character seems to have been forged in the
fire of rejection and disapproval from her family. As a grown
woman, health challenges, isolation, poverty, and lack of
support from her husband for her beliefs, were difficult for
her. While it is clear that she suffered, it appears she did not
sink under the weight of her sorrows for any length of time,
and that she chose service to others to provide meaning to her
life. Nursing was a definite avenue for her service, but she also
found purpose in being a true friend and providing a listening
ear to those who were in pain and difficulty. Her daughter said:

*"Ideas were more important than places, and materialism
did not appeal to Mabel. She was sincerely interested in
the people she met and was a great listener. People told her
their life stories and shared their problems. Perhaps this is
why people were attracted to her. She was introspective but
could be very vocal if someone was being hurt and needed
an advocate."*

In 1941, when Allison finished high school and planned to attend normal school in Edmonton, Mabel's husband got a job in St. Albert to be nearby, and Mabel became the only Bahá'í in Edmonton. A fellow Bahá'í from Vancouver, Ruby China, visited soon after she settled in to discuss establishing a Bahá'í community in Edmonton. According to Allison:

"This must have been a monumental task, but Mother had enthusiasm and determination, and she accepted the challenge. The place [their home] was small but many spirited gatherings were held there, and good fellowship resulted. Mother had continued her correspondence with Mrs. Collin and Mrs. Joyce, who had introduced her to the Faith. I found out that Mrs. Collin, Mrs. Joyce and her sister Mrs. Harvey, as well as Austin Collin, became Bahá'ís when they met Jenabi Fadl in Vancouver in 1921. Mother probably corresponded with other Bahá'ís as well. The National Teaching Committee was based in California and was responsible for expansion in British Columbia and the northwest United States. The National Spiritual Assembly of the United States and Canada was in charge of Canada and its territories, but they lost contact with mother. I received brightly colored pictures and stories from 'auntie' Victoria Bedikian[157], a Bahá'í from the United States. At that time, I did not know who Auntie Victoria was."

Mabel and her husband moved to two more small towns before their marriage disintegrated. Allison speculates they stayed together for as long as they did, for her sake. Commenting on her mother's move back to Edmonton at the

---

157 Victoria Bedikian became a Bahá'í in New Jersey in 1919. She and her husband established an orphanage and a school for children and adopted a son. She started a magazine for children and kept in touch by letter with children from all over the world. Allison Stecyk in Alberta was one. 'Abdu'l-Bahá praised Victoria's efforts saying, "Helping the poor and the orphan is service to the Kingdom of God. No benevolent deed has or will ever surpass it in merit." *https://brilliantstarmagazine. org/articles/shining-lamp-auntie-victoria-bedikian-1879-1955*

                                            Mabel Pine

age of sixty-five, and all the losses she experienced, Allison said, "Mother had lost her husband, her daughter, and her home all in one summer."

When Mabel was seventy, the Ten-Year Crusade[158] swung into action and she 'pioneered' to Vernon. Thereafter, she moved to Calgary where she kept working to supplement her insufficient pension. In 1975 at the age of ninety-three, Mabel was living in New Westminster and becoming increasingly frail; a concern for all who knew her. Her daughter brought her back to Alberta to live with her before moving her into a Sherwood Park nursing home. Forbes Campbell[159], a young Bahá'í in the Edmonton community, used to drive out to Sherwood Park to give Mabel a ride to Feasts in Edmonton. I can only imagine how much she appreciated it.

According to Allison, John Robarts made a special trip to Edmonton to see her mother near the end of her life as well. She recalled the visit being made after the 1968 National Bahá'í Convention, which was held in Regina, Saskatchewan. It occurs to me that Allison may have

Mabel Pine later in life. Photo source: Allison Stecyk.

158 The Ten-Year Crusade was launched by Shoghi Effendi in 1953 for the organized expansion of the Bahá'í Faith throughout the world. It involved the development of the World Centre, consolidation of the national communities where the Faith was well established, consolidation of other territories already 'open', and the opening of the remaining 'chief virgin territories' around the globe.

159 Forbes Campbell became a Bahá'í as a youth in the 1960s and was known as a passionate supporter of the Sylvan Lake Bahá'í Centre in the early days, doing significant amounts of labor to build it up. He also drove a 'big rig' (semi-trailer truck) which he converted into a mobile display of information about the Bahá'í Faith.

confused which Convention the visit followed, because her mother would not have been living in the senior's residence as early as 1968. Also, a report in *The Canadian Bahá'í News* on the 1968 Convention in July of that year, says that Mr. Robarts was unable to attend the Convention so sent Peggy Ross and Fred Graham as his representatives instead. Whatever the occasion for his visit to Mabel in Sherwood Park, her daughter was most grateful and spoke of it saying,

> *"… He presented her with an Indian necklace, and a bouquet of flowers from those attending the Convention. She knew him and responded. The hospital sent for me shortly before she passed on. With tremendous effort, she managed to speak to me. She asked me to carry on her Bahá'í work and told me she was leaving all her money to me, to spend on the Cause. I gave her my promise… Mother slipped over to the other world on January 20th, 1982. She did not quite make it to her hundredth birthday. I received a call the night she passed away, but there was not enough time to get into town, so I sat and prayed at home. As mother was making her journey to the other world, she spoke to me, 'What are you doing sitting there, when you have so much work to do?' She had quite often said those same words to me, throughout our time together. She was a person of action, and the years of inactivity in the nursing home must have been intolerable for her.*
>
> *Mom was spared—to lie in that hospital bed—month after month, and year after year. Many Bahá'ís visited her bedside during this time. I know that the Ball family from St. Albert, were often there with their children. I was told that a young man used to drop in and feed her.*
>
> *I am glad that people honoured her. I believe that the Edmonton Bahá'í School is named for her as well. I still feel my mother's presence, every day in my life. Mom was tiny*

in stature, but vast in spirit. Time alone will reveal her great contribution to the Bahá'í Faith, and to all the lives she touched."

I join her daughter in wondering what time will reveal. What new developments will occur in the growth of her beloved Bahá'í Community? What new friendships will be forged? How will the community's growth begin to affect the overall culture in terms of relations between settlers and the original inhabitants of our land? How long will us settlers take to learn about a history of Canada that genuinely includes Indigenous people and their experience?

I leave you with my thoughts turned towards justice, the possibility of enduring unity, and the beauty of the human family.

Afterword

The people whose stories I have featured from Treaty Seven Territory, are only a handful of the Bahá'ís who lived there during the 1950s and '60s. Much of what I have shared about them relates to their activities within the Bahá'í community, but they were also vital members of their communities at large. The significant strand that ties them together is the manner in which they befriended people of other backgrounds; insisting on seeing the humanity and nobility in the people they met regardless of race. They did so at a time when racist policies and practices were rarely challenged in their country. They seem to have done their utmost to take the counsel of 'Abdu'l-Bahá to heart regarding how to approach their fellow humans:

> "...rise up in such wise, and with such qualities, as to endow the body of this world with a living soul, and to bring this young child, humanity, to the stage of adulthood. So far as ye are able, ignite a candle of love in every meeting, and with tenderness rejoice and cheer ye every heart. Care for the stranger as for one of your own; show to alien souls the same loving kindness ye bestow upon your faithful friends."[160]

As I travelled the highways of the region to visit people with knowledge of my subjects, there were days I glanced westward and became so filled with exhilaration that I would pull over to take a longer look. The Rocky Mountains are their most

160 'Abdu'l-Bahá, *Selections from the Writings of 'Abdu'l-Bahá.*

Nancy Healy and Joan Young on a road trip through the Porcupine Hills, 2023. Photo source: Joan Young.

dazzling on a sunny winter day when they are glistening with snow. The contrast of brilliant snow with bleak rock inclines that rise to the sky, can take your breath away. For me, the vistas became increasingly infused with memories and thoughts of the people I was learning about, and the landscape became a doorway through which I sensed an unseen, spiritual realm.

These years of listening, laughing, and sharing over coffee and sometimes a casserole, have been rich in experience. I met new people and realized connections between others that left me astonished. I was introduced to new worlds of sport and culture, including the thrill of Indian Relay Racing. I learned to love the smell of sweet grass and sage in a smudge. I learned of

 Afterword

an ancient trail called the Old North Trail, which runs through
Treaty Seven Territory from the Yukon to the deserts of Mexico,
used by the original people of the continent for 11,000 years or
more. I discovered that remnants of that deeply rutted trail pass
through the Rosebud Coulee within four kilometers of Carstairs,
where I live. Prehistoric sandstone formations are clustered in
that coulee, formations my friends and I explored in the 1960s as
teenagers while munching on hot dogs we had roasted. We were
blissfully unaware of the area's use before Europeans arrived.

More difficult was the discovery of the legacy of my country's
history of colonialism as it had infused my own life and
consciousness. I realized how much relative ease my skin colour
and background afforded me in all areas of life. I realized how
easy it was for me to speak out in public meetings, to apply
for any job for which I was qualified, to rent an apartment, to
be treated with respect in stores and businesses. None of my
ancestors were forcibly removed from their homes as young
children, and the mere threat of that in Stalinist Russia in the
1920s sent them fleeing here—to this land—where their white
children were safe in their homes. Perhaps the relative trauma
of my family's past, haunted as it was by incidents of uncles
being shot in the street in Stalinist purges, man-made famine,
two of my mother's younger siblings dying of malnutrition,
and the pillaging of their village, helped me to be as receptive
as I was to learning of another group's suffering and allowing it
to affect me. But I did so from a privileged position, and I still
have a very long way to go in understanding the Indigenous
experience and culture. I also have a long way to go in
understanding the blind spots within myself.

My human sources who taught me so much have become
dear, close friends. They inspired me to stay in touch, nurture
bonds of friendship, love my 'mother' the earth, and be
grateful to the Creator. I have learned to see qualities such as
courage, humility, and generosity, as wealth. I have learned
how very little I know, despite how much I have learned. To

the people who shared their knowledge with me, and to those
who I have written about, whether living or dead, I extend my
gratitude and love. My hope is to have honoured them with
remembrance, and to have made some small contribution to
the national dialogue on Truth and Reconciliation with the
examples of their lives. They taught me about true friendship
and love, and a way of relating to Creation itself.

Acknowledgements

I want to acknowledge the encouragement and assistance of numerous people in bringing this book into existence. I am grateful to my adult children, David and Dermai, and to the other family members who provided me with the warmth and support of a small but mighty family. My friend, Donna Coey, was my frequent companion, heading out with me on the open road in search of people, places, and stories. Dale Lillico and Bev Knowlton spent many hours patiently providing me with an understanding of people and events which they had direct knowledge of, and in correcting me on things I had gotten wrong. I am grateful to Bev for helping me re-frame my colonial understandings of First Nations life and culture. She graciously took me under her wing and read and re-read segments of the manuscript. Dale hosted me in her home with immense kindness on my travels and provided numerous documents and photos for my use.

I am also deeply appreciative of Amy Singh who put much time into answering my questions, searching through old *Canadian Bahá'í News* issues, and sharing letters from her youth as well as her recorded memories.

The Alberta Bahá'í Council provided the initial stimulus for me to begin collecting the accounts of trailblazers in the Bahá'í community of this province. Elaine Zavitz, the Council's administrative assistant, became a dear friend in the process of responding to my requests for information, and she supplied welcome encouragement for the efforts I was making. Pat Verge responded generously to my questions. Long-time friends, Judie and Michael Bopp, often added to what I knew. My brother-in-law, Glenn Cameron, frequently directed me to points of information from his database at *https://Bahá'í-library.com/ chronology*.

The Canadian Bahá'í Archives, under the direction of Ailsa Leftwich sent wonderful photographs and information on people I was interested in. The United States Bahá'í Archives shared letters they possessed. Maureen Burhoe provided a starting point for further research with her website, *A Selected timeline related to the History of the Bahá'ís of Alberta*. Many other individuals who spoke with me provided precious insights. Among them are David Sherwin, Eleanora McDermott, Reggie and Cindy Newkirk, Miriam Nicholls, Dawn Nicholls, David Nicholls, Jean Hedley, John Sargent, Del Craig, Earlene Healy, Paul Bujold, Jack McLean, Diana Melting Tallow and Catharina Ankersmit. My apologies to others I have neglected to mention. Special thanks to my initial editor, Ellen Kelly, who often asked just the right questions. And finally, to those who listened to me read segments of my work and provided encouragement to keep going, I give my heartiest thanks. These include my sister Darlene Cameron, Donna Coey, Elaine Zavitz, May and Howie Cummings, May's mother Mehri Afsahi, Sandy Taylor, William Hawkins, Ed Muttart, Donna Zoller, Dale Lillico, David Sherwin, Eleanora McDermott, Brian Berteig, Bev Bliss, and Mavis Edey.

My final thanks go to individuals in the next world, including my parents, Gordon and Sue Dyck. From time to time, they seemed to whisper just the inspiration I needed to keep going—or a clue of where to look next. Without them this book could never have been written.

Note: The documents in the Appendices were written many years ago. They use terms like 'natives' and 'Indians' which are offensive to many in the 21st century. At the time they were written, these terms were common and the newer terms not yet in use.

Appendix A

History of the Bahá'í Faith on the Peigan Reserve (1958 to 1995) **by Dale Lillico**

In 1958 I paid my first visit to the Peigan Indian Reserve in southern Alberta. I came with Dr. Arthur and Mrs. Lily Ann Irwin from Calgary. We visited the families of Allen and Maggie Prairie Chicken, Jim and Mary Small Legs, Samson and Rosie Knowlton, Ben and Louise White Cow, Sam and Agnes Yellow Face and others.

We made several monthly visits and showed films and slides to a packed community hall, before that hall burned down.

It was during one of these visits early in spring, while they were showing slides at the hall, that Alfreda Knowlton, (Clarence's wife) who was sitting with me suggested I move to Peigan permanently. She said there was a job opening at the agency (Indian Agent) office. I left the hall and went over to see the agent, Harold Woodsworth.

After a brief discussion with him that night, I applied to Indian Affairs in Calgary the next day. Within three days, I was advised that my application had been accepted. God truly works in mysterious ways. In June of 1959, I moved to Peigan with my few belongings in a small U-Haul trailer.

Many visitors from all over the world came to visit the Bahá'ís and their friends over the years. Some of these visitors were John Robarts, Hasan Balyuzi, Amatu'l-Bahá Rúhíyyih Khánum (from Haifa Israel), Angus and Bobby Cowan, Doug Crofford, Hooper Dunbar (from California), Chester Khan, as well as many others from around the United States and Montana.

Amatu'l-Bahá Rúhíyyih Khánum came to visit twice. She had a great deal of love and admiration for the Peigans. During her first visit in 1960, she was given the Indian name Natu Oksist (Blessed Mother) by Elder Charlie Crow Eagle, a band Councillor.

Also present on that occasion were John Yellow Horn (chief), Pat and Susie Bad Eagle (Pat was a Councillor), Samson and Rosie Knowlton, (Samson was a Councillor), Walter Bastien, (Councillor), Joe Crowshoe (Councillor)[161], and a great crowd of others. The ceremony took place outdoors at the home of Samson and Rosie Knowlton in the area called High Bush, down in the river valley below the town of Brocket.

We nearly always met at the Knowltons' home, though sometimes at Ben and Louise White Cow's which was nearby. (Louise was Rosie's sister). The Knowlton's home would be packed full, and many times over the years, we met in the summer, outdoors. Picnics and meetings with visitors were plentiful and attended by all who heard the news of such forthcoming happenings.

Clarence and Alfreda Knowlton would come to hear their parents' Bahá'í friends too. As they did some entertaining, they would bring their talents and musical equipment.

Particularly vivid in my memory was a man from California, Hooper Dunbar, who had a message of love and hope and news from all over the world.

We were anxious for everyone to hear him so Clarence came to the aid of the Bahá'ís and rigged up his loudspeaker, hanging it from a tree near the house. We all sat on benches or chairs and the grass.

As visitors from so far away were very rare, the occasion was well advertised and attended. Few people on the Reserve had cars, so visitors with vehicles picked up residents for several hours beforehand. The afternoon of prayers and stories concluded with lots of good food and all went home spiritually and physically contented.

---

161 John Hellson said that Joe Crowshoe was the son of the holy woman who performed the necessary ceremonies for the setting up of the Sundance. He conducted the pipe ceremony for Rúhíyyih Khánum when she came to Peigan in 1986, for which her letter to Clarence Knowlton expresses such gratitude. (Second letter in Appendix D)

As there was no activity for the young, children's classes on behaviour, attitude, and spiritual well-being were started. They called it their Sunshine Class and Dale Lillico taught. They continued for a few years during nice weather. Children from the families of the Big Weasels, Holloways, White Cows, and Knowltons—to name a few—attended. Also, some of their friends who came to visit would attend. They were very shy at first but opened up as the months went by. If a ball game was held down in High Bush, we would all go over after our class.

The first Local Spiritual Assembly of Peigan was formed on April 20, 1961. The members of that Assembly were Sam Knowlton, Rosie Knowlton, Ben White Cow, Louise White Cow, Guy Yellow Wings, Dale Olivier (Lillico), Joyce McGuffie, Charlie Strikes With A Gun, and Sam Yellow Face.

Bahá'í assemblies are elected once a year from the registered Bahá'ís of the area who are 21 years of age or older. There are special spiritual qualifications to guide the voter and the election is done by secret ballot. The Spiritual Assembly guides the affairs of the Bahá'í community.

Our assembly met once a month usually in High Bush. Many times, Guy Yellow Wings would wait for me at the top of the hill to accompany me down—past Holloways—whose dogs who would lie in wait in the tall grass and bark ferociously. They never bit me, however they certainly succeeded in frightening me. Everyone would know by the noise of the dogs, that someone was coming down the hill.

Ben and Louise White Cow, very active Bahá'ís with a large family, lived between Frank and Cecil Holloways and the Knowltons. Despite their poverty, their doors were always open to everyone who came. Louise had a way of making a meal out of very little and always found a place for the weary to sleep. Their large family gathered many friends, and these remained friends until their death.

One year a son passed away and the White Cows wanted to have a Bahá'í funeral. We all put our resources together and the service was held from their humble home, for a packed crowd. There was country music played on a record player and Dale Olivier conducted the service for them.

We experienced many growth problems over the years—jealousy of one another—when we were trying to teach love and respect for one another.

The introduction of alcohol was a tremendous setback for all the Peigans, a very sad day for us. Wealthy people on the reserve lost nearly everything they had and poorer people were tempted to try liquor and became addicted. Many deaths and suicides resulted over the years from overindulgence in alcohol and drugs.

Because alcohol is prohibited in the Bahá'í teachings, much effort was made by Joyce McGuffie, a schoolteacher in Brocket and a Bahá'í, to introduce Alcoholics Anonymous on the reserve. She arranged meetings and brought in speakers. It was a small healing for a rampant disease. Joyce spent her time on Peigan encouraging all her friends there to be proud of themselves and show the people their successes.

She was also instrumental in encouraging and helping set up the first handicrafts outlet by Madeline Good Rider and her family and friends, who were good leaders. This became a great enterprise and kept a lot of people busy and feeling good about themselves. The business still grows, a tribute to many Peigans.

The Bahá'í Faith continued to grow and we were very fortunate to acquire the old Anglican Day School in 1984 because of the quick thinking of Clarence Knowlton. He approached the band's public works manager and asked that rather than tearing it down which is what was about to happen, that it be given to the Bahá'ís for their activities. After consultation with his Bahá'í friends who had construction and building knowledge, and a visit from David Hadden of the National Spiritual Assembly in Toronto, it was thought money could be found to restore and rebuild the old day school.

Consultant Bob Pilbrow and Dan Telfer were contacted, as well as others who advised that there was a definite potential. Following this, the delegation appeared before Band Council and a B.C.R. (Band Council Resolution) was passed dated April 12, 1985 which stated the following:

"At a duly convened meeting of the Chief and Council of Peigan Nation, the Chief and Council do hereby resolve and concur with the following:
- ◊ *whereas many Peigan Band members who are Bahá'ís and*
- ◊ *whereas the old school has been abandoned and is now unused (NW ¼ – Twp 7 –Sec 8 – Range 28 – W4M)*
- ◊ *be it resolved that the Peigan Band council grants the Spiritual Assembly of the Bahá'ís of the Peigan Reserve and the Bahá'í Community, the right to restore the building and use it for religious activities and community service projects, and*
- ◊ *the Bahá'ís shall have continuous and exclusive use of the building for as long as they require the facility.*
Signed: Chief Peter Yellowhorn, Councillors, Faron Strikes With a Gun, Patsy English, Jessie Scott, Leonard Bastien, Floyd Smith, Glen North Peigan, Peter Strikes With a Gun, and Norman Grier."

We were all very excited to think that with the quick thinking of one person (Clarence) and the long-term vision of his father and mother (Samson and Rosie Knowlton) a great opportunity to have a Bahá'í Center would be realized. Several committees were set up by the National Spiritual Assembly to assist with the planning and actual construction.

The initial development committee consisted of Michael Bopp, Peter Rempel, Clarence and Alfreda Knowlton, and Dale Lillico, with Peter Rempel being asked to serve as construction supervisor. Everyone worked very hard to first clean the premises of broken debris, and then the grounds of broken glass and pieces of wood which lay everywhere.

Many Bahá'ís from Lethbridge, Calgary, Pincher Creek, Brocket, Medicine Hat, Coaldale, High River, Edmonton, and even parts of eastern BC volunteered their assistance with the work. They came with trucks, tools, and whatever ability they possessed, to do what they could to assist the hired contractors. This was done in order to save money, given that the funds were being donated by Bahá'ís from all across Canada. Rúhíyyih Khánum herself sent a contribution from Israel for the Centre—which she specifically wanted to be spent on the doorknobs that needed to be purchased.[162]

Other volunteers that come to mind are a dear Persian Bahá'í lady who came many times and cooked for everyone and Valerie Good-Rider McFarland who designed and painted the big sign on the outside of the building.

There was a lot of discussion about an appropriate name for the Centre and the consensus was 'Naat Owa Pii Bahá'í Centre'. Naat Owa Pii is a Blackfoot word meaning "sacred things".

Carloads of Bahá'ís would arrive on Friday evenings after a week's work with their bedroll and food. Mornings would begin with prayers, and then work began with the brooms, paint, building supplies etc, that had arrived. Sunday evening most people would leave—very tired but happy be have been able to assist with the building project.

Several construction stages followed. In April 1986, the Canadian Bahá'í community received word that Rúhíyyih Khánum, whom the Peigans had previously given the name Natu Oksist, (Blessed Mother), was returning to Canada for a visit. She wished to see her friends at Peigan again.

---

162 Joan Young's note: Eleanora McDermott has a memory of going to the Centre during its restoration and seeing Dale herself, down on the floor with a power saw, cutting up lumber in a cloud of flying sawdust. Numerous Bahá'í men were standing around watching her, looking rather helpless. Eleanora still gets a chuckle out of this... Dale herself has no memory of this.

It was decided this would be an ideal time to have the dedication of the Bahá'í Centre, even though the final stages were not complete. The date was set for July 20, 1986. The National Spiritual Assembly of Canada would hold their meeting at the Centre that day as well.

Invitations were sent far and wide. An information booklet was drawn up to inform visitors of the itinerary and was given out as they arrived. We soon ran out of booklets, there was such a large turnout that beautiful, sunny, Sunday afternoon.

It began with the assembling of dignitaries and special guests outside, followed by the flag song. This is a traditional Indigenous song with drummers and their own flag. The dignitaries were introduced by Peter Strikes With A Gun, who acted as Master of Ceremonies. He was accompanied by Phil Lane (Instructor of Native Studies at the University of Lethbridge) and Blandine Bastien, who all did a memorable job in organizing and carrying out of the day's events.

The ribbon-cutting was done by Rúhíyyih Khánum outside the eastern door of the building, where everyone was able to witness the great event taking place.

This was followed by a spiritual program and traditional native ceremony. Elder Joe Crowshoe, burned sweet grass and prayed in Blackfoot. Then Bahá'í prayers and readings with music followed. A memorial service for the early Bahá'ís from Peigan was held, with several of their family members participating.

The dignitaries then addressed the gathering. Rúhíyyih Khánum, standing in the ceremonial shawl she had just been given, called native Bahá'ís to spread the message of cooperation and world peace to other Canadians.

"You have values we need," she said. "Among these, are the Indians greater spiritual awareness of the land they inhabit, and their respect for elders."

She reminded people of the prediction that spiritually awakened aboriginal people of North America would become, "…the source of illumination for the whole continent."

Chief Peter Yellowhorn responded with the following comment, "It is good to feel the friendship you project… the once condemned building has grown spiritually." He noted the positive impact the various faiths active on the reserve have had over the years and acknowledged the Bahá'ís respect for older world religions and for the Indians' traditional beliefs.

The afternoon culminated in a spiritual unity feast and a musical variety show. Several newspapers carried articles about the visit of Rúhíyyih Khánum and the opening of the Bahá'í centre.

The building still had some stages to complete, and this would come between 1986 and 1989.

It was an expensive undertaking. $71,738.01 was given to the Centre by the National Spiritual Assembly as well another $10,500 in 1985, and $4000 was received from Joyce McGuffie. This did not include the labour which was largely donated by the Bahá'ís. After that, there was on-going sponsorship by the National Spiritual Assembly to cover more repairs and utilities, though some money was received from rentals of the Centre as time went on.

We experienced some difficulties with renting the facility. There was money that was received and not turned over to the Treasurer, and some parties rented it and then refused to pay the previously agreed-upon fee, saying they felt the Bahá'í Centre should be free of charge.

Having groups use it for free was not possible because the cost of utilities was high, and the Bahá'ís couldn't afford to offer it for free. It was always thought by the committee, that the rental fees they charged were very fair compared to other facilities available on the Reserve.

Diverse activities took place at the Centre over the years. Bahá'ís organized and held Feasts, Local Spiritual Assembly meetings, study classes, weekend seminars, children's classes, youth classes, women's study groups, Bahá'í retreats, unity gatherings, memorial gatherings, yoga classes, Blackfoot language lessons, Unit Conventions, family dances, Bahá'í winter schools, and a performing arts presentation by Maxwell Bahá'í School students.

The Centre also hosted ballet and tap dance lessons, singing and drum group workshops, educational upgrading groups, life skills program courses, a severely disadvantaged employment course, an early childhood education program, carpentry course, morality classes, drama program, retreats for women and men's groups from the Catholic Church, kindergarten graduation exercises, and fundraising groups.

While most activities were very successful and a joy to host, some were not—such as when guests were drinking alcohol. Because Bahá'u'lláh prohibits the use of alcohol and drugs (for the Bahá'ís), the committee felt great concern in sponsoring events where liquor would be present. There was concern for both the damage that could be done to the building, as well as for the good name of the Faith.

The local priest on one occasion approached the caretaker of the Bahá'í Centre to say he was saddened at the 'activities' going on there. He was referring to a dance where some intoxicated individuals were making a scene on the property. The Bahá'ís had a good relationship with the priest and felt that some positive action needed to be taken. Dances were stopped for a period of time, and only traditional native dances were allowed.

Numerous custodians looked after the Centre over the years including Joyce McGuffie, Charles and Sylvia Jardine, Doug and Diane Gray, Angel Knowlton, Ahmad Motlagh, Bill Brewer, Caroline McKay, Deb Clement, Dolores and Doris Many Guns and Barbara Healy.

Valuable and memorable occasions resulted from the volunteering of these Bahá'ís to stay at the Centre. It was difficult for new, incoming caretakers at times, as new rules were set by new committees that were put in. However, all of them left with valuable understandings of working with people in a spirit of cooperation and respect—something we constantly need to develop more of—and how to continue to be a loving friend to the community around us.

Signed: Dale Lillico

Appendix B

Early Native Teaching in Canada by Arthur B. Irwin

Introduction

Friends have urged me to record early events in native teaching in Canada. I hope this account of experiences that my wife, Lily Ann, and I shared, will not only be of historical value but will encourage the friends, both native and non-native, to arise to teach.

Lily Ann and I were privileged to receive encouragement and guidance from our beloved Guardian, Shoghi Effendi. Without it I doubt we would have been the instruments for achieving the teaching successes that we did. We were visited and encouraged also by Hands of the Cause, Rúhíyyih Khánum, John Robarts and Hasan Balyuzi. Our greatest direct guidance came in a letter from Hand of the Cause, Enoch Olinga.

In 1950 I was successful in obtaining a job as a resident geologist for the Northwest Territories with headquarters in Yellowknife. Accompanied by our children, Wayne and Norvena, aged 5 and 4 years, we moved there in the summer of that year. We were the first resident Bahá'ís in the Mackenzie, and second only to Jameson Bond in the whole of the Northwest Territories. The National Spiritual Assembly of the Bahá'ís of Canada which was first formed separate from the United States in 1948, had general goals under the Five Year teaching plan which called for the participation of Eskimos and Red Indians in membership, to share administrative privileges in local institutions of the Faith in Canada.

There were however, no specific locality goals for natives. In all Canada there were only three native believers, James and Melba Loft at Tyendinaga Reserve in Ontario and Noel Wuttunee in Calgary.

A short time after we arrived in Yellowknife I joined the local radio station as a volunteer announcer. As a result, we were able to obtain thirty minutes per week of prime time for a Bahá'í program. We also ran ads and submitted news releases on the Faith. Within a few months of our arrival, we are sure that most everyone in Yellowknife and the surrounding region, was acquainted with the name Bahá'í. However, only a very few expressed even mild interest in the Faith, and the radio program appeared to engender resentment and a measure of ostracism from our white, middle-class associates. During our three years in Yellowknife, there was only one declarant, Fran Bachynski (now Fran McLean, an Auxiliary Board member) who had been introduced to the Faith in Winnipeg before coming to Yellowknife.

In those days we sent contributions to the International Fund directly to the Guardian at the World Center. Sometimes we enclosed a message. We were thrilled to receive a letter from Rúhíyyih Khánum, 31 October, 1951, on behalf of the Guardian which stated in part:

> "He is delighted to see you settled in such a virgin region
> (from our Bahá'í standpoint), and although the teaching
> work will no doubt go very slowly at first, the effects of your
> labors will sooner or later be felt and fruitful.
>
> He will pray that the way may open for receptive souls to
> be found, especially amongst the Indians, and that you may
> soon claim at least one Bahá'í.
>
> He sends his loving greetings and urges you never to feel
> discouraged.
> With Bahá'í love,
> R. Rabbaní"

And in the handwriting of the Guardian:

> "Assuring you of my deepest appreciation of your
> contribution and of my fervent prayers on your behalf.
> Your true brother,
> Shoghi"

From that time on we focused our minds on reaching the Indians. However, we were timid and we did not seem able to communicate the Teachings to the natives. While in Yellowknife we did serve on the National Eskimo Teaching Committee, but as the nearest Eskimos were over 500 miles further north, our service was limited to compiling information on their location and numbers, their culture, and on employment opportunities for prospective pioneers in Inuit country.

In 1953 my job was transferred to Edmonton, so the family moved south, not fully realizing the importance of maintaining the outpost in the Mackenzie. That year marked the beginning of the Ten Year Crusade, the first world embracing teaching plan established by the Guardian. At this time we were encouraged by Jameson and Gail Bond and others to think in terms of winning homefront goals among the natives of Canada. In those days only a few Bahá'ís made occasional teaching visits to reserves.

In Edmonton we set our minds to meeting Indians and joined a group where we could find them, The Friends of the Indians Society. We also read books on Indians and compiled the first map of Canada showing the size and location of bands, tribes and linguistic families of the Indians. Years later I persuaded the Departments of Indian Affairs and Northern Development to use our manuscript map as a pattern for the government map published in 1967.

In 1954 we were both appointed to the National Indian Service Committee and served on it and its successor, the National Indian Teaching Committee, until 1960. Our services included compiling information on the Indian people and on the teaching of Indians across Canada; keeping in touch with the friends teaching Indians and encouraging them through letters and bulletins; compiling material for pamphlets suitable for use in Indian teaching, much of which was obtained from Africa and adapted for use in Canada; arranging for the translation of the Bahá'í message into Blackfoot and Mohawk;

arranging for the printing and distribution of the teaching literature. We became immersed in books on the Indian culture and actively cultivated the friendship of Indians. All this was in addition to our teaching visits to the Indian communities.

The names of those active in bringing the Faith to Indian people in the mid 1950s that come to mind include: Jim and Melba Loft, Gerda Christofferson, Mabel and Leslie Silversides, Gary Rea-Airth, Doug Crofford, Ted and Joan Anderson, Noland Boss, Angus Cowan, Laura Davis, and Amy Putnam.

In 1955 the Irwin family offered to pioneer anywhere in the world. The Guardian advised us to contact Hand of the Cause John Robarts in Bechuanaland (now Botswana) for assistance in locating in that part of Africa. Although Mr. Robarts did contact a former employer of mine (I had worked in central Africa from 1937 to 1941 before hearing of the Faith), there were no jobs open at that time. Instead, a position in Calgary with Indian affairs was offered to me and approval to accept was received in a letter from Rúhíyyih Khánum dated 21 October, 1955:

> *"The beloved Guardian has received your letter of September 25 and has instructed me to answer you on his behalf. As he has already cabled you, he approves of your moving to Calgary, from which point you will be working with the Indians in Alberta and Saskatchewan, and at the same time reinforcing the efforts of the friends in Calgary.*
>
> *The teaching of the Indians is of utmost importance. Although much contact work has been done, yet the red Indian believers are very few in number. The Guardian would be very happy indeed to see a large number of the Indian race become Bahá'ís, so that the Indians may be properly represented within the Faith.*
>
> *He is most happy that you will be engaged in this work, for which you are evidently so well-qualified.*

*He deeply appreciates your spirit of devotion, and assures
you of his prayers for the abundant success of your labors
for the Faith.
With warm Bahá'í greetings,
R. Rabbaní"*

And in the handwriting of the Guardian:

*"May the Beloved bless, guide and sustain you, and enable
you to promote the vital interests of his Faith.
Signed: Your true brother,
Shoghi"*

Meanwhile in the Yukon, Knights of Bahá'u'lláh, Ted
(subsequently appointed Auxiliary Board member) and
Joan Anderson, were anxious to respond to the urging of the
Guardian to teach the natives. They asked our advice how
they might be of service to the natives to promote the Faith.
We've told them of our experience with the Friends of the
Indian Society which gave us the opportunity to meet Indian
people, although the group was 'Indian rights' oriented, with
the Indians being only honorary members. We cautioned
them to avoid the political overtones of the F.I.S. and instead
to emphasize improvement of the social relations between the
Indians and the whites.

With active participation of government and church leaders,
including the commissioner of the Yukon Territory, they were
instrumental in forming the Yukon Indian Advancement
Association. Through this Association, several natives were
attracted to the Faith.

Peigan Reserve

In April, 1956, our family moved south to Calgary where I
started my new job of managing the petroleum and mining
resources of the Indian bands of Western Canada. This work
entailed meeting many reserve Indians, particularly the band
chiefs and councillors. On one of my trips to the Peigan Reserve

in southwestern Alberta, an Indian guide was assigned to lead me to a reported petroleum seep. Although the seep proved to be not a find of petroleum but weathered bird dung, the guide, Allan Prairie Chicken, proved to be a real find. He wanted to hear about the Faith and invited Lily Ann and me to his home for a 'prayer' meeting. In the late autumn of 1956, firesides commenced at Allan's home and continued once or twice each month. Allan introduced us to many of his friends and they joined in the firesides.

At that time the qualifications for accepting new believers included the reading and understanding of the Guardian's compilation, *The Dispensation of Bahá'u'lláh*, *The Will and Testament of 'Abdu'l-Bahá*, and the *Kitáb-I-Àhd*. At one time I reviewed and paraphrased the Teachings in these publications and spent many hours attempting to instruct the ready souls in the meanings. None of the Indian seekers could qualify. However, about a year and a half after firesides started at the Prairie Chicken home, Hand of the Cause John Robarts joined us on a trip to the reserve.

In March 1958, in response to his invitation, Allan and Maggie Prairie Chicken enrolled. Following a meeting between Mr. Robarts and the National Spiritual Assembly later that year, policy was changed to allow enrollment of those who simply accepted Bahá'u'lláh as the Messenger of God for this age and were prepared to obey His teachings. Additional enrollments followed at the Peigan Reserve: Samson and Rosie Knowlton, Ben and Louise White Cow, Sam and Agnes Yellow Face.

At the time of Mr. Robart's visit we asked him about literature effective for teaching the Africans, which he felt might be adapted for use among the Indians of Canada of limited education. He advised us to write to Mr. Andrew Mofokeng, Secretary of the National Spiritual Assembly of the Bahá'ís of South Africa, and Hand of the Cause, Enoch Olinga. From Mr. Mofokeng we received samples of simply worded teaching pamphlets which were subsequently adapted for teaching the

Indians. Mr. Olinga, on the other hand, did not send literature but wrote us an inspiring letter which became a guide for our teaching. Here is a portion of this letter:

"Dear Bahá'í friends:

Thank you ever so much for your loving and spiritual letter, dated April 6, 1958. Its thoughtful contents have brought much joy and delight to our hearts.

We are happy to hear of your plans to carry the Holy Message to the Red Race there and are praying for your guidance and confirmation in this great undertaking.

The Beloved Master constantly urged the friends to advance the Kingdom of Bahá'u'lláh, and to occupy their hearts always by mentioning His Holy Name. Therefore, the most important thing is to center all our attention on this: the guidance of the peoples and nations of the world. Our deliberations, our consultations and talks must revolve around this focal center: teaching the cause of God.

Our Beloved Master said that this is not the time of decoration. It is the time of laying the foundation, which means, we must gather brick, stone, wood, iron and other building materials. We must be engaged in enrolling the masses under the luminous banners of the triumphant Cause of God, asking ourselves the question: "What can I do that may bring results?" This is very important, particularly at this hour when the villages and slums of the red Indians are to be penetrated.

We must try all the methods of teaching various people and races, and must adopt the easiest if we can find it. What the Red Indians need is LOVE! They will react more to this than logic.

In fact, they will be magnetized! If we are to redeem these down-trodden children of our Lord, Bahá'u'lláh, we must be ready and prepared to forget ourselves for their sake. This not only illumines the horizon of their spiritual understanding, but fires our physical and mental bodies with spirituality, unless we do this, that is, unless we die to ourselves for the sake of God and his loved ones, shall we be called his disciples? This condition is very essential for the accomplishment of definite results there."

Then, Hand of the Cause, Enoch Olinga, uses the analogy that the large rivers and the oceans are much more powerful than the mountain streams because they are below them. He continues:

"Therefore, humility, gentleness, and true love must be our adorning. These will attract the Indians to the Faith. Further, the teacher must lower himself if he is to rise, and must yield to others if he is to direct them. The importance of the teacher listening to, and appreciating the views and understanding of the seekers, particularly so with simple minded people, cannot be overestimated. Allow them to empty themselves before taking in the new wine. After all, this is the stage they have reached in their evolution. They are not evil at all, and their understanding is a stepping stone to higher planes of consciousness.

When we make friends, we must be on the watch never to lose them. We must be sincere and honest with them. If they lose confidence in us it is difficult to regain it. They will not trust us, and, like a snail after its feelers have 'foreseen' danger, they will shrink!

In Africa although the friends have successfully tried to reach the minds of the people, giving them rational proofs of the mission of Bahá'u'lláh, they however feel, that in order to convert the masses—the thing to which the beloved Guardian attached great importance—they must try to reach the hearts of the people and not their minds. The masses live in villages. This means the application of universal love—the magnet which will attract its like. The simple hearts are the essence of purity and love, that is why

  Appendix B

they are easily attractable by the rays of love.

The Beloved Master said that the greatest gift of man is universal love, "…for if this love penetrates the heart of man, all the forces of the universe will be realized in him, for it is a divine power that transports him to a divine station. It is this power of the magnet which diffuses life with infinite joy." "Strive," said our Master, "to increase the love-force of reality, to make your hearts greater centres of attraction, to create new ideals and relationships."

In his many letters to the friends here, the beloved Guardian said to them that if the fire of the love of Bahá'u'lláh blazes in the heart of the teacher, it is certain that that fire will catch the heart of his hearer.

We should select a few and teach these thoroughly, and after their conversion and deepening, they must be encouraged to teach their relatives and friends. As we all know, without first acquiring true love for, and faith in Bahá'u'lláh it is difficult to spread the message. Therefore, endeavor day and night to ignite in the hearts of the people the fire of the love of Bahá'u'lláh, which alone can inspire and lead them along the luminous path of servitude.

Although the administration is the fortress of the Cause, we should allow them to grasp its principles gradually. This must not be forced, but it should be a gradual process. As far as this matter is concerned, we must be flexible and supple. We must teach them the Message, encourage and urge them to ascend the numberless steps of service, making mistakes until they become masters. What therefore, should qualify them for membership in the Bahá'í World Community is the knowledge of the divine station of Bahá'u'lláh, and His being the promised world educator. Once they are attracted to Him we have not the right to deny them their birthright. They should be enrolled. Administration will come later on."

Lily Ann and I were privileged to escort Hands of the Cause several times on visits to Peigan reserve. John Robarts visited

the second time in April, 1960 followed by Rúhíyyih Khánum
a month later. She had requested a meeting with the Chief and
Council. After invitations were extended, the chief and five
Councillors attended, as well as other interested people. At that
time only one Councillor, Samson Knowlton, had enrolled.
Later, three more of those Councillors who heard Rúhíyyih
Khánum accepted Bahá'u'lláh, two of whom were medicine
men, Charlie Crow Eagle and Pat Bad Eagle. Pat did not enroll
but stated on his deathbed to his family that the Bahá'í Faith was
the true faith. The third Councillor to accept, Joe Crowshoe,
was for several years a lay preacher in the Anglican church
before accepting Bahá'u'lláh.[163]

In May 1961, Hand of the Cause Hasan Balyuzi visited the
Peigan reserve. He was deeply touched by his experiences.
Another visiting teacher was young Hooper Dunbar (now
Continental Counsellor serving at the International Teaching
center in Haifa). Hooper was very much loved by the Peigans
and was given an Indian name. A few of the National Spiritual
Assembly members visited the Peigan community about this
time: Michael Rochester, Douglas Martin and Roland Estall.

One of the most significant visits by a National Spiritual
Assembly member occurred in early 1960. A number of
the friends from Saskatchewan and Alberta gathered for a
teaching conference in Calgary. Two of those attending from
Saskatchewan, NSA member Angus Cowan and Tom Anaquod
(who later was elected to the NSA) decided after hearing
reports of teaching experiences on the Peigan reserve, to
make a special trip there. They were so inspired by the Indian
community there, that they immediately started teaching
on reserves in Saskatchewan, resulting in the message of
Bahá'u'lláh spreading like a prairie fire in that province.

Starting in late 1956 and continuing through until well after
the first Assembly was formed at Ridván 1961, we journeyed

---

163 Members of Joe Crowshoe's family dispute that he enrolled as a Bahá'í,
    though he remained a life-long friend to the Bahá'ís. (Insertion by
    author, Joan Young)

                                          Appendix B

from Calgary to the Peigan reserve and return, on a Sunday, once or twice each month. Typically, we would leave home at 7 am, arrive at the appointed time, say 10:30, to find the host family having breakfast or occasionally absent from their home—we had to adjust to any eventuality. Pickups at various homes on the reserve would often take two hours. Then the gatherings for prayers, readings, talks and discussions would last until late afternoon. Then we would rush home for our Sunday evening fireside in Calgary!

We are convinced that we learned more from the Peigan Indian people about spiritual matters such as attitude toward prayer, respect for each other, the importance of silence, and the tenacity of their faith, than they learned from us. We served only as postmen, to bring the Message to them.

The greatest dedicated service that began in the early years was from Dale Lillico (nee Olivier) who pioneered there in 1959, Joyce McGuffie (the Anglican residential school-teacher who enrolled in January 1960), and from Councillor Samson and his wife Rose Knowlton. In the early stages Allan Prairie Chicken, the first Blackfoot speaking Indian to enroll in the Faith, was untiring in his enthusiasm to recruit new seekers amongst his fellow Peigans and to host them for firesides in his home.

Other visiting teachers besides those mentioned above were Jenabe and Elaine Caldwell, Beatrice Ashton, Mary Burroughs, Tom Anaquod, Dorothy Francis, John Dixon, Dick Stanton, Peggy Ross, Bob and Daphne Beattie, Ken Jeffers, Tom Matechuck, Henry Kaye, Harvey Iron Eagle, Charles Hinton, Ed and Jean Many Bears, Jack and Esther Bastow, Mildred Mottahedeh, Don and Mary Kidd, Ted and Joan Anderson and Reg Wilson.

At Ridván 1960, there were 19 adult native Indian believers in Canada, nine of whom were in Alberta. Of those nine, seven were in the Peigan community. At Ridván 1961 when the first Assembly was established at Peigan reserve, there were 15 enrolled adults of which ten voted. On the Assembly were: Samson Knowlton, Chairman; Guy Yellow Wings, Vice-chairman; Dale Olivier, Secretary; Joyce McGuffie, Treasurer; Rosie Knowlton, Charlie Strikes With a Gun, Ben White Cow, and Louise White Cow. Other community members were councillor Charles Crow Eagle, James and Mary Small Legs, Allan and Maggie Prairie Chicken, and Sam Yellow Face.

From time to time questions arose which required answers. The National Spiritual Assembly of Canada was not always able to provide answers so some were referred to the Hands of the Cause in the Holy Land (following the passing of the Guardian, but before the first Universal House of Justice was elected). Two of the earliest Peigan believers had lived in a common-law marital relationship because the Roman Catholic Church did not permit the wife to become divorced from her first husband who had battered her. The Hands advised the common-law couple could be accepted as Bahá'ís providing all possible efforts were made to normalize the marriage. Over a period of a year this was achieved with the help of many people. The Needy Litigants Committee of Alberta provided free legal aid and the Alberta Court waived court charges. When the divorce was finalized, Ben and Louise White Cow, who had born to them seven children, registered by law in the name of Louise's first husband, were married in July 1960. Earlier that year the province of Alberta gave legal recognition to Bahá'í marriage and the White Cows were the first Bahá'ís in Canada to have a legal Bahá'í wedding.

One of the Indian believers continued to attend the Roman Catholic Church because he was afraid that if he did not, on his death his body would not be permitted to be buried in the Catholic cemetery near other family members. The Hands in the Holy Land advised that this member should be allowed to retain his church affiliation but the Bahá'í community should become strong and active so that gradually he would be weaned away from his church.

Teaching at the Peigan Reserve was often beset with difficulties, frequently caused by fellow Bahá'ís. Some of the believers in our Calgary community wanted to join us in our teaching project because it was so successful. On one occasion I reluctantly consented to one of the Bahá'ís coming with me who had different ideas about teaching than mine. In those days we had a dearth of authoritative advice on teaching approaches. On another occasion a female Bahá'í who joined us insisted on her right to wear what she wished, even though she shocked the conservatively dressed Peigan men and women.

Amongst some of our Calgary Assembly members, our teaching successes appeared to engender a measure of jealousy because they were not invited to join us, and our teaching methods were, at times, openly criticized in the Assembly. After a time when RTC's (Regional Teaching Committees) had budgets to financially assist fruitful teaching projects, funds were withheld. We prayed for strength, love and unity, and carried on with our own resources which were occasionally supplemented by direct contributions from friends. On two occasions the National Spiritual Assembly sent representatives to Calgary to attempt to dispel the disunity. But it was not dispelled until several years later when the couple who appeared to be the cause of the disunity, dropped out of the Faith when they were no longer able to command a following.

During the early part of the Ten Year Crusade, very few of the believers in Canada were interested in the teaching of Indians, or realized its importance. I recall that for many years a Summer School was held at the Banff School of Fine Arts, which was attended by the Bahá'ís from much of western Canada and the northwestern United States. Unless one of the ardent teachers of Indians was a member of the school committee, Indian teaching was left off the agenda despite requests. During school sessions we would organize impromptu gatherings during free time to discuss our favorite topic with others interested and we recruited teachers from Alaska, United States and Canada. At two or three of the Banff Summer Schools we sponsored the attendance of natives.

Other Indian Teaching

In July 1960, there were 19 Indian believers in Canada. In the Yukon, Sally Jackson, a Tlingit; Joseph and Dorothy Francis in Calgary of the Saulteaux tribe; Tom and Sophia Anaquod in Regina of the Saulteaux and Cree tribes; Noel Wuttenee in Winnipeg, Cree; James and Melba Loft and their daughter Evelyn Watts of the Tyendinaga reserve, Mohawk and Ojibway; Robert Jamieson of the Six Nations reserve near Hamilton; and Kelly Ritchie an Ojibway in the Georgian Bay area. Teachers of note in regions outside of Alberta were Knights of Bahá'u'lláh Joan and Ted Anderson, Angus Cowan in southern Saskatchewan, the Lofts at Tyendinaga Reserve and Amy Putnam of the Six Nations Reserve.

1960 was a milestone for beginning accelerated Indian teaching in Western Canada. As mentioned earlier, Angus Cowan and Tom Anaquod were inspired after visiting the Peigan Bahá'ís, to begin teaching on the reserves of southern Saskatchewan, particularly Tom's home reserve, Pasqua. By this time Lily Ann and I had compiled, among other teaching pamphlets, a booklet entitled *Thoughts on Teaching Indians*. *Thoughts* contained a listing of the similarities between the practice of the Indian religion and the Bahá'í Faith, as well as advice on teaching approaches and preparation for teaching. It served to help build a bridge between the two faiths. In July 1960, I was invited to speak at the Pasqua Reserve in the Qu'Appelle Valley near Regina, together with two Indian speakers. I was accompanied by two of our new Bahá'ís, Dorothy Francis and John Hellson. The occasion at Pasqua reserve was a feast for the departed, conducted by the medicine man including prayers, the feast of food, peace pipe ceremony and the open-air public meeting near the beach. As one of three speakers, I spoke on the beauty of the Indian religion and its similarity to the Bahá'í Faith. There were no Bahá'ís on Pasqua Reserve then, but a week or so later the enrollments came one after another through the efforts of our Regina friends, Angus, Tom and others. At Ridván 1961, two Indian assemblies were formed in Saskatchewan, Pasqua and Piapot.

In the fall of 1960 Lily Ann and I consulted with our Indian friends, Dorothy and Joe Francis and with Indian acquaintances through my work at Indian affairs, on the formation of a social club where Indians and non-Indians could come together. At this time, there were strong prejudices amongst most non-native Calgarians expressed against the Indians. They were excluded on racial grounds from some of the hotels and restaurants, and qualified Indians had difficulty finding employment. By early 1961, the club, later known as the Native Friendship Club, attracted gatherings of 50 to 150 people, more or less equally divided between Indians and whites. We met monthly for dances, speakers, movies, addresses and just visiting. Meetings were held in Calgary or on one of the three nearby reserves: Sarcee, Blackfoot and Stoney. Through this club we became friends with many lovely Indian people, a few of whom became Bahá'ís.

Notable amongst these were Councillor Ed Many Bears and his wife Jean, of the Blackfoot Band, the first Bahá'ís of their band. Through the Many Bears, a teaching program was carried out on the Blackfoot Reserve at Siksika.

The Blackfoot teaching was assisted by two teachers from distant places. Jim Walton, a Tlingit Indian from Alaska came to southern Alberta and remained for a month or two in 1962. About this time, several of our Blackfoot friends were hospitalized following a serious car accident. A team of teachers including Jim, took turns visiting them in hospital and before too long, they were confirmed in the Faith. Ken Jeffers, a non-native from Minneapolis made several lengthy trips to Alberta and Saskatchewan. Others who came to assist were Henry Kaye, Tom Matechuk and Harvey Iron Eagle from Saskatchewan; and from Alaska came Willy Willoya, an Eskimo, and Agnes Harrison who was part Indian and part Eskimo. By Ridván

1962 when the first Assembly was formed, there were some 15 or more adult believers. By Ridván 1963 there were many dozens of Bahá'ís on the reserve. However, I believe that it was the summer of 1962 when Mabel Robinson pioneered to the town of Gleichen near the reserve boundary, where she rented a tiny, abandoned storefront on the main street. From here she carried out much of her teaching of the adults and children on the reserve, occasionally trudging on foot to the Reserve homes. Through her brave and steadfast efforts the Blackfoot Bahá'í community, with the help from the weekend visitors from Calgary, was consolidated and expanded.

We commenced teaching at the Stoney Reserve at Morley, west of Calgary, in 1961. Some earlier contacts had been made by Noel Wuttunee and Gerda Christofferson. The first Indians of the Stoney (sister tribe to the Assiniboine in Saskatchewan) to accept the Faith were Moses and Mary Jane Chiniquay.

About this time Mary Jane was chosen as the Holy Woman for the Stoney Sundance. She was the only woman living who was qualified for this honour. Lily Ann and I were invited and it turned out that we and our visiting Bahá'í from Central America, Hooper Dunbar, were the only non-Indians attending this religious observance, where we camped for two or three days. We were invited to say prayers and give thanks to the Great Spirit. By 1962 there were nine adults and two youth in the Bahá'í community. The Stoney community was not united and an Assembly could not be formed. Two of the early believers, Horace Holloway and Judea Beaver, who remained steadfast Bahá'ís till their deaths, led the way for many of their children and grandchildren to accept Bahá'u'lláh at a later time.

On one occasion on a business trip to the Blood Reserve, I picked up an Indian man named Eddie Little Shields on the highway and I stopped at his home where I met his wife Nellie. Later we visited Eddie and Nelly, returning several times to their home for firesides. The Little Shields were the first of the Blood tribe to accept Bahá'u'lláh—in 1962 I believe. We became friends with many of the Bloods including their head chief, Jim Shot-Both-Sides and Senator James Gladstone, but the Little Shields were the only Bloods confirmed in the Faith during the Ten Year Crusade.

Lily Ann and Jean Many Bears made several teaching trips together—sometimes it was a foursome including Ed Many Bears and me. We helped with teaching visits to the Louis Bull, Samson, and Pigeon Lake reserves. Some of the other teachers were Corol Found, Jean Bleiler, Maxine Fraser, Baptiste Shortneck of the Louis Bull (Cree) Reserve and Pam and David Sherwin. We also made trips to the Rocky Mountain area—the Sunchild and O'Chiese reserves—and to the Wabamun Reserve of Paul Band where we renewed our acquaintance with the Bird and Burnstick families. A great supporter of the Indian teaching work at this time was NSA member, Glen Eyford.

At times the administration had to adjust to the Indian way of doing things. On one occasion in Calgary, Indian believers brought an Indian woman into a 19 Day Feast. It was her first Bahá'í meeting. She was so inspired by the devotions that she asked to enroll at the end of the Feast. On another occasion, Ed and Jean Many Bears made one of their frequent trips into the United States to visit Indian relatives and friends. They didn't hesitate to enroll ready souls using Canadian cards. Our teaching committee had its knuckles rapped via the United States NSA and the Canadian NSA, for failing to train our Indian believers in the proper procedure for contacting the American teaching committee. The Indian Bahá'ís disregarded the border and were not concerned about administration when there was teaching to be done amongst their tribesmen across the line.

Because of our friendship with the Indians, our home became a place to visit when they were in the city. We encouraged these visits. But sometimes our Indian visitors, both Bahá'í and non-Bahá'í, were in trouble. They were drunk, they had no place to sleep, they needed bus fare to get back to the reserve, and so on. We at first tried to accommodate all of these visitors but found that we were getting to be known as easy marks for handouts and free hospitality. Those that were drunk and needed a place to sleep we took to the Salvation Army. These pressures were taken care of later in the city of Calgary when the Indian Friendship Centre came into being through the efforts of a number of interested groups and government services, including our native friendship club. In fact, one of the ardent members of the club who was also a Bahá'í, Ed Many Bears, was chosen as the first director of the Indian Friendship Centre.

One of the first Peigan couples to accept Bahá'u'lláh, Sam and Agnes Yellow Face, brought their lovely 17-year-old daughter, Annabelle, to us to look after and help. Annabelle had taken most of her high school but had not completed her final exams because her place of residence while in school was noisy and it disrupted her studies. We took Annabelle into our Calgary home and in about two weeks' time, after consulting with educators and hospital authorities, she was accepted for nursing aid training. We continued to give her friendship and encouragement until she completed her course with honours and was accepted into a hospital near the Peigan Reserve. According to the Indian affairs administrator, Annabelle was the first Peigan student to successfully complete a vocational training course and to qualify for employment in that vocation.

Mention was made earlier of the surge of teaching on the reserves of Saskatchewan. One of the outcomes of the teaching there was the number of Indian teachers that came to the fore. A few that come to mind are: Thomas Asham (stepfather to Tom Anaquod, Jane Asham (Tom's mother), Alec Poorman, J. B. Redwood, Harvey Iron Eagle, and Henry Kaye.

At Ridván 1962, six Indian assemblies were formed in Saskatchewan: Pasqua, Piapot, Poorman, Mosquito, Okanese and Cote. In Alberta three were elected: Peigan, Blackfoot and Wabamun, and in the Yukon, the Whitehorse Flats Assembly. At the end of the Ten Year Crusade at Ridván 1963, eleven Indian assembly goals were won in the provinces of Québec,

                                        Appendix B

Manitoba, Saskatchewan and Alberta. In addition, two or three assemblies in the Yukon Territory had substantial numbers of Indians serving on them.

Canada's Assembly goal for the Ten Year Crusade was 60. By Ridván 1963, Canada had won 64 Assemblies, four more than the goal, due in no small measure to the Indian Assemblies.

During the latter part of the 10 Year Crusade, Lily Ann and I were able to contribute assistance to teaching in provinces outside Alberta and Saskatchewan. Lily Ann made a teaching tour of reserves in British Columbia in 1961. That same year I gave a course at the Alaska Summer School on native teaching, and travel taught on Baranof Island. I made several trips to reserves in Ontario and Québec: Curved Lake, Six Nations, Tyendinaga, and Caughnawaga. The teaching of Amy Putnam on Six Nations and the Lofts on Tyendinaga has already been mentioned. On the Curve Lake Reserve, Richard and Gladys Tranter established the first Bahá'í community, after years of steadfast teaching. On the Caughnawaga Reserve, Dorothy Walsh commenced regular teaching visits which were brought to fruition after John and Jim Milne pioneered to the reserve before the end of the Crusade.

Since 1963, Lily Ann and I have continued in native teaching in Ontario and Québec and often returned to visit our Bahá'í children on the Alberta reserves and to travel teach to the Yukon, Northwest Territories, Saskatchewan and the Atlantic provinces.

Two successes in which we take great pride: confirming the second and third Canadian Inuit to accept Bahá'u'lláh; and bringing in the first Carib Indian assembly in Dominica in the West Indies. Lily Ann is continuing to perform valuable teaching of natives, now in the Okanagan Valley, while I am turning to teaching amongst the blacks in St. Lucia, Dominica and other countries in the Caribbean.

Signed: Arthur Irwin, July 1983

*Transcribed by Joan Young in September of 2017, from a typed
document signed by Arthur Irwin in 1983, and passed on to Joan
by Dale Lillico of Pincher Creek.*

Appendix C
Ruhyíih Khánum's 1994 reply to Lily Ann Irwin

PO Box 155,
31001 Haifa, Israel
13 November 1994

Dear Lily Ann,

I enjoyed very much your recent long letter, not only the news of yourself and your family but also of the Peigan Reserve, which is always dear to my heart. The memories associated with my visit to the Indians on my trip to Canada in 1960 and again in 1982 and 1986 are always fresh and the source of deep satisfaction. I think that a special effort should be made to enable the Indians to understand that not only are they the original inhabitants of Canada but that they have a duty to this position in history not only to ensure that their native race is not forgotten but to share many of the Indian concepts, especially their deep spiritual convictions, with the rest of the population. I hope the Bahá'ís can be instrumental in encouraging them to do this.

I think that we Bahá'ís lack imagination; love, devotion and sacrifice we certainly have.

But we are weak on imagination, thinking up new ideas and applying the possibility of doing something through ourselves personally. It seems to me it would be a good idea if some of the Canadian Bahá'í communities would make a point of inviting some of the Indian Bahá'ís from a place like the Peigan Reservation, where there have been many firm believers for many decades, to come and visit their local Bahá'í communities and talk about themselves and how perhaps visiting Bahá'ís (not to be a burden on the local Indian community) could visit them, encourage them,

*and deepen them in their understanding of the Faith and
bring them up to date, so to speak, with what is going on
all over the world Bahá'í-wise at a rapid pace nowadays.
I am sure that with your many contacts with the Bahá'ís
you could further such a type of teaching activity and of
encouragement of the Indian believers.*

*I am, thank God, in good health and often travel as much
as half of the year. The Faith is rapidly growing everywhere,
so rapidly that when Mrs. Nakhjavani and I were in
Yakutsk in northeast Russia, in Siberia, we actually met
a Canadian Bahá'í Indian—very appropriate and very
encouraging!*

*With warmest Bahá'í love,
Signed: Rúhyíyyih*

Appendix C

Appendix D

Rúhíyyih Khánum Message of Condolence to Samson Knowlton: A handwritten sympathy card

Haifa, Israel
June 25, 1981

Dear Samson,
Through Jamie Bond, I heard of the death of dear Rosie and want to write to express my loving sympathy. When we have been together for a lifetime, separation is very hard—as I well know from my own life.

My visit in your home in Peigan so long ago, and the giving of my name, Natu Okcist, is always fresh in my memory and one of the great events in my life. So many times I have spoken of it, in many countries of the world. If there is anyone who still remembers me, please give them my warm greetings, to them and your family my love.

Ruhiyyih

P.S. Enclosed is a recent photo of me—to remind you how I look—older! Also a picture of the Panama Temple, the second Bahá'í Temple in this hemisphere

1986 Letter from Rúhíyyih Khánum to Clarence Knowlton, expressing her gratitude to Joe and Josephine Crowshoe and her appreciation of Indigenous spirituality

My very dear Clarence,
Your letter dated 2 Sultan 143 on behalf of all the Bahá'ís associated with the Peigan reserve and the Naat owa'pii Bahá'í Center was received and read with great joy. So often my thoughts and my heart are back on the Peigan Reserve and I recapitulate in my mind the wonderful occasion of the opening of the Bahá'í center there.

Again, I ask you to tell Chief Joe Crowshoe how profoundly stirred I was by the Pipe Ceremony, and that I shall always be deeply grateful to him—and you and the other Bahá'ís who persuaded him—for that wonderful spiritual occasion. I often think of Josephine and I firmly believe that inwardly we have a profound bond. I felt it that day, and all I have to do is think of her to feel it again.

I have spoken many times about my visits with the Indian friends during that memorable tour in Canada and to Pine Ridge in South Dakota, and tried to bring a sense of the deep spirituality of the Indians and their conception of God and man and nature, to others. Incidentally, have you received a copy of the tape I recently sent regarding these convictions of mine? Around the middle of December a copy of this taped message to the Indians was sent to the International Bahá'í Audio-visual Center, and they were informed that it could be duplicated and distributed as widely as they wished. If you have not received a copy, I think you should write to the international Bahá'í Audio-visual Center, 7200 Leslie Street, Thornhill, Ontario L3T 6L8, and ask for it. We are very weak on communications in the Bahá'í Faith. We do not teach enough and we do not communicate quickly enough! Everything else seems to be fine. Enclosed is a typed transcript of the tape.

I was delighted to hear about the improvements to your Center and that through the Canadian government's Job Creation Program you are able to employ non-Bahá'í workers from the Reserve to help with the Bahá'í Center work. This is just the sort of thing we like to have happen.

However, the most exciting news was the calling together of the traditional sacred societies on the reserve by Joe Crowshoe for consultation and to produce united action towards harmony, peace, and unity. It was certainly highly befitting that the Bahá'í Center should be used for this purpose, and that through this and similar activities

Appendix D

towards creating loving cooperation and understanding the Bahá'ís on the Peigan Reserve are able to sustain and assist their fellow Indians in every meritorious and praiseworthy activity.

Please give my love to all the dear friends there—Bahá'í and not Bahá'í—especially your own family and tell them I remember them in my prayers at the Holy Shrines.

With warm Bahá'í love,
(signed) Rúhyíyyih

Appendix E

Rúhíyyih Khánum's 1986 letter to NSA: Reflections on her experiences with Indigenous people

PO Box 155
31001 Haifa, Israel
28 October 1986

The National Spiritual Assembly of the Bahá'ís of Canada
7200 Leslie St.
Thornhill, Ontario, L3T 2A1, Canada

Very dear Bahá'í friends,
Since our return to Israel on the 6th of October, there have been a great many things to attend to, as you can imagine, hence the delay in writing to tell you what a joy the whole Canadian trip was to me, how happy I was to meet with your Assembly in Pincher Creek, and to have the opportunity of being with various members of it on different occasions, particularly with dear David Hadden, who made the wonderful trip to the North, and various Indian centers, possible—indeed, proposed it!

I particularly want to write you my feelings regarding the Indian Bahá'ís (and to a lesser extent the Eskimos as they are much smaller group). I think the most valuable part of my trips to the Indian reservations after Frobisher Bay was that they developed and strengthened in me certain ideas that had been growing for a long time. I am so seldom in North America and so seldom have any chance to think about these matters once I leave it, that it has taken far too much time to come to my present conclusions, which I feel it important to share with you. I have already shared them with the Universal House of Justice in my meeting with them upon my return to Haifa.

The significance, the explanation if you like, of the extraordinary prophecy of 'Abdu'l-Bahá in the Tablets of the Divine Plan: *"You must attach great importance to the Indians, the original inhabitants of America... should these Indians be educated and properly guided, there can be no doubt that through the Divine teachings they will become so enlightened that the whole earth will be illumined..."* *has been brought home to me during this last trip. As far as I know, this highly significant passage is the only 'racial' prophecy in the Bahá'í teachings. It is a pretty challenging thing to state that if a certain group of people accept the message of Bahá'u'lláh they will become so enlightened that the whole earth will become illumined! An idea has been growing in my mind, greatly strengthened by the experiences of this last contact with the Indians; it is hard to put into words, but I think I should try and express it to you.*

The Indians have a triangle, this is the way I express it in my own mind: the Most Great Spirit (God), man, and nature; they seem to have a profound inner understanding of this fundamental relationship in the universe; I think this relationship is supported in our Teachings, if we perhaps read them with a more understanding concept of the subject. The Indians are profoundly spiritual people—particularly those least affected by our civilization—with a tremendous orientation to prayer, to the Creator on the one hand, and a deep rapport with nature on the other. The words of Bahá'u'lláh quoted by Abdul Baha, "...the city is the home of the body, the country is the home of the soul..." do not mean much to our race and certainly nothing to our civilization, but to the true Indian they are a deep reality. If you take the concept of this triangle, God, man, and nature, and you insert one more factor, between God and man, in other words the principle of the Ray, the Intermediary or Prophet, that carries communion with the Great Spirit to us, the Indians entire theology, if you like, or concept of life and the cosmos, becomes complete from the Bahá'í standpoint. I think we should approach the Indian

                                              Appendix E

teaching in this way. Too often, at least we white Bahá'ís are preoccupied with trying to place Indigenous people, in this case the Indians, inside our own framework of what we think the Cause is. I think very few Bahá'ís of our type ever think much about theology! We think about the administration, goals, plans, etc. Obviously all these things are important, but to attract the Indians by this approach is not working at all. Maybe in the end, with the insertion of the principle of the Manifestation of God, this Indian fundamental concept of theology is closer to the teachings of Bahá'u'lláh than the way most of us understand them at present!

I need not tell you what a profound experience the pipe ceremony on the Peigan Reservation was. It was probably the most moving thing that happened to me in my whole trip, and one of the most moving things that has happened to me in my whole life. As I could neither understand the Indian words nor clearly see what was happening, it was undoubtedly the profound spiritual feeling of the Indians connected with this most sacred ceremony that affected me.

You also know that the behavior of many of the Bahá'ís, particularly of some of the Persian friends, was totally lacking in either patience or respect for this most holy ceremony of the Indians and showed no consideration for their feelings. When I spoke to the Bahá'ís in Regina, they asked me to say something in Persian at the end of my talk, and I spoke as strongly as one can humanly do on the subject of not going near the Indians or approaching them or going to the Reservations, unless they could treat them with respect and honour their customs and feelings. I pointed out that while some of the most active, successful and much-loved Bahá'í teachers in the whole of Canada amongst the Indians are Persians, the conduct of some of the others in Peigan was very detrimental to the Faith, that they as Bahá'ís would be very offended if people showed disrespect when visiting our Holy Shrines at the World Center, but we saw no reason why we should respect something that meant as much to them as that does to us. The talk was recorded, and if you want to get someone to translate these Persian remarks of mine, they might be of some use to you, if used in the right way.

The Tablets of the Divine Plan were given to us in 1919, almost 70 years ago; unlike South and Central America, we have done almost nothing to teach the Indigenous people of the Americas in North America. In the meantime, I heard from Phil Lane that some of these Indian swami movements are very active now amongst the Indians, in other words, **they are doing what we should be doing.** *It says in the Bible you cannot put new wine into old bottles which I have always understood to mean that when something was full there was no place to add to it. If these people are going to fill the spiritual vacuum in the lives of the Indians, their longing for recognition of their culture and inner spiritual fulfillment, then would you mind telling me when we are going to fulfill the prophecy of 'Abdu'l-Bahá? We Bahá'ís—and I am certainly old enough to assert this authoritatively—do nothing but miss buses; one bus after another whizzes by, and for one reason or another we are always going to catch the bus; too often we do not. Are we going to miss this Indian bus for the whole period of the Bahá'í Dispensation? I think you have to ask yourselves this very seriously. I know you have a tremendous amount of work, limited resources, and all the rest of it, but I firmly believe that every Bahá'í individually, and the administrative bodies of the Faith as such, are obligated* **to consider priorities and to judge what should be done now or it will never be done.**

Your Assembly has done a great deal more in recognizing the native believers of Canada than ever before, witness giving them a session at the Montréal conference in 1982, your Assembly in toto meeting with them recently on the Peigan Reservation, your giving them an evening at the London, Ontario Association for Bahá'í Studies conference. All of us who were there remember how profoundly Dr. and Mrs. Lazlo were affected by the simplified pipe ceremony, and when I crossed the stage afterwards I saw how profoundly they were moved, she had tears in her eyes. Obviously this does not mean we must grace all the Bahá'í occasions with a pipe ceremony! But it certainly should be an eye-opener to us. But my dear friends, it is not enough! I remember Shoghi Effendi telling the American pilgrims at the dinner table in the Western pilgrim house, that the American Bahá'ís were tainted with race prejudice; he said, "They do not know that they are, but they are." I think that this holds true also of the whole situation vis-à-vis the Indians in North America.

I am greatly preoccupied with the subject. I wonder whether, amongst the Persian Bahá'ís, cannot be found teachers for these people. I remember, I think it was Phil Lane, the subject coming up of how deeply the Indians crave prayer. Why could not a Persian friend, preferably middle-aged or elderly, go to various Reservations, stay for a period and just hold Dawn prayer gatherings? Many of these good Persian Bahá'ís, particularly the older ones, are sad at heart because they see no field in which to serve the faith, they often have no command of English, but the love of the Faith in their hearts, their loyalty and grasp of the Teachings, their oriental warmth and demonstrativeness, can I believe be put to a marvelous use in this field. In the cities their capacities are never drawn upon for obvious reasons, but with the Indians love, faith, prayer, courtesy, respect for the elders—all could work, hopefully, miracles. You have this reservoir to draw upon.

With warmest Bahá'í love to all of you,
Signed: Rúhíyyih Khánum
Cc: The Universal House of Justice
The International Teaching Center
National Spiritual Assembly of the United States

Appendix F

Reggie Newkirk's 2015 letter to National Spiritual Assembly of the Bahá'ís of Canada

P.O. Box 962
Lumsden, SK, S0G 3C0
August 24, 2015

National Spiritual Assembly of the Bahá'ís of Canada,

Re: Contribution to the National Fund in name of James W. Wonders III

Dear Friends,
This past April 2015 I flew to Corpus Christi, Texas to attend the funeral of my dearest friend—my "brother in the Cause of Bahá'u'lláh" James W. Wonders III commonly known as Jim. He and I met as youth Bahá'ís in 1962 as we both were stationed at the then Lowry Air Force Base in Denver, Colorado. I am writing to request prayers for Jim and to make a contribution to the National Fund in his name.
Jim was a staunch advocate of participation of young people in the Cause from those days in the 1960's to present. Here is a little background information of his service to Canada during the '60s.

- *December 1965 he and I organized a group of youth from New Mexico, Colorado, Wyoming and Montana to travel to Calgary to attend a youth conference that was held at the University of Calgary.*
- *In the spring 1966 a group of youth from Alberta and Saskatchewan travelled, as an exchange group, to a youth conference that was held in Albuquerque, New Mexico. Encouragement for this project came from Jim and other youth in the Western states.*
- *Jim became a member of a planning committee for a youth conference that was to be held at the International*

Peace Park (Waterton). The conference was held July 7,8,9 and 10, 1967 on the U.S.-Canada border at the Belly River campsite. We had the honour of the presence of Hand of the Cause of John Robarts and Audrey.

· *Late fall 1967 Jim organized a group of American youth to attend a youth conference near Fort Qu'Appelle that was attended by youth from Alberta, Saskatchewan and Manitoba. The adult organizers, with a team of youth, were Ken and Barbara Eaton. It, too, was a terrific occasion during which youth friendships were strengthened and they were inspired to make greater effort to teach their peers upon returning to their home communities.*

In memory of Jim's service in western Canada, the enclosed $500 contribution to the National Fund is made in his name. I'd like this amount to be earmarked and divided equally ($250) for the Framework for Action in Saskatchewan and Alberta to facilitate efforts to reach Canadian Indigenous youth and junior youth.

Yours truly,
Signed: Reggie Newkirk

Appendix G

Recollections from Mr. Samandari on the Occasion of Attaining Bahá'u'lláh's Presence in 'Akká Garden

Translated by Marzieh Gail and framed in a wall-hanging in the reception area at the Junaynih garden near 'Akká. I took a photograph of it while on pilgrimage. Portions of the photograph were hidden by reflections of sunlight on glass. Most of it was legible and is included below. [Joan Young]

"… Toward morning (of Naw Rúz), we were told that Bahá'u'lláh would be visiting Junaynih that day, and that He had summoned all the settlers and pilgrims to that spot. They provided us with conveyances and brought us there. It is quite a long way from Haifa to Junaynih, and in those days people went by carriage. Junaynih is near the Mansion of Mazra'ih; not far from there, in fact quite near. We came to Junaynih, where we found Bahá'u'lláh. So there, too, I entered his presence… They had prepared a lamb for our luncheon; cooked it in the stove; and brought it on a large tray, placed on the table in Bahá'u'lláh's room…

They took it to the other room where they had laid the luncheon cloth on the floor. We had bread too, with the lamb. We all ate luncheon in there. Following the meal, it seems to me there was a revelation of verses. …. I heard a little. Then, that afternoon, Bahá'u'lláh was to return to the Mansion at Bahjí. There was a white donkey which, I know, Haji Ghulam Ali Kashani had brought to Bahá'u'lláh at that time. The Blessed Beauty mounted, and a servant held an umbrella over Him, for a light rain was falling. I also accompanied Him. On his right-hand side, the servant held up the umbrella while I was on His left. And thus we came from Junaynih to the Mansion of Bahji."

Appendix H

2020 Letter to Swedish Bahá'í History Committee re Catharina Ankersmit from May Cummings who grew up in Sweden (the daughter of Persian pioneers)

Additional notes: Sandy Taylor (friend and collaborator in Canmore activities)

Dear Bjorn and Liss,
Allâh'u'Abhá.

Here is the story of Catharina Ankersmit and her connection to Norway. I hope that you can add this to the historical Bahá'í archives of the Bahá'í Norwegian community. Catharina heard about the Faith in 1950 in Norway through the American pioneer Elinore Gregory and became a Bahá'í. It was as if Elinore dropped a pebble into the Ocean of Bahá'u'lláh's revelation and its ripple effects are now being felt in Canada. We feel so grateful to get to know Catharina, and through God's grace her journey can be told as an inspiration to others. Her story teaches us that our work as Bahá'ís is to mention the name of Bahá'u'lláh and He will find the hearts in which His living waters can flow to others.

My husband Howie and I were asked by Sandy Taylor to join a Bahá'í teaching team to the town of Canmore, 100 km west of Calgary where we live. Canmore is just at the foot of the Rocky Mountains. We met this lovely lady, Catharina, who is an isolated believer in Canmore since 2003. I have included Sandy Taylor's description and thoughts about Catharina at the end of this document.

In my conversation with Catharina, I discovered that she became a Bahá'í in Norway and that we knew many of the same Bahá'ís from the 1950s, such as Ms. Amelia Bowman, a staunch American Bahá'í pioneer who lived in Norway for 25 years. I remember as a young child the

*visits that Ms. Bowman made to my hometown of Uppsala,
Sweden. Catharina met other Norwegian Bahá'ís such as
Rita van Sombeek and the American pioneer Dagmar Dole
to Denmark. She attended Dagmar's funeral in Montreux.
Catharina met many Bahá'ís in her travels to Lausanne,
Geneva, and Montreux. She attended (in September of
1951) the 4th Bahá'í teaching conference in Scheveningen
and in 1952 in Luxembourg-ville.*

*In 1952/1953 the Canadian Government offered to
welcome any Dutch farmer who wanted to come and settle
immediately. Catharina applied to emigrate. On Monday
August 24, 1953, she arrived in Montreal, lived in Toronto
and met many of the staunch Canadian Bahá'ís. In 1955
she moved to Calgary where she met her future husband,
Erik. In 1958 they bought a farm in Rimby, 200 km north of
Calgary. She and her family lived in isolated communities
such Bowden, Olds and, since 2003, in Canmore.*

*When my mom Mehri Afsahi who lives in Uppsala,
Sweden visited us in Calgary in January 2020, Sandy Taylor
arranged for a luncheon to meet Catharina. So she drove
my mom and me to Canmore January 22, 2020. We were
very excited to have a visit together with Catharina. My
mom and Catharina reminisced about the Bahá'í world in
the 1950's in Europe.*

*On July 8, 2020, I participated in the 100th celebration
of the first Bahá'í pioneer, August Rudd's, arrival to
Sweden, and it inspired me to add Catharina's journey of
discovering the Faith, becoming a Bahá'í in Norway and her
immigration from Holland to Canada. Here in the province
of Alberta her dedication to the Faith and steadfast service
will be appreciated and known for generations to come.*

*Catharina wrote an autobiography about her life titled
The Nut from Nijmegen, published in 2018 for her 90th
birthday. It became a Bow Valley Bestseller. Bow Valley
includes the areas of Canmore, Banff and Lake Louise. Her*

discovery of the Faith is copied from her autobiography [below]. Her 90th birthday was celebrated by her children, grandchildren, great-grand children and many Bahá'ís. A celebration of a life lived to the fullest in the path of God.

With loving regards
May Cummings (Afsahi)

Excerpts from Catharina's autobiography *The Nut from Nijmegen* published in 2018:

In 1949…I felt restless and decided to go to Norway. I wrote a letter to the Dutch embassy in Oslo, asking if there were any jobs for secretaries or domestic help. They wrote me back that they were not an employment agency. Nevertheless shortly afterward the Embassy forwarded a letter from a doctor in Oslo who wanted domestic help. Geertrui (my sister) found a cheap flight for me on a Norwegian plane and I had just enough money for the flight, so off I went. It was the second of June 1950. The plane to Oslo was full of sailors returning home, and the stewardess and I were the only females on board with sixty men. I tried to read a Norwegian paper and was surprised that I was able to guess and understand what I read, using my English and German and Dutch.

In Oslo the doctor met me at the airport and took me to his home. His wife and I did not really gell and I resented the housework. I did not last long with them. But in Oslo I soon felt home. It is a city with a beautiful view of the Oslo fjord and I loved the main street, Karl Johans Gate. The doctor and his wife lived at Holmenkollen, halfway up a hill north of Oslo and close to a hotel in the neighbourhood of Frognerseteren. One evening I walked over to the hotel, and tried to order a cup of coffee and a piece of apple cake. From the table next to me a lady asked, are you from Holland, and I answered yes. The lady was Dutch too, married to

*a Norwegian and mother of two beautiful little children.
Jeanette and I hit it off right away and she invited me
to her home nearby. Jeanette gave me a cotton bunad, a
Norwegian national dress, which did not fit her anymore. I
wore that dress at special occasions for many years.*

*From the doctor's family I moved to another family. Mr.
Falkenberg was Norwegian and his wife was German. We
got along well and I stayed there till I returned to Holland
at the end of the following summer. I had every weekend off
and went skiing or hiking with the International Friendship
Club branch in Oslo.*

*On the September long week-end a trip was organized to
Drammen, south of Oslo on the Fjord. We met at the East
Railway Station and there with others was an American
girl, Elinor, who was very happy to talk to me. We both were
not very good at speaking Norwegian at that stage, and
she was in love with a young Dutch man. On the train we
talked and I told her about my trying to figure out how the
world could live in peace. She was immediately interested
and had some very good suggestions and before long the
world "Bahá'í" came up. Finally I asked what it meant
and she told me all about the Bahá'í Faith. I think, maybe
a week or a couple of weeks earlier I was climbing up the
hill from Holmenkollen to the hotel and walking through
the forest when I decided that Christianity as a religion
had failed, but the teachings of Jesus could not be denied
even though people who called themselves Christians, like
the Germans, did not follow those teachings. Bahá'u'lláh
had come to reinforce and renew the teachings of Jesus and
blow a new breath into society for equality and peace. I
was dumbfounded that a religion existed that had all those
ideas that I had accumulated since I was seventeen as its
basic teachings. I asked Elinor for a book by "that man" and
when I started to read the* Book of Certitude, *I was soon
convinced that this was it, and I became a Bahá'í. But no*

*one I talked to about this new-found Faith was interested,
and I could not understand that.*

*The winter in Norway was so dark and dreary that I did
not want to spend a second one there. From the seventeenth
of December till the tenth of February there was no
sunshine, it got daylight at 10 am and got dark at 3 pm, and
there was lots of snow. When the sun finally broke through
the clouds in February, Fru Falkenberg gave me the day off
and I went for a tour on the skis to enjoy the sun.*

*I loved Norway. I still do. It is so beautiful there; the
landscape is like paradise with green fields on the rolling
hills, the forest on the higher mountains, and fast-flowing
streams in the valleys. It looks like the background from a
fairy tale. I could never get enough of looking down on the
Oslo Fjord from Holmenkollen."* (Pages 30-33)

Catharina visited Norway with her daughter Kirsten in 2016. It
was part of a longer trip to Stockholm, Estonia, St, Petersburg
in Russia, and Germany. She writes on page 130 in her
autobiography:

*When we got to Oslo we walked down Karl Johans Gate, the
main street, to our hotel in a nearby street. The following
day we found the electric train up to Holmenkollen and
Frognerseteren. Frognerseteren has not changed in sixty
years, the same log hotel. Kirsten went in and asked if they
still had eplekake, or apple cake and by golly here, sixty
years later we enjoyed a coffee and an enormous piece of
apple cake with an inch and a half of whipping cream on
it. I was in heaven, looking out over the Oslo Fjord with so
many memories coming back.*

Additional notes re Catharina Ankersmit
[Sandy Taylor Aug 2, 2020]

Catharina, who was among the first Bahá'í friends I met after moving to Alberta in December 2016 welcomed me warmly into her home and introduced me to the other friends in the small Bahá'í community in Canmore, through enthusiastically hosting deepenings and gatherings with a generosity and comfortable lack of formality. She has been a steadfast believer in this small community for years and her dedication to the Faith remains unshakeable.

As well as being impressed by her twinkling sense of humour, and her unassuming manner, I am so very taken by her bright mind and the way she can speak fluently about almost any broad and varied topic that is raised in general conversation, and can frequently follow up this conversation by retrieving a relevant book from her large and extensive library. Her knowledge of the Faith also seems grounded in personal experiences and a deep understanding of the principles of the Faith, which she shares with conviction, but even more impressively, through a life well-lived.

This 'well-lived life' was especially evident when her family and friends held a birthday celebration for Catharina two years ago in 2018, which was attended by well over 100 people; a sign of just how much she is loved. Friends and family members—young and old—shared stories that reflected her sense of adventure, playfulness, generosity, courage and joie-de-vie. Although it was her 90th birthday, those close to Catharina never think of her in connection with her age; she seems ageless. Catharina remains an ideal role model for me as example of a life well-lived, and an example of a well-grounded principle of the Bahá'í Faith, "Let deeds, not words, be your adorning."

Lovingly shared,
Sandy Taylor (August 2020)

Bibliography

Achuff, Peter L. *Assessment and Status Report on the Limber Pine in Canada*. COSEWIC. 2014. Committee on the Status of Endangered Wildlife in Canada. Ottawa. ix + 49 pp. *http://www.registrelep- sararegistry.gc.ca/default_e.cfm*

Anderson, Ted. Audio interview [cassette recording of Lily Ann Irwin], 1993

Ankersmit, Catharina. *The Nut From Nijmegen*, 2018. self-published

Ashton, Beatrice. London World Congress 1963, *The Bahá'í World* Vol XIV 1963-1968, 1974

Bahá'í Perspective, Bahá'í World Congress 1963, Fred Murray - *Enrollment of the Masses* [audio recording) 1963, available on *YouTube: https://www.youtube.com/watch?v=jgBkLn-R5j0*

Bahá'í Faith (The), official website *https://www.bahai.org*

Bennett, Betty J. *Montana Bahá'í History*
https://Bahá'ílibrary.com/pdf/b/bennett_montana_Bahá'í_history.pdf

Bishop, Katie. *Shining Lamp: Auntie,* Victoria Bedikian (1879-1955)" updated 4/01/2020, *https://brilliantstarmagazine.org/articles/shining-lamp-auntie-victoria-bedikian-1879-1955*

Bahá'ípedia.org, *The Ten Year Crusade, https://Bahá'ípedia.org/Ten_Year_Crusade*

Burhoe, Maureen. *A Selected timeline related to the history of the Bahá'ís of Alberta, https://hdcommittee.wordpress.com/be-anxiously-concerned/deepening-themes/history-of-the-Bahá'í-faith/a-selected-timeline-related-to-the-history-of-the-Bahá'ís-of-alberta/*

Craig, Del. *Twenty Years in Africa,* unpublished memoir

Crowshoe, Reg and Geoff Crow Eagle. *Piikani Blackfoot Teaching, http://www.fourdirectionsteachings.com/transcripts/blackfoot.html*

Hellson, John and Dave Melting Tallow. Interview with George First Rider, October 25, 1968. Provincial Archives of Alberta, *https://ourspace.uregina.ca.* Copyright: Diana Melting Tallow

Horton, Chelsea. *All is One: Becoming Indigenous and Bahá'í in Global North America.* UBC Doctoral thesis, 2013. *https://open.library.ubc.ca*

Indigenous Foundations.arts.ubc.ca, *Terminology, https://Indigenousfoundations.arts.ubc.ca/terminology/*

Irwin, Arthur. *Early Native Teaching in Canada,* unpublished account, 1983

Joe, Stephanie. *The Story Behind Elbow River Camp,* 2019. *https://www.avenuecalgary.com*

McClintock, Walter. *The Old North Trail.* Macmillan and Co. 1910

Nakhjavani, Violette. *The Maxwells of Montréal: Early Years.* George Ronald, 2011.

Pemberton-Pigott, Andrew. *The Bahá'í Faith in Alberta, 1942–1992: The Ethic of Dispersion,* University of Alberta Graduate Studies Thesis, 1992

Perkins, June. *A Tribute to Fred Murray: Retracing the Story of Uncle Fred,* Bahá'íblog.net, April, 2020. *https://www.Bahá'íblog.net/2020/04/a-tribute-to-fred-murray-retracing-the-story-of-uncle-fred/*

Ross, Michael. *Weasel Tail: Interviews with Joe Crowshoe.* Newest Press, 2008

Sargent, John. *Stumbling in the Half-Light*. Friesen Press, 2018

Savage, Candace. *Geography of Blood*. Greystone Books, 2012

Singh, Amy. *Miriam Nicholls*, [Audio interview recording] 2013

Singh, Amy. Unpublished Memoir and letters to her parents

Stark, Peter. *The Old North Trail*, 1997. *https://www. smithsonianmag.com/*

Stecyk, Allison. *Mabel Harriet Pine: Unsung Heroine of Canada*, unpublished diary of her mother

van den Hoonaard, Will. *The Origins of the Bahá'í Community of Canada*, 1898–1948. Wilfred Laurier University Press, 1996

Verge, Pat. *Honouring Blood and Bahá'í Traditions: Allison and Earl Healy*, *https://www.nativeBahá'ís.com*

Verge, Pat. *History of the Bahá'í Faith on the Peigan Reserve, Yeares 1956–1995*, (document prepared for Band Council background information, at the time of the closing of the Bahá'í Center, 1995)

Verge, Patricia. *Angus from the Heart*. Springtide Publishing, 1999

Wall Kimmerer, Robin. *Braiding Sweetgrass*. Milkweed Editions, 2013

Wente, Jesse. *Unreconciled: Family, Truth, and Indigenous Resistance*. Penguin Canada, 2021

White, Roger. *Edmund and Jean Many Bears*, In Memoriam article, *The Bahá'í World* Vol XIV 1963-1968, 1974

Yellowhorn, Dr. Eldon, *Digging up the Rez: Piikani Historical Archeology,* [documentary film] SFU Faculty of Arts and Social Sciences, 2014

About the author

Joan Young has lived in the shadow of the Rocky Mountains near Calgary most of her life. Her professional life was spent teaching young children, but her passion outside the classroom has been exploring the cultural and physical landscapes around her. Spending long hours adventuring in the eastern slopes of the mountains, travelling the backroads of the prairies, and meeting the people who live there, she first met members of the Blackfoot nations in her early twenties. Their mutual membership in the Bahá'í Faith allowed her to begin spending significant time with them. Some of these individuals became close personal friends, significantly affecting the way she viewed the history of the land around her. She began recording stories of lifelong friendships between Blackfoot and settler individuals in 2013.